Chinese
Christians
in
America

Fenggang Yang

Chinese Christians in America

Conversion, Assimilation, and Adhesive Identities

The Pennsylvania State University Press
University Park, Pennsylvania

Library of Congress Cataloging-in-Publication Data

Yang, Fenggang
    Chinese Christians in America : conversion, assimilation, and adhesive
identities / Fenggang Yang.

        p.   cm.
    Includes bibliographical references and index.
    ISBN 0-271-01916-6 (cloth : alk. paper)
    ISBN 0-271-01917-4 (pbk. : alk. paper)
    1. Chinese Americans—Religion—Case studies.   2. Chinese Christian Church
of Washington, D.C. (Washington, D.C.)   I. Title.
BR563.C45Y36   1999
280'.4'0899510753—dc21   98-37365
                                                                                          CIP

Copyright © 1999 The Pennsylvania State University
All rights reserved
Printed in the United States of America
Published by The Pennsylvania State University Press,
University Park, PA 16802-1003

It is the policy of The Pennsylvania State University Press to use acid-free paper for
the first printing of all clothbound books. Publications on uncoated stock satisfy the
minimum requirements of American National Standard for Information Sciences—
Permanence of Paper for Printed Library Materials, ANSI Z39.48-1992.

Contents

Preface

Until recently, Christianity was a foreign religion to the Chinese. Even worse, since the Opium War (1840) the Chinese have regarded Christian missions as an integral part of Western imperialism and Christian religion as the spiritual opium and means to conquer the Chinese nation. In spite of intense missionary work for more than one hundred years since the early nineteenth century, Christians remained a negligible minority in China, less than 1 percent by 1949 when the Communists took power. Under the rule of the Chinese Communist Party, which exhorted an atheist ideology, Western missionaries were expelled, Chinese believers were persecuted, and all religions were subject to complete elimination during the radical Cultural Revolution (1966–76).

Since the 1980s, however, hundreds and thousands in the People's Republic of China have turned to Christianity. On the other side of the globe, since 1989, the year when student-led prodemocracy movements in Beijing and other cities of China were violently crushed by the government, large numbers of mainland Chinese students and scholars studying in the United States began to flock into Christian churches. More importantly, these Chinese newcomers found many Chinese Christian churches readily and enthusiastically welcoming them into their congregations. These Chinese churches in America had been established mostly by immigrants from Taiwan and Hong Kong since the 1960s. Some of these Chinese had become Christian in Hong Kong and Taiwan after fleeing the Communist mainland, and many more converted after immigration to the United States. These Chinese from diverse social, cultural, and political backgrounds gathered together in America and claimed Christianity as their own religion.

Indeed, Chinese Christian churches have become the predominant religious institutions among the Chinese in the United States. Some surveys report that as many as 32 percent of the Chinese in metropolitan areas of Los Angeles and Chicago are Christian, a higher percentage than that of Buddhists and other religions. If these surveys reflect the reality, the high proportion of Christians among the Chinese is in remarkable contrast to the old image. In the past Chinese converts were chastised with the popular sarcasm "one more Christian, one less Chinese." Why have these Chinese converted to Christianity? What kind of Christianity do they believe in? Do these Christian converts still preserve Chinese cultural and religious traditions? Gathering together from diverse origins and cultural backgrounds, how do these church people reconstruct their Chinese identity? Living in the United States as immigrants and ethnic minority people, how do these Chinese construct their American identity? How do Chinese Christians in the United States integrate conflicting identities of being Christian, Chinese, and American? These questions were so intriguing to me that, when considering my Ph.D. dissertation research, I could choose nothing else but a study of Chinese American Christians, even though I foresaw myriad difficulties in methodology, theory, and my own knowledge backgrounds.

These questions are also theoretically important in the studies of immigrant assimilation, religious conversion, identity construction of Chinese diaspora, and ethnic studies. However, almost no scholarly research on Chinese American Christians exists in the literature. Considering the significant proportion of Christians among Chinese Americans and the theoretical relevance, such an empirical study of Chinese American Christians is overdue.

Identity constructions in the immigrant Chinese church are the focus of this sociological study. I would like to bring readers into a typical Chinese immigrant church. I will examine their symbols, discourses, and behaviors and will examine layers of meanings in them with in-depth ethnographic description and sociological analysis. Obviously, such a project would have not been possible without intimate contacts with Chinese Christians in the churches. I want to express my appreciation for the cooperation and generous help from many pastors and lay leaders in Chinese churches in the greater Washington area as well as in Chicago, New York, Miami, Houston, Los Angeles, and San Francisco. I am especially grateful to the people at the Chinese Christian Church of Greater Washington, D.C. They opened not only their files and homes to me, but also their lives and hearts. They provided me not only an ethnographic field for this study, but also a warm home for a deeper understanding of myself.

Doing an ethnographic study of a Chinese American church was a great challenge to me. This study could not have been completed without the

generous help of many scholars and the financial support of several organizations. I am very grateful to my professors at the Catholic University of
America, Dr. Dean H. Hoge, Dr. Che-Fu Lee, and Dr. William V. D'Antonio,
for their consistent encouragement, invaluable advice, and warm friendship. I can never adequately express my appreciation and gratitude to
Dr. R. Stephen Warner of the University of Illinois at Chicago for his understanding of my research and his critical comments on my writings about Chinese American churches. The New Ethnic and Immigrant Congregations
Project (NEICP), funded by the Lilly Endowment and the Pew Charitable
Trusts and directed by Steve Warner, provided me a fellowship in 1994–95.
More important, Steve Warner, Dr. Judith G. Wittner of Loyola University
in Chicago, and other research fellows, and the NEICP training workshops
and conferences helped me to become an ethnographer and scholar. I also
want to acknowledge the support of the Society for the Scientific Study of
Religion (SSSR). An SSSR research award in 1993 served as a boost for me to
initiate field research on Chinese American churches. I thank the Louisville
Institute and its Executive Director, Dr. James W. Lewis, for awarding me a
dissertation fellowship in 1995–96.

Between the beginning of 1997 and the end of 1998 I worked as a post-
doctoral fellow on the Religion, Ethnicity, and New Immigrants Research
(RENIR) project, funded by the Pew Charitable Trusts, directed by Dr. Helen
Rose Ebaugh, and hosted at the Center for Immigration Research of the University of Houston. The RENIR project provided me further ethnographic
research opportunities on various immigrant religious groups, which helped
me to refine some ideas in this book and also provided me precious time
for preparing the manuscript. Dr. Ebaugh has been an excellent mentor,
supportive colleague, and trustworthy friend, to whom I am forever grateful.

I am also indebted to Dr. Wing Ning Pang and Rev. James Chuck, two
pioneer researchers of contemporary Chinese churches in North America,
and to Dr. Timothy Tseng of Colgate Rochester Divinity School, Dr. Sze-
Kar Wan of Andover Newton Theological School, and Dr. Samuel Ling, for
their generous advice and scholarly comments on this study. There are many
others whose names I have left out, not because of lack of appreciation, but
because they are so numerous.

Finally, I wish to acknowledge my gratitude to members of my family. My
parents and brothers, who may never set their feet in the American land,
instilled in me the tenacity of spirit that helps me to accomplish my goals
in life. My deepest and most heartfelt appreciation is to my wife, Juan He,
for her unwavering confidence, understanding, patience, and love, which
encouraged me and sustained me throughout this study. Our daughter,

Connie, was born when I had just started the research on Chinese American churches. Since the days of her learning to prattle sentences we have talked about identities, languages, and cultures. She enjoys going to the Chinese church and learns to speak both English and Chinese. Our second daughter, Minnie, was born when I was finishing the final manuscript. I hope that some day they may find this book helpful for understanding various people around them.

Introduction

A Chinese Christian church in the United States is probably an eccentric enigma to most Americans and most Chinese. Chinese are from the Far East, whose religious traditions are Confucianism, Daoism (Taoism), and Buddhism, whereas Christianity has been the religion of the West (Europe and America). When the East and the West meet in a Chinese Christian church, what happens to the distinct cultural and religious traditions? This was a question that came to my mind on a sunny spring day in 1989 as I was stepping, for the first time, into a Chinese church in the United States.

In January of that year I had come to the United States as a visiting scholar, intending to spend the year of 1989 gathering various materials for my teaching of Christianity at the People's University of China in Beijing.[1] Since the mid-1980s, some Chinese universities had offered courses of religious studies in part because of a growing interest in Christianity and other religions among college students and young scholars. However, books on Christianity were hard to find, and Christians were hardly accessible in the People's Republic of China back then. Upon arriving in the United States, I engulfed myself in reading and visiting various churches—Catholic, Episcopalian, Methodist, Baptist, Presbyterian, large and small, white and black. I had a dinner with Catholic monks at a Benedictine monastery in Washington, D.C., spent a week at a Catholic-run charismatic center in New York, and stayed a weekend with people of diverse denominations at a Mennonite-run retreat center in the mountains of West Virginia. All these were very American to me.

On Palm Sunday 1989, after visiting a predominantly white Presbyterian church in a suburb of Washington, D.C., my American host dropped me at a Chinese church in the same neighborhood. Fortuitously, this church became a major site of my ethnographic study of Chinese Christianity in

America and the central stage of this book for reasons that I will explain later in this introduction. But for now, let us take a close look at this ordinary Chinese church.

Surrounded by low-rise brick houses, small blocks, quiet streets, and a middle-school playground across the street, the church compound of three steepleless brick buildings fit plainly into the neighborhood. A passerby would hardly notice anything distinct without stopping to look at the ungarnished church sign that reads, in both English and Chinese, "Chinese Christian Church of Greater Washington, D.C." On Sundays, however, it would be hard not to notice large sedans and minivans cramming the small parking lot in front of the church buildings and spilling over into the nearby streets.

When I got out of the car, the Sunday service was already over. Several people were still lingering around in the pathways connecting the buildings. A casually dressed man greeted me, warmly yet gingerly. We exchanged information about each other's name, place of origin, job, and school. He was from Taiwan, a computer programmer. Coincidentally, he worked at the university where I was a visiting scholar. As we were finding more commonalities, we exchanged phone numbers and addresses. Then he suggested picking me up the next Sunday to attend the Sunday service. I gladly agreed and came on the following Sunday.

A first-time visitor to the Sunday service is greeted by ushers with a welcome package that includes a general schedule of Sunday services, Sunday school classes, and fellowship group meetings, and a statement of faith. The "Synopsis of Our Church" reads:

> The Chinese Christian Church of Greater Washington, D.C. is a nondenominational church. We believe in God's inspiration of the whole Bible that is the standard measure of our faith, our daily living, and our ministry. We believe in the triune Godhead. . . . We believe in the unity of the church, with Christ being the Head. The Church is composed of believers born of the Holy Spirit and baptized into the name of Christ for the purposes of worshiping God, fellowship with the saints, and witnessing and ministering to the world.

In the vestibule to the sanctuary, a rack on the wall holds a variety of English and Chinese newsletters, magazines, and pamphlets from Christian organizations. A bulletin board on another wall displays letters from missionaries supported by this church, flyers announcing evangelistic meetings and retreat camps, and minutes of the monthly Official Board meeting. Two ushers stand at the stairway leading to the upstairs sanctuary, handing out a photocopied bulletin to everyone. It contains the order of worship, with inserts of a long list of prayer requests and a long list of various fellowship group meetings and activities in the following week.

The main sanctuary is on the second floor. A center aisle with red carpet divides the straight rows of hardwood pews into two columns, which can comfortably seat about three hundred people. Unadorned walls, amber-colored glass windows, and the pitched open ceiling amplify conspicuously the organ pipes symmetrically built into the front wall. In the recessed hollow under the organ pipes hangs a large metal cross. Below it is the baptismal pool. The organ console stands on the right and a grand piano on the left like cupping hands holding the raised platform in the center. Two rows of choir stalls are symmetrically arranged at an angle spreading out on both sides of the baptismal pool. At the center of the platform is the communion table. To the front left of the platform stands the pulpit, a large wooden desk equipped with two adjustable microphones. During Sunday services, two men stand behind the wide pulpit, one a preacher, the other an interpreter. The preacher often preaches in Mandarin, while the interpreter translates it, sentence by sentence, to Cantonese or English. An identical desk is on the front right, which is used by the song leader. The whole setup is very balanced and steady, and accentuates the centrality of preaching and hymn singing. The lack of ornaments or icons in the sanctuary reflects puritanical simplicity, very much like those Congregationalist churches in the New England area that I visited.

The Sunday service follows a simple order. Hymn singing and preaching take most of the time. There is no recitation of creeds and no responses between the preacher and the congregation. Its lack of liturgical formality resembles many churches of the Reformed tradition. The service does not create an atmosphere of sacraments like in a Catholic or Episcopal church. During the pastoral prayer following the first hymn, the pastor prays to the Lord for taking care of various church ministries, and for healing the sick and giving jobs to the jobless among the congregants. An image of a living and caring God emerges out of this prayer. In the prayer, he refers to "Sister so and so" (e.g., Sister Cindy Chang) if the needy person is a female, or "Brother so and so" (e.g., Brother David Wong) if a male. If the person is a senior, however, he would mention him as "Uncle so and so" (e.g., Uncle Yao) or her as "Aunt so and so" (e.g., Aunt Leung). This creates a sense of a big family caring for each other.

On most Sundays a separate English service is concurrently held in the Fellowship Hall of another building, which also serves as the dining hall for lunch each Sunday. The participants at the English service are younger, from teens to thirties, and a few in their forties and fifties. They wear jeans and T-shirts. The singing time is livelier and longer, lasting more than thirty minutes, pausing only for a spontaneous prayer by a song leader. The song leaders are five or six boys and girls standing on the front stage, holding guitars in arms, tambourines in hands, and microphones close to their mouths. In gloomy light they lead a continuous singing while the congregation remains standing all the time. Congregants follow the song leaders to clap hands or hold up arms while they sing. After this a short gospel drama sometimes precedes the sermon. Surprisingly, the preacher is always a white man, the "assistant pastor" who independently ministers to the English-speaking people. In his preaching he cites no Chinese stories, refers to no Chinese cultural values or customs, but he often shows conservative Christian concerns for the social and cultural problems in American society. From the form to the content, there is hardly anything distinctively Chinese in the English service except for the skin and hair color of the participants. Similar worship services of contemporary style can be easily found in many evangelical or fundamentalist churches throughout the country.

Around the time of my first visits, this church was starting a new ministry, the Ark Fellowship, to evangelize mainland Chinese students and scholars. I became one of the first mainland Chinese to attend the lectures of the Ark Fellowship and later joined its first evangelistic Bible study group. At the end of 1992 I was baptized and became a member of the church. Then I began to try to find scholarly studies of Chinese Christians in America. Unfortunately, almost nothing existed then, except for an anthropologist's account (Palinkas 1989) and passing fragments in studies of American Chinatowns.

Beginning in 1993, I began to collect data about Chinese churches in the greater Washington area systematically, later extending my study to other areas of the country. My preliminary research found that the history of Chinese churches in the United States goes back as early as the 1850s, that the growth of Chinese churches since the 1960s has been rapid, that most Chinese churches are heterogeneous in membership, and that many church members are adult converts from non-Christian family backgrounds. When the time came for me to choose a dissertation topic, nothing could interest me more than a sociological study of some aspects of Chinese Christianity in America. After visiting many churches, I eventually chose the Chinese Christian Church of Greater Washington, D.C., for in-depth ethnographic research. It is a typical Chinese church in many ways, as I will explain below. It is also my own church, so I have full access to its members and documents.

But before discussing my research methods and my role in the church, a brief overview of Chinese Christian churches in the United States is in order.

Chinese Christian Churches in the United States

The history of Chinese Christianity in America is almost as long as that of Chinese immigration. However, unlike European immigrants who transplanted their Protestantism and Catholicism to the New World, earlier Chinese Christian churches were missions started by American denominations (Lau 1933; Cayton and Lively 1955; Woo 1983; Tseng 1994). The first Chinese church was established in San Francisco in 1853, with the support of the Presbyterian Board of Foreign Missions, by a medical missionary, William Speer, who had been in China. Four Chinese who had been converted in China became the charter members of this first Chinese church in America. Other denominations then started their own missions for Chinese laborers: Methodists in 1868 and Baptists, Congregationalists, and Episcopalians separately in 1870. By 1892 eleven denominations had established ten Chinese churches (including three in Canada), ten Chinese Christian associations, and 271 Chinese Sunday schools and missions in thirty-one states (Condit 1900). Not until the early 1900s did the Catholic Church start its mission to the Chinese in San Francisco. Not surprisingly, the pastors of all the churches were Caucasian (Cayton and Lively 1955, 41); Chinese Christians could only serve as assistants to white missionaries (Woo 1988). During the decades of the Chinese exclusion acts (1882–1943), and in line with the exclusionist sentiments and policies toward the Chinese in the United States, these mission churches were treated mostly as extensions of China missions (Woo 1991). The goal was to Christianize the "heathen" Chinese and send them back to China to help American missionaries there. These early missions were not very successful in terms of converting the Chinese. "[I]t was clear that, as in the case of nineteenth-century China, the ratio of converts to the whole population was minuscule" (Woo 1991, 217). Meanwhile, the Catholic mission was hampered by the fact that strongly Catholic Irish and Italian groups were active in California anti-Chinese crusades, and identification of Catholic elements with the drive for exclusion slowed down Catholic evangelism until after World War I (Cayton and Lively 1955, 46).

In the first half of the twentieth century, most Chinese churches were still missions aided and supervised by American denominations. However,

despite social, political, and economic hardships, some of these Chinese
mission churches gained financial and leadership independence within the
denominations, and a few nondenominational churches were established
(Lau 1933). By 1952 there were sixty-six Chinese Protestant churches in the
United States: forty-seven were denominational, five were interdenominational (sponsored by several denominations or a council of churches), and
fourteen were independent of any denominational body (Cayton and Lively
1955). In addition there were Catholic missions in Hawaii (begun in 1925),
Philadelphia (1939), Chicago (1941), Boston (1946), and New York (1949)
(Cayton and Lively 1955; Johnson 1976). During this period, a majority of
Chinese church ministers were born in China. Most churches were small:
the average membership size was 155. However, some churches began to
grow fast after World War II.

Since the 1950s the number of Chinese Protestant churches has rapidly
increased, reaching nearly 700 by 1994 (Pang 1995). Some Chinese Catholic
groups also emerged in Washington, D.C., Houston, and other metropolitan
areas. Table 1 clearly shows this trend of fast growth in the number of
Chinese Protestant churches in the United States.

Table 1. The Growth of Chinese Protestant Churches
in the United States, 1853–1994

Year	Number of Chinese Churches
1853	1
1890	7
1931	44
1952	66
1979	366
1984	523
1994	697

SOURCES: Pang 1980, 1985; Lau 1933; Cayton and Lively 1955;
AFC 1984, 1994.

In contrast to early mission churches, most new Chinese churches were
founded by Chinese immigrants themselves. Beginning in the late 1950s
and early 1960s, Chinese students studying in American universities formed
many campus Bible study groups (BSG). Many BSGs later evolved into
churches as many students adjusted to permanent resident status under the
new immigration act of 1965. More churches then came to exist through
their efforts of church planting and schisms.

Contemporary Chinese churches in America have two general characteristics—theological conservatism and organizational independence. On the
West Coast, where earlier mission churches *for* the Chinese concentrated,

many Chinese churches are affiliated with mainline American denominations. For example, in 1996 there were 158 Chinese churches in the San Francisco and Bay area. Among them, 10 were Presbyterian (PCUSA), 7 United Methodist, 6 Episcopal, 5 American Baptist, and 4 Lutheran (Missouri Synod). However, a great number of new churches established *by* Chinese immigrants are independent, and those new churches that do affiliate with American denominations tend to favor theologically conservative ones (see Chuck 1996; S. W. Chan 1996). Nationally, about half of all Chinese churches have no affiliation with American denominations (Pang 1995). Furthermore, denominational churches tend to maintain a high degree of independence. The denominations most attractive to Chinese Christians are conservative in theology and less centralized in organization. The largest group of Chinese churches belongs to the Southern Baptist Convention (SBC), which claimed about 150 Chinese churches in 1995. The second largest is the Christian and Missionary Alliance (C&MA) with about 60 Chinese churches in the United States.

More important, Christian churches have evidently become the predominant religious institutions among the Chinese in America. The last count reported about 700 Chinese Protestant churches (AFC 1994), whereas the number of Chinese Buddhist temples and associations was less than 150 (Yu 1996). In the Washington area, there were twenty Chinese Christian churches, but only three Chinese Buddhist centers in 1995. Meanwhile, some surveys in certain metropolitan areas show that as many as 32 percent of ethnic Chinese are Christian, but only 20 percent Buddhist (Hurh and Kim 1990, 20; Dart 1997).[2] This is in remarkable contrast to the situation in China, where Christians remained a tiny minority of between one and five percent.[3] Although the exact percentages of various religious believers among the Chinese cannot be decided without further survey research, Christianity has evidently become the most practiced institutional religion among the ethnic Chinese in the United States.

Chinese Churches in the Greater Washington Area

Chinese churches in the Greater Washington area share the national characteristics of organizational independence and theological conservativeness (see Table 2).

The first Chinese church in Washington, D.C., was the interdenominational Chinese Community Church, which was formed in 1935 by pooling together Chinese Sunday school students in several denominational churches.

Table 2.   Denominational Affiliation of Chinese Protestant
Churches in the Greater Washington Area, 1995

Churches	Number
Independent	8
Southern Baptist Convention	3
Christian & Missionary Alliance	3
United Presbyterian Church U.S.A.	2
United Methodist Church	1
Free Methodist Church	1
Evangelical Formosan Church[a]	1
Interdenominational	1
Total	20

[a] The Evangelical Formosan Church (EFC) was started in 1970 in Los Angeles by a group of Taiwanese-speaking immigrants. By 1996 the EFC claimed 25 churches in the United States and half a dozen churches in Canada, Central America, Australia, and New Zealand.

Located at the border of Chinatown and sponsored by American churches in the city, this Chinese mission served mostly pre–World War II Cantonese immigrant laborers and their descendants. Until 1972 this Chinese church was under the control and supervision of the General Board of Managers, which consisted of 50 members from the sponsoring churches of various denominations.

In 1958 a group of Chinese students who were studying in several universities in this area established the second Chinese church and named it the "Chinese Mandarin Church." Mandarin was chosen because it was the common language that every educated Chinese was supposed to be able to speak. In 1970 this independent church renamed itself the "Chinese Christian Church of Greater Washington, D.C." to signify greater inclusiveness to all Chinese regardless of the language spoken. At the beginning, Sunday services were held at a downtown office building of the International Students, Inc. Then the church bought its own property on 16th Street Northwest, which was not in the vicinity of the Chinatown. In 1971 it moved to a near suburb in Maryland. The church continuously grew both by membership transfers and by baptizing converts. Sunday attendance peaked at more than 400 in the mid-1970s.

Following a period of conflicts, a schism in 1976 took away about half of the members at the Chinese Christian Church of Greater Washington, D.C. (CCC). Those walkouts established the independent "Chinese Bible Church of Maryland," which has become the largest Chinese church in this area with nearly 700 people attending Sunday services in 1995. Around the time of this bitter split and soon thereafter, several Chinese churches emerged in the suburbs in Maryland and Virginia. When I visited these churches in 1993 and 1994, I frequently met people who were former members of the CCC. The rest of the twenty Chinese churches were established after 1980.

Because of its history and close relationships with other Chinese churches, the CCC is a strategic site for an ethnographic study. Moreover, it is a typical Chinese church in terms of theological conservativeness and organizational independence. It is also an average church in membership size, with about 300 adult and youth members and about 270 in Sunday attendance in 1995. Also, the CCC is one of the churches with a high proportion of adult converts from non-Christian family backgrounds. (My interviews in 1993–94 with leaders of Chinese churches in the greater Washington area reveal that the proportion of converts is high in most Chinese churches, ranging between one-third and two-thirds of all members in these churches.)

Research Questions: Religious Conversion and Identity Construction

For Chinese immigrants going to Christian churches in the United States, three important identities undergo construction and reconstruction. As converts, they achieve a Christian identity; as immigrants, they achieve an American identity; and as Chinese, their identity is challenged by their emigration away from China and their diverse diasporic experiences. Each of these three identities has its own complexity. In other words, there are very different kinds of Christians, Americans, and Chinese. Furthermore, these three identities are not easily compatible with each other. There have been cultural, political, and social conflicts between Chinese and Christian identities, and between Chinese and American identities. Chinese are from a nation with rich cultural and religious traditions. Then why do these immigrants convert to Christianity? Have they forsaken their own religious traditions to accept the dominant religion of the host society? What Chinese traditions have they inherited, if any? How does the church help these Chinese Christians in their identity constructions? Does the immigrant church function mostly as an assimilation agency in American society or as a bastion for preserving ethnic culture?

Struggles of identity construction and tensions between diverse identities are pervasive and obvious in most Chinese churches. These questions and the focus of this study gradually emerged during my ethnographic research on Chinese immigrant and ethnic churches. In other words, this research project was not theoretically driven, because scholarly research on Chinese Christians in the United States has been scarce. This allowed me to take the utmost concerns of these Chinese Christians as the primary issues for my scholarly analysis. Meanwhile, there is a rich literature from which I could draw theoretical references for this study, including assimilation and ethnicity, immigrant and ethnic religious organizations, and Chinese identity construction in the contemporary world. In return, this ethnographic study of the Chinese Christian church contributes to the theoretical development in these areas. My theoretical arguments include (1) that assimilation is selective in the segmented and pluralist American society, (2) that the ethnic church, even with a majority of adult converts, serves both to selectively assimilate its participants into American society and to selectively preserve ethnic culture, (3) that Christian conversion in the immigrant church helps to retain Chinese identity and Chinese traditional culture, and (4) that identities can be adhesive and multiple for some individuals in the immigrant church.

Research Methods and My Roles at the Church

Religious conversion and identity construction are changing processes. To understand the people who are undergoing these processes, an intimate look is necessary—to observe their behaviors and interactions in natural settings and to hear their discourses in various situations. Ethnographic methods are thus appropriate for such research. In order to achieve an in-depth understanding about Chinese Christians in their identity construction, I focus on one church for in-depth research and for presentation in this book. However, the empirical data have a larger base. Between 1993 and 1994, I visited all of the twenty Chinese Christian churches in the Greater Washington, D.C., area. I conducted participant observation in their Sunday services and Sunday school classes; interviewed their pastors and conversed with members at lunch tables; and collected their bulletins, newsletters, and anniversary memorial publications. Since then I have also visited Chinese churches, Buddhist temples, and other Chinese groups in Boston, Chicago, Houston, Miami, New York, Philadelphia, and San Francisco; attended some Chinese Christian camp meetings and national conferences; and read dozens of Chinese Christian periodicals, conference proceedings, and ministry reports.

My ethnographic research focused on the Chinese Christian Church of Greater Washington, D.C. (CCC). Beginning in September of 1993, I conducted (1) extensive participant observation in CCC's various gatherings and meetings, including sitting in at the Official Board (*zhang-zhi-hui*) meetings and various committee meetings; (2) many informal conversations and formal interviews with pastors, lay leaders, members, ex-members, and former pastors; and (3) a thorough search and examination of membership records, church magazines and other publications, and several boxes of church documents, all that I could find. Participant observation, informal conversations, and a variety of church documents are the most important data for this research. Formal interviews were mostly for the purpose of clarification. These were semi-structured, conducted either in Mandarin or English at homes or the church. Most church documents were in Chinese, though some had both Chinese and English versions. Many quotations throughout this dissertation are my own translations, and although I have sometimes upgraded the English in order to smooth the text, I have been very careful to avoid distorting the original meaning and tone.

I chose the CCC for in-depth research because it is a typical, average Chinese immigrant church with a relatively long history. Another important consideration was the level of accessibility. As a sociology student from the People's Republic of China, I experienced some difficulties in the 1993–94 study of Chinese churches in the Washington area. At a monthly gathering of all Chinese pastors in the Washington area, I introduced my proposed research project. Immediately, a pastor bluntly questioned me: "How can we know that you are not doing the investigation for the Chinese Communist government?" Although I tried hard to explain the academic nature of this study, this pastor was very reluctant to be interviewed and simply refused to show me any written materials of his church. Later I found out that he had served in the Chinese Nationalist (Kuomintang) army, immigrated from Taiwan several years ago, and seemed to have a continuing fear of mainlanders from "Communist China."

Chinese church leaders tend to be very protective for their churches. An outsider may find it hard to gain their trust and access. Of course, I had successful interviews with most pastors—some were very informative—but most of the pastors showed various degrees of reservation for my accessing their church records and documents. However, the CCC received me both as a member (participant) and as a researcher (observer). The church opened its cabinets of records and documents, and many members welcomed me to their homes and spoke honestly in the interviews.

Being a Chinese Christian was helpful for me in studying Chinese Christian churches. Proselytization is often the first priority at these evangelical churches, especially to Chinese visitors to their churches. A common question they ask first-time visitors is "Have you believed in the Lord?" or "Are you a born-again Christian?" Without an affirmative answer, they may not discuss anything else seriously but try to convert the visitor first. I have heard complaints of frustration by Chinese doctoral students who tried to study Chinese churches but were heavily proselytized. In comparison, as a Christian myself, I had smoother entries. During my 1993–94 study, I interviewed a Chinese pastor who had been living in the Washington area for twenty years. Before the interview, he asked me whether I was a Christian. I could honestly say yes. Toward the end of the nearly five hours of a very informative interview, he said, "If you were not a Christian, I would have not told you all the conflicts in these Chinese churches, because you would misinterpret them. And if you were not a Chinese scholar, I would have not explained to you the historical and social connections between these churches here and Christian movements in China, because you would not be able to understand whatsoever."

Being a member of the church has many advantages, including an insider's understanding of the church, its organizational structure, its symbols, and its members. I share many thoughts, feelings, and experiences with these immigrant Chinese Christians, especially those converts who are struggling in their identity constructions. On the other hand, being a member of the church may have the danger of biases in understanding and interpretation. Although "value free" is no more than an ideal in social science research, my sociological training has helped me to stay as neutral and detached as possible during research and analysis.

However, the dual roles of participant and observer occasionally caused me anxiety and ambivalence. After a period of conscious and intense observation of Sunday services, meetings, and activities, I wanted to be an ordinary participant in the church. Unlike anthropologists and many sociological ethnographers who can formally "exit" their fields at some point, I had nowhere to go. I and my family attended this church. Many friends of mine were also there. Sometimes I wanted to be able to relax among my friends, to have casual conversations with people at my church, and to enjoy activities together with my family. However, at meetings or activities that I did not plan to "observe," interesting things frequently popped up and seemed very relevant to my sociological mind. I had to grab a pen and paper quickly and begin taking notes; consequently, some of my field notes were written on napkins or scrap papers in various shades. Although I was delighted to catch some unexpected and exciting movements as a researcher, I sometimes felt sorry about not being able to be an ordinary and full participant, simply "one of them." A sudden "mental withdrawal"—from being a participant to becoming a detached observer—requires shifting gears of thinking and ways of mental processing. When I put aside my conscious observer's role, I often enjoyed the fellowship time more, although the sociologist observer was always in the back of my mind.

More challenging to my dual roles were situations in which I wanted to be an observer but was dragged into greater participation. During the time of my field work, I was very careful in trying to reduce my intrusive interventions to the natural processes at the church. Since I decided to focus my research on this church, I was determined to be a watchful member, a silent observer in church meetings, and an empathetic listener in informal conversations and formal interviews. However, remaining silent at all meetings was impossible. Every gathering at church or in someone's home would start and conclude with prayers. Not only was there social pressure for every participant to say a prayer, but sometimes I was unexpectedly assigned to lead or conclude a round of prayer. In those situations, I was truly a participant-observer or observer-participant.

Like many new converts from mainland China, I was invited to be involved in "co-workers" meetings of the Ark Fellowship. Co-workers were volunteers who could be decision-makers of this evangelistic ministry or simply helpers with assigned tasks, such as giving a ride to prospective converts or preparing snacks at special gatherings. At co-workers meetings I refrained from expressing distinctive opinions or initiating actions. But in Bible study or evangelism meetings I often asked questions, like other new converts did. When I was approached for taking up leadership responsibilities at the fellowship group or on the church level, I declined. However, to remain a member in good standing, I eventually accepted a volunteer task of editing the newsletter for the Ark Fellowship in 1995. I also contributed essays to the quarterly church magazine, which was simply appropriate for me as a "scholar" member of the church. However, I made it clear on various occasions that my stay in the Washington area would be transient and that I had no intention of becoming a leader or power-player in this church. Thus I could dodge most of the limits to a person classified in the newcomer's category, and I enjoyed opportunities to attend various activities and have candid conversations with church members of various backgrounds. Overall, I have been well received both as a participant and an observer.

There were more difficult situations to maintaining the double roles of participant and observer. For example, sitting in at official board meetings and special committee meetings as an observer, I sometimes became un-easy with the opinions expressed or with misunderstandings toward certain groups of people. Suppressing the urge to speak out in defense or opposition was hard for me, but now I am glad that I managed to keep steadfastly quiet on those occasions. My investigations uncovered overt conflicts and disgraceful fights that caused the schism in 1976 and that left painful scars in the hearts of many longtime members. After almost twenty years, they still did not want to discuss it, hoping to maintain harmony and preserve the unity of the church. In 1995 there were again tensions and conflicts between various fellowship groups. The congregational meeting even fired the senior pastor. Some unhappy newcomers heard rumors about the bitter split of 1976, sensed its continual impacts on current issues, and demanded to know what really happened twenty years ago and why the church had its present organizational structure. After they failed to get details from old-timers, some turned to me, the known researcher. This put me in an awkward situation. My personal opinion was that open discussions could lead to better understanding of both the church's past and the present, and would thus be helpful to the church's unity and ministries. However, I was well aware of the old-timers' wish and concern for protecting church unity. Thus, I painfully persuaded myself to stay detached as an observer and not tell the stories then and there. Only after completing my dissertation and before leaving for a job in Houston at the end of 1996, did I finally agree to present some of my findings and analysis at two Sunday school class sessions and some fellowship group meetings.

In various parts of this book I describe and discuss some past and present tensions, conflicts, and problems in this Chinese church. Obviously, as a limited person with limited time, hearing everyone who was involved in the conflicts and fights, especially those that happened more than twenty years ago, was impossible for me. Nevertheless, I can honestly say this: I made sincere efforts to interview people in various factions who either remained at CCC or left this church. I succeeded in interviewing some who had been pastors and lay leaders before the schism as well as several people who dropped out of the church. During the process of my field research, I encountered people who saw many problems as personality conflicts, which is a psychological interpretation, or as struggles between genuine and false Christians, which looks like a "Christian" interpretation. In this book I present a sociological interpretation: given the social and historical contexts in which the church exists, and given the diverse social and cultural backgrounds of the members, most tensions and conflicts in the immigrant Chinese church result from confusions and conflicts in the process of identity construction and reconstruction. By putting these in proper social and cultural contexts, I hope to help people at this and other Chinese churches to understand their own history and present situation. Of course, throughout the process of my research, fundamentalist leaders and members questioned the value of sociological research. Certainly I would not wish to argue that a sociological analysis has greater validity than their logic of reasoning, and I am aware that "accepting multiple explanations is not a comfortable position for the people [in conservative churches]" (Ammerman 1987, 11). Nonetheless, I hope they can give a serious reading to this analysis of the issues from a sociological perspective.

Plan of the Chapters

This study explores the church's construction of three identities—Christian, American, and Chinese. Historical developments are important for understanding the changing process of identity construction. However, instead of chronologically documenting historical changes and events of this church, I want to describe and analyze the three identities one by one, and then the relationships of the three together. The historical developments of this church are interpolated throughout the chapters. I provide a briefly illustrated chronicle of the church in the appendix, to which a reader may want to refer from time to time while reading the chapters.

Earlier in this introduction, I briefly introduced the history and current status of Chinese Christian churches in America and in the Greater Washington area. To situate this Chinese Christian church in broader social and historical contexts, in Chapter 2 I summarize the historical changes of Chinese immigration, Chinese ethnic organizations in the United States and in the Washington area, and Chinese cultural traditions. Chapter 2 also reviews the rapidly growing literature about the reconstruction of Chinese identity in the contemporary world.

The patterns of identity construction at this Chinese immigrant church bear theoretical importance. To put this study in a theoretical framework, Chapter 1 reviews the literature of assimilation, ethnicity, and religion. Recent scholarship is leading toward a theoretical integration of assimilation and ethnic pluralism. Multidimensional pluralism in the segmented American society and growing transnationalism makes it necessary for new immigrants to carry out selective assimilation and selective preservation of ethnicity. The immigrant and ethnic religious community is an important mechanism for constructing adhesive identities.

Following the reviews of theoretical and historical backgrounds, in Chapter 3 I will first describe the Christian identity as it is reflected in the CCC's public rituals, practical theologies, and ministry emphases. This is an evangelical church in the Reformed tradition, and its most important mission is evangelism or proselytization. Consequently, it can be characterized as a church of converts. The various conversions to evangelical Christianity mostly result from dramatic social and cultural changes in China, immigrant experiences in the pluralistic American society, and active proselytization of evangelical Christians.

Although assimilation is not the major motivation for their Christian conversions, the immigrant church does help these immigrants to achieve an American identity. Selective assimilation is the focus of Chapter 4. The CCC is not the major assimilation agency for its members in terms of learning English and adopting American lifestyles. Immigrants need the ethnic church in part because of structural assimilation in public spheres of school and workplace. On the other hand, however, the church promotes certain "American" values and proclaims the conservative Christian version of American civil religion.

Chapter 5 describes selective preservation of Chinese traditions. Becoming Christian and becoming American, however, does not mean abandoning Chinese culture and ethnic identity. To the contrary, the Chinese church helps to selectively preserve Chinese cultural traditions, including the Chinese language, cultural customs, and Confucian values. Church members try to separate Chinese religious traditions from nonreligious traditions, rejecting the former while accepting the latter.

Moreover, through deconstructing Chinese identity into political, cultural, and primordial dimensions, these Christian Chinese in America are moving toward greater universalism. Meanwhile, the church helps to integrate three identities. In the process of constructing and reconstructing various identities, tensions and conflicts are abundant. Chapter 6 analyzes various Chinese identities and patterns of multi-identity integration among CCC members. The most theoretically intriguing and practically interesting pattern is "adhesive integration," which embodies two or three identities harmoniously. Those who follow this pattern are truly bicultural or multicultural.

The concluding chapter summarizes empirical findings of this ethnographic study and makes further theoretical reflections on the identity constructions of new immigrants.

1

Assimilation, Ethnicity, and Religion

"Is Assimilation Dead?" This question posed by a renowned scholar of immigration and ethnicity (Glazer 1993) marks the beginning of revived debates on immigrant assimilation in the United States. Before the 1960s assimilation was the canonical concept in the study of immigrants. Ethnic pluralism then became dominant for three decades. In the 1990s scholarship has been moving beyond the perceived contradiction of pluralism and assimilation. Ethnic pluralism and assimilation are both realities in American society. For many contemporary immigrants becoming American and retaining ethnic identity are simultaneous and cohesive processes. This chapter reviews the theoretical developments in immigrant studies and presents the theoretical arguments underlying the descriptions and analyses in the following chapters.

Strictly speaking, the classic conceptualization of assimilation expects complete disappearance of ethnic distinctiveness. It presumes the existence of an American core society and core culture to which immigrants are expected to assimilate. In contemporary American society, however, the core has been eclipsed and pluralism has become more acceptable. Accordingly, recent conceptualizations of assimilation and ethnicity are leading to the construction of an integrated theory that recognizes immigrant assimilation as occurring within American pluralism and increasing transnationalism. Within the new context, assimilation or Americanization has to be selective. Selective assimilation is also the process of selective preservation of ethnic identity and traditional culture. Instead of choosing *either* American *or* ethnic identities, immigrants may construct adhesive identities that integrate both together. In the process of attaining American identity and retaining ethnic identity, religion may play an important role because religion itself is a powerful source of personal identity, and because particular religions are often closely associated with particular ethnic and American identities. The religious community, where face-to-face interactions are regular and frequent, serves as a major social mechanism in the construction of adhesive identities.

Assimilation and Pluralism

Assimilation

The term *assimilation* came into general use around 1900, although the idea itself has a much longer history (Gleason 1992, 49). In the first half of the twentieth century, assimilation became a scholarly canon as well as an ideological norm for American society (e.g., Park 1950; Wirth 1928; Myrad 1944; Warner and Srole 1945; Handlin 1951; see also Alba and Nee 1997). Milton Gordon summarized various assimilation theories into three models, namely, Anglo-conformity, the melting-pot, and cultural pluralism:

> [T]he "Anglo-conformity" theory demanded the complete renunciation of the immigrant's ancestral culture in favor of the behavior and values of the Anglo-Saxon core group; the "melting pot" idea envisaged a biological merger of the Anglo-Saxon peoples with other immigrant groups and a blending of their respective cultures into a new indigenous American type; and "cultural pluralism" postulated the preservation of the communal life and significant portions of the culture of the later immigrant groups within the context of American citizenship and political and economic integration into American society. (Gordon 1964, 85)

Both the "Anglo-conformity" and "melting pot" models presumed the essential Anglo-Saxon core and expected immigrants to give up their ethnic identities in order to achieve a complete American identity. Gordon believed that people in various ethnic groups had been substantially acculturated or culturally assimilated, so that there was not "*cultural* pluralism" but "*structural* pluralism" based on race, ethnicity, and class. The opposite of structural pluralism was structural assimilation—the large-scale entrance of newer groups into cliques, clubs, and institutions of the host society on the primary group level. "Once structural assimilation has occurred, either simultaneously with or subsequent to acculturation, all of the other types of assimilation will naturally follow" (1964, 81).

Following Robert Park's progressive and irreversible "race relations cycle" of contacts, competition, accommodation, and eventual assimilation (Park 1950), Gordon proposed a seven-stage model of assimilation, including cultural assimilation (acculturation), structural assimilation, marital assimilation (intermarriage), identificational assimilation (lost original sense of ethnicity), attitude receptional assimilation (no discriminatory attitudes), behavior receptional assimilation (no discriminatory behaviors), and civic assimilation (no conflict of values and power) (1964, 70–71). Like Park, Gordon believed in the inevitability of the eventual "disappearance of the ethnic group as a separate entity and the evaporation of its distinctive values" (1964, 81). Overall, the classic conceptualization of assimilation "foresees the progressive weakening and ultimate disappearance of the primordial traits and bonds of ethnicity as succeeding generations adopt the general society's unitary system of cultural values and become absorbed into economic, social, and political networks that are blind to ethnicity" (Morawska 1990, 189). However, this classic assimilation theory has fallen into disrepute since the 1960s. Instead, the ethnic pluralism model arose and became the dominant model in theory and politics.

Ethnicity

The term *ethnicity* was first applied to groups of immigrant descent by W. Lloyd Warner in 1941 (see Sollors 1989, xiii). In the 1960s and 1970s the ethnic revival movements amidst the Civil Rights movement showed the persistence and vitality of ethnicity as a source of group solidarity (see Fishman et al. 1985; Royce 1982; Thompson 1989). These movements stimulated an enormous amount of research on the nature of ethnicity, and the debates are continuing today. Many studies (e.g., Vecoli 1964; Bodnar 1985) showed that "old-country ways" and institutions were not receding and giving way to the new American ways of life. Traditional cultural values and institutions were resilient and persistent in the New World. Some scholars (e.g., Novak 1972; Greeley 1974) rose to celebrate the new and old ethnics against assimilation.

Four definitions of ethnicity have appeared in discussions of immigrant adaptation. The first is "primordial ethnicity" (Geertz 1973; Isaacs 1975; Swidler 1986), which holds that people have an essential need for "belonging" that is satisfied by groupings based on shared ancestry and culture.

Such primordial ethnicity is found to continue to powerfully influence the descendants of immigrants even into the third and fourth generations. Contrary to the "primordial" claim, Herbert Gans (1979) argues that ethnic identities are becoming mostly "symbolic," mere vestiges of immigrant cultures and doomed to fade away before the irresistible forces of assimilation. The third understanding is "situational ethnicity," which regards ethnicity mostly as situational and instrumental for social political interest (Glazer and Moynihan 1963; Yancey, Ericksen, and Juliani 1976; Espiritu 1992).

The fourth and newest conceptualization is the "invention of ethnicity," a phrase first used by Werner Sollors (1989) and developed by a group of scholars of ethnic studies (Conzen et al. 1992). After nearly three decades of mostly pronouncing the persistence and resilience of ethnicity, these scholars have finally arrived at a position intending to encompass ethnic pluralism with assimilation. They claim that ethnicity is neither "collective fiction" nor mere preservation of old-country ways; rather, it is an ongoing process of invention that "incorporates, adapts, and amplifies preexisting communal solidarities, cultural attributes, and historical memories" (Conzen et al. 1992, 4–5). In this process, ethnic group boundaries are repeatedly renegotiated and expressive symbols of ethnicity are repeatedly reinterpreted. This theory continues to emphasize the transforming role of immigrants in the larger American society and to underline the incorporation of elements of ethnic cultures into changing definitions of what is American. However, the word *invention* clearly communicates a sense of subjective innovation and flexibility. The protean nature they assign to ethnicity makes it hardly distinguishable from the classical "melting-pot" model. It very much resonates with assimilationist claims that ethnicity is becoming mostly "symbolic" (Gans 1979), entering into the "twilight" (Alba 1985), or becoming "optional" (Waters 1990). Herbert Gans rightfully declares that what looks like invention to one school appears to be acculturation to the assimilationists (1997, 881). John Higham had argued that the process of ethnic group formation itself was a "very successful, intermediate level of assimilation" (1981, 9). Theorists of the "invention of ethnicity" also agree that "ethnicization *is* Americanization" (Gerber, Morawska, and Pozzetta 1992, 60). Therefore, assimilation eventually seems to have prevailed over ethnic pluralism.

Race

Ethnic studies from the 1960s to the early 1990s focused almost exclusively on European immigrants and their descendants. They either completely left the race factor out of the research or reduced it to ethnicity or class. Michael Omi and Howard Winant (1986, 1994) have strongly contested these reductionist theories of race. Although race is not simply something fixed, concrete, and objective, they argue, the sociohistorical race concept continues to be "a fundamental *organizing principle* of social relationships" in the United States (1986, 65).

The race factor poses the greatest challenge to assimilationist theories. Facing this impediment, Robert Park in his later writings backed away from viewing assimilation as preordained and conceded that the "race relations cycle" could also end in a system of castes or one that included a permanent racial minority (Park 1950, 194–95; see also Kazal 1995, 445). There are ample evidences of race leading to structural separation of groups (Warner and Srole 1945; Glazer and Moynihan 1963; Gordon 1964). Recently, Nathan Glazer has argued that the discredit of the idea of assimilation since the 1960s was primarily due to the failure to include blacks (1993, 134).

However, racial group formation is not limited to the blacks. In the 1960s and 1970s the "Black Pride" or "Black Power" movement gave positive affirmation to black racial identity (see Vecoli 1985; Kazal 1995, 453). Some researchers have also raised the issue of "whether European immigrants and their children became American by being redefined as 'white' " (Kazal 1995, 468). Irish immigrants at first, then Jews, Italians, and Slavs who came to the United States around the turn of the century all managed to pass the progression from "not-yet-white ethnic" to the white race (Roediger 1991). Recent sociological research confirms a decline in ethnic differences among Americans of European origin, evidenced especially by a rise in intermarriage among non-Hispanic whites across both ethnic and religious lines (Alba 1990; Kazal 1995, 468–69). In other words, these descendants of European immigrants did not simply become *the* American, but became *white* Americans.

Moreover, experiences of non-European minorities are not simply a recapitulation of those of European immigrants or blacks. Children of European immigrants could choose as individuals to leave the ethnic community and blend in with the larger society (Child 1943; Whyte 1955). However, such individualistic assimilation is not viable for people who are members of racial minorities: blacks, Native Americans, Hispanics, and Asians (Takaki 1987). Because of phenotypical differences, few contemporary immigrants from Asia, Mexico, and Central America can "pass" as "white" in the same way as European immigrants did. Nor do they simply become the "colored" and readily join the blacks, as evidenced by the Mississippi Chinese in their struggle to achieve better status (Loewen [1971] 1988). The same social forces leading to the racial formation of black and white have also pushed for the emerging "Latino identity" (Moore and Pachon 1985) and "Pan-Asian American identity" (Espiritu 1992).

On the other hand, racial formation is a process of homogenization as well as diversification. Racial formation must involve a certain level of homogenization and integration beyond the limits of ethnic-group boundaries. Therefore, racialization *is* Americanization. However, this understanding of mid-level assimilation takes racial pluralism as an indispensable component and is thus a significant departure from classic assimilation theory that foresees immigrants melting into one common pot.

The Core Society and Culture

Classic theories of assimilation held a notion of the core into which the immigrant and minority groups were expected to assimilate:

> If there is anything in American life which can be described as an over-all American culture which serves as a reference point for immigrants and their children, it can best be described . . . as the middle-class cultural patterns of, largely, white Protestant, Anglo-Saxon origins. (Gordon 1964, 72)

However, the size of the core society and the significance of the core culture have greatly declined in the sea of pluralism in contemporary American society. Gordon used "the host society" to stand for the dominant subsociety composed of the Old Yankee families of colonial Anglo-Saxon ancestry (1964, 72). However, this center had acquired the status of an ethnic group by the 1960s, leaving little for other immigrant groups to assimilate to (Glazer and Moynihan 1963, 17–20). This has become even more evident today because of the increasing volume and diversity of new immigrants from Asia and South and Central America. By 1980 the "core society"—those who claim English ancestry—had shrunk to 22 percent of the total U.S. population (Lieberson and Waters 1988).

Nevertheless, the "core culture" may still persist to be the norm in the American society. Some people believe that no ethnic group has yet challenged the preeminence of the Anglo-Saxon core culture (Barkan 1995). Any influence of non-English populations on American culture is mostly on extrinsic rather than intrinsic features: "The basic Anglo-American core culture, shaped in the colonial era and modified by the new nation, has remained the guiding inspiration and ultimate standard of acceptance for two centuries" (Barkan 1995, 98). However, many other scholars disagree. They think that few people still believe in the unchanging cultural hegemony of an Anglo-Saxon core. Historian Russell Kazal succinctly pronounced: "The concept of an unchanging, monolithic, Anglo-American cultural core is dead" (1995, 437–38). He argues that the core culture collapsed amid the turmoil beginning in the 1960s, including the Civil Rights movement, the Vietnam War and the ensuing domestic turmoil, and the social movements of black separatism, feminism, sexual revolution, and gay liberation (1995, 453). Very different value systems have emerged, all claiming legitimacy in contemporary American society.

American Identity and Unity

Within such a reality of racial, ethnic, and cultural pluralism, what holds American society together? Responding to the challenges and turmoil in the 1960s, Robert Bellah (1968) articulated an American "civil religion," which would serve as the legitimating and unifying myth of the American nation. However, many scholars argue that the American civil religion has fallen into deep division: "Religious conservatives and liberals offer competing versions of American civil religion that seem to have very little of substance in common" (Wuthnow 1988, 244). Tensions of diverse value systems contending in the American mainstream have escalated to "culture wars" (Hunter 1991; see also Green et al. 1996). The culture wars are wracking America and leading to "the twilight of common dreams" (Gitlin 1995).

Many people instead emphasize political and ideological ideas. Will Herberg (1960) delineated "the American way of life" as the common faith of American society. This includes beliefs in democracy, free enterprise, and a social egalitarianism entwined with high mobility. Others called it the "American creed" (Myrdal 1944) or the "American idea" (Kallen 1956). Hans Kohn, a scholar of American nationalism, argued that American nationality rested on a structure of ideas about freedom, equality, and self-government (1957, 13). Many contemporary scholars also stress the unifying role of a common ideology (Gleason 1980; Glazer 1993). They believe that "America was held together by political allegiance alone. The wish to be free, the allegiance to the institutions of a free nation, made one American.

Consequently cultural differences were irrelevant to the nation" (Conzen et al. 1992, 10).

In the meantime, some scholars contend that American identity has never been fixed or complete, but has always been an arena subject to competition, contention, and conflict. They claim that the essence of Americanness is to "be different" and that people gain a sense of being American "by turning aspects of a carefully nurtured sense of separate identity against a vaguely defined concept of mainstream or dominant culture" (Moore 1986, xi). Jews and Catholics have been most American when they have resisted the process of blending into an "American way of life." Without necessarily becoming more typically American in their values than they ever were, Catholics, Jews, and Mormons have been granted mainstream status after World War II (Moore 1986, 100). The so-called civil religion is no more than "an arena of contested meanings where Americans make assertions about what makes them different from other Americans" (Moore 1986, 203). Moore's suggestions may be radical. However, in contemporary American society there are evidently diverse versions of American identity rather than one singular Americanness.

American society has become increasingly pluralistic in many dimensions—ethnic, racial, cultural, political, and religious. More importantly, pluralism has become more acceptable and appreciated. The diversification of American value systems and the segmentation of American society place new immigrants in a difficult situation. The "core culture" or the "American way of life," the referent point into which immigrants are supposed to assimilate, has become no longer perceivable or hardly accessible for contemporary immigrants. Instead, upon their arrival new immigrants encounter diverse value systems and multiple subsocieties. Making choices or selective assimilation becomes life's exigency, and different choices will lead to divergent destinies in the segmented American society.

Constructing Adhesive Identities Within Pluralism and Transnationalism

Recent theoretical developments in the research on new immigrants and their children are moving beyond the polarities of assimilation and pluralism. Three independently innovated concepts are important to this study, including "segmented assimilation," "transnationalism," and "adhesive pattern of adaptation." These are building blocks toward an integrated theory that recognizes the necessity and possibility of constructing adhesive identities among contemporary immigrants.

Segmented Assimilation

Focusing on the "new second generation" of post-1965 immigrants, a group of researchers (e.g., Portes and Zhou 1993; Portes and Rumbaut 1996) argue that the assimilation of contemporary immigrants and their children has become "segmented." Compared with pre–World War I European immigrants and their descendants, post-1965 immigrants face very different problems:

> First, descendants of European immigrants who confronted the dilemmas of conflicting cultures were uniformly white. Even if of a somewhat darker hue than the natives, their skin color reduced a major barrier to entry into the American mainstream. For this reason, the process of assimilation depended largely on individual decisions to leave the immigrant culture behind and embrace American ways. Such an advantage obviously does not exist for the black, Asian, and mestizo children of today's immigrants. (Portes and Zhou 1993, 76)

Second, the structure of economic opportunities has changed. The gap between minimally paid menial jobs and high-tech professional occupations has widened, which consequently reduces the opportunity for children of immigrants to move up the ladder of social mobility gradually through better-paid occupations. Under these new conditions, assimilation becomes divergent for different immigrants:

> Instead of a relatively uniform mainstream whose mores and prejudices dictate a common path of integration, we observe today several distinct forms of adaptation. One of them replicates the time-honored portrayal of growing acculturation and parallel integration into the white middle-class; a second leads straight in the opposite direction to permanent poverty and assimilation into the underclass; still a third associates rapid economic advancement with deliberate preservation of the immigrant community's values and tight solidarity. (Portes and Zhou 1993, 82)

Among these divergent paths, the first two are not completely new phenomena in the racial stratification structure (cf., Warner and Srole 1945; Glazer and Moynihan 1963); they are also called "whitening" and "blackening" processes by other scholars (Ong 1996). Beyond the contradiction of "black" and "white," however, the most theoretically intriguing is the third path in the "segmented assimilation" theory. Gordon (1964) believed that "cultural assimilation" would precede or concur with "structural assimilation." However, some new immigrant groups and their second-generation children achieve "structural assimilation" in their socioeconomic life but resist "cultural assimilation" in their private life—religion and the family. More important, within the contemporary context remaining securely ensconced in their ethnic community can be advantageous for immigrant minorities in achieving better socioeconomic status because it helps to capitalize on otherwise unavailable material and moral resources (Portes and Zhou 1993, 96). "Selective acculturation where learning American ways combines with continuing strong bonds with the ethnic community" may lead to positive outcomes in socioeconomic mobility (Portes and Rumbaut 1996, 250).

Structurally speaking, assimilation in contemporary America is "segmented" with divergent paths and destinies into various subsocieties. From the vantage point of immigrants, assimilation must be "selective"—they must choose the desired aspects of assimilation. Within multidimensional pluralism, making choices is a necessity, not a luxurious pleasure. Of course, different immigrants enjoy varied levels of resources and cultural and social capital, and they suffer from various obstacles.

Transnationalism

The segmented assimilation theory narrowly focuses on factors within U.S. borders. However, increasingly integrated economies and politics across nation-state borders, and advancements of communication and transportation technologies have created *transnationalism*, "the process by which immigrants forge and sustain multi-stranded social relations that link together their society of origin and settlement" (Basch et al. 1994, 7). An increasing number of contemporary migrants maintain dual or multiple "citizenships"—culturally, socially, and sometimes politically—such as among Caribbean and Filipino immigrants (Basch et al. 1994), Korean Americans (Min 1998), and Hong Kong and Southeast Asian emigrants in Canada, Australia, and the United States (Skeldon 1994; Ong and Nonini 1997). They build strong social networks linking their country of origin, their country of settlement, and sometimes extending the network to such settlements in several countries. Instead of being "uprooted" from the old world and "replanted" permanently in the new land, they are migrating back and forth between the host society and the original country. For transnational migrants who live lives across national borders and/or have family members living in different countries, complete assimilation into the host society by abandoning traditional culture and ethnic identity is neither desirable nor possible. Traditional culture and ethnic identity can be social and cultural capital transmutable into economic benefits and political opportunities. Meanwhile, given enough time and proper social environments, many transnational migrants or immigrants with transnational ties will learn the culture of, and achieve a certain level of identification with, the host society.

Adhesive Identities

The segmented assimilation and transnationalism theories point to domestic and international factors for the coexistence of assimilation and ethnic preservation. Kim and Hurh (1993, 700) use the phrase "adhesive pattern of adaptation" to describe the growing Americanization among Korean immigrants in some dimensions of social and cultural life while retaining or reinforcing significant parts of their ethnic lifestyle and social network. These immigrants "adhesively" attach certain forms of American identity to their existing ethnic identity.

The conceptualization of constructing "adhesive identities" brings a breakthrough in the study of assimilation and ethnicity. Instead of either assimilating by abandoning ethnicity or simply preserving ethnicity in sacrifice of assimilation, this new concept opens the possibility of holding both American and ethnic identities simultaneously. In reality, many immigrants desire subgroup belonging while striving for interaction with other Americans. Contemporary immigrants may not form separate ghettos isolated from the larger society. Many people join several and overlapping groups. Besides the more visible ethnic and racial groupings, new immigrants also join or create new social, political, and religious groups. For example, Haitian middle-class immigrants may willingly or involuntarily identify with blacks racially, but with middle-class Americans in lifestyles. Meanwhile, they also create their ethnic and cultural identity, and seek out a political or civil identity.

Americanization takes effect as immigrants join the processes of ethnicization, racialization, and so on. However, the traditional culture of the old country will not evaporate soon, and the original national or ethnic identification will not be easily replaced by an American identity. Within the increasingly integrated world system, the government of the country of origin, the globalizing world market, and the receiving country are all players influencing the identity construction of contemporary immigrants.

However, existing studies do not articulate how immigrants integrate these seeming polarities of becoming American and remaining ethnic. What is the mechanism for constructing adhesive identities? Segmented assimilation theorists point to the importance of the family and the immigrant community (Portes and Rumbaut 1996); some even clearly indicate the importance of ethnic community involvements for successful adaptations among second-generation children (Zhou and Bankston 1994; Bankston and Zhou 1995); but none of the empirical studies has investigated the dynamics of acculturation and ethnicity within well-defined immigrant communities—those that provide regular and frequent face-to-face interactions beyond the family.

Among various immigrant communities, the religious institution has been a fundamental organizational form among many immigrant groups (see Pozzetta 1991, vol. 19), including new immigrant groups such as Koreans (Hurh and Kim 1990; Min 1992) and South Asians (Fenton 1988; Williams 1988). Because religion is closely related to ethnic and American identities, and identification problems are frequently encountered in immigrant religious communities, the local religious congregation may serve as a major mechanism for constructing adhesive identities. However, researchers of new immigrants are often ill-equipped in theory and methodology to study religious communities, and frequently even have an antireligious bias (Warner 1998; see also Leong 1996; Yoo 1996).

Religion and Ethnicity

The close relationship between religion and ethnicity has long been recognized by sociologists (Durkheim 1947; Weber 1961), but not appreciated until the 1970s (Marty 1972; Dolan 1975; Smith 1978). Only recently has the complexity of the relationship become a focus of analysis (Hammond and Warner 1993; see also *Ethnic and Racial Studies* 20, no. 2, 1997). However, virtually no research has been done about assimilation and ethnicity among religious convert groups, although Latino Pentecostal and Asian American

Protestant churches have been a growing phenomenon in contemporary American society.

Classical theories of American religion have proclaimed "religious pluralism" over and against ethnicity. Will Herberg, its best-known advocate at the midcentury, believed that immigrants and their descendants would retain their traditional religion but abandon everything else of the old country:

> Sooner or later the immigrant will give up virtually everything he had brought with him from the "old country"—his language, his nationality, his manner of life—and will adopt the ways of his new home. Within broad limits, however, his becoming an American did not involve his abandoning the old religion in favor of some native American substitute. Quite the contrary, not only was he expected to retain his old religion, as he was not expected to retain his old language or nationality, but such was the shape of America that it was largely in and through his religion that he, or rather his children and grandchildren, found an identifiable place in American life. (1960, 27–28)

However, ethnic and racial pluralism did not go away just because religious pluralism was able to serve some social purposes. Many people found it impossible or undesirable to define themselves merely in terms of one of three religions—Protestantism, Catholicism, and Judaism. Actually, according to Marty (1972, 9), "ethnicity is the skeleton of religion in America." Ethnicity or national origin is one of the main sources for denominationalism in the United States (Niebuhr 1929; Pozzetta 1991, ix).

Amid the ethnic revival movements in the 1970s, many people began to emphasize the role of religion in creating and maintaining ethnicity. Some scholars argued that both ethnicity and religiosity are somewhat primordial and could mutually reinforce each other. For example, the identification of Catholicism and Irish nationalism or ethnicity in the United States is inseparable: "A more fruitful way of viewing the situation is to acknowledge that religion and ethnicity are intertwined, that religion plays an ethnic function in American society and ethnicity has powerful religious overtones" (Greeley 1971, 82). Dolan (1972, 360) found that "Religion and ethnicity were intimately bound up together in the national [Catholic] parish, and one supported the other." Timothy Smith (1978) believes that ethnic grouping is determined by the immigrant's identification with a particular religious tradition more than any other factor, such as common language, national feeling, or belief in a common descent. Traditional religious beliefs, customs, and loyalty "have been the decisive determinants of ethnic affiliation in America" (1174).

The religious factor in ethnic formation is further strengthened by the migration experience. The acts of uprooting, migration, and repeated resettlement produce the intensification of the psychic basis of religious commitment in the minds of new Americans, which reinforces attachments to the traditional religion (Smith 1978, 1174–75). Some even went further, claiming the indistinguishable oneness of ethnicity and religion and suggesting the term *ethnoreligion* (Stout 1975). However, the inseparability of ethnicity and religion might be applicable to certain groups, but not to others.

In reality, the relationship between religion and ethnicity varies among different groups. Andrew Greeley (1971, 42) first identified three types of the relationship: some religious people do not hold an ethnic identity; some have an ethnic identity but are not religious; but in most cases, religion and ethnicity are intertwined. Hammond and Warner (1993) further explicate the types of "intertwining relationships": The first is "ethnic fusion," where religion is the foundation of ethnicity, as in the case of the Amish and Jews. In this pattern ethnicity equals religion. The second is "ethnic religion," where religion is one of several foundations of ethnicity. The Greek or Russian Orthodox and the Dutch Reformed are examples. In this pattern, ethnic identification can be claimed without claiming the religious identification, but the reverse is rare. The third is "religious ethnicity," where an ethnic group is linked to a religious tradition that is shared by other ethnic groups. The Irish, Italian, and Polish Catholics are such cases. In this pattern religious identification can be claimed without claiming the ethnic identification. Hammond and Warner suggest that the relationship of religion and ethnicity is strongest in "ethnic fusion," and least strong in "religious ethnicity." Furthermore, in the case of "ethnic religion" it is more likely that ethnicity helps to uphold religion, while in the case of "religious ethnicity" it is more likely that religion helps to uphold ethnicity.

These typologies and analyses represent significant progress in the study of religion and ethnicity. However, the static typologies fail to encompass changes, especially the change of achieving nontraditional religions among some ethnic groups, such as Latino Pentecostals, Korean and Chinese Protestants, and Vietnamese Catholics. Existing theories and studies of general relationships between religion and ethnicity do not provide a base for postulating about convert groups. Common sense might lead us to assume that the newly achieved religious identity among immigrants would more likely help them to move away from their traditional culture and ethnic identity. However, it is also possible that the local religious community, where face-to-face interactions are frequent, may serve to uphold ethnic culture and identity. In other words, besides religious identity, religious institutions may exert powerful influence on assimilation and ethnicity.

The Roles of Immigrant Churches in Identity Construction

Empirical studies of various immigrant groups show that the immigrant church may serve both as an assimilation agency and a bastion for preserving traditional culture. These two functions seem contradictory, but they are not necessarily exclusive to each other. The real question for the empirical research is, what are the mechanisms of the assimilation function and the ethnicity function?

The Mechanism of the Assimilation Function

The mechanism of the assimilation function of the religious organization lies in the denominational hierarchy on the regional and national levels and in the American-born generations. Other forces for assimilation may come from the needs of the immigrants to accommodate the social, legal, economic, and religious environment in the United States.

Denominational hierarchy can impose policies either for religious uniformity or for Americanization. This is especially evident in the history of the Roman Catholic Church. According to Buczek (1976), most of the Catholic hierarchy, particularly between the two wars of the twentieth century, believed that "to Catholicize America we must Americanize the immigrants." Between 1870 and 1924 the number of Polish national parishes in the United States increased dramatically. Up to the 1930s there was unabated fervor to maintain the "Polishness" of the Polish national parishes. However, most Polish national parishes disintegrated after World War II. The dynamism for preserving Polish identity came largely from immigrant Polish clergy and immigrant parishioners, but the Irish-dominated hierarchy of bishops made efforts to promote the English language against the usage of Polish and other old country languages. The oft-repeated notion was that "We are in America, we should be Americans." A cardinal cited by Buczek stated:

> The American people in general, and the government of the United
> States in particular . . . expect the various nationalities to become

one people, one race, loyal to the government of this country. . . . It will be a disaster for the Catholic Church in the United States if it were ever to become known that the Polish Catholics are determined to preserve their Polish nationality and that there is among their clergy and leaders a pronounced movement of Polanization. (1976, 57)

The pressure to adopt English and American ways not only came from the hierarchy, but also from American-born generations. As the younger Polish-Americans questioned the usefulness of the Polish language, bishops were watchful for signs of disintegration in the national parishes. In 1938 the Holy See issued a declaration: "When foreign immigrants and their children speak the English language and do not wish to belong to their own national parishes, they must affiliate with the American territorial parish in which the English language may be spoken." This papal declaration was widely regarded as a blow to the future of the ethnic parishes by the Polish-speaking clergy, and a victory by the English-speaking clergy of America (Buczek 1976, 59–60). Protestant denominations may have played similar roles when they have tried to implement policies for ethnic integration and for uniformity of religious practice (see Alexander 1987).

In addition, there are other forces for assimilation beyond the control of the church. Coming from villages in the old country to cities in America, the early European immigrants often had to accommodate their life to the changed social, economic, political, and religious environments. The accommodation measures in the immigrant church would facilitate assimilation in the larger society.

The Mechanism of the Ethnicity Function

The effectiveness of the assimilation efforts of the denominational hierarchy should not be overstated. Rudolph Vecoli (1964, 1969) first questioned the efficacy of the role of the Catholic Church in Americanization by citing widespread anticlericalism among Italians and persistence of old religious practices. Following Vecoli, the research emphasis shifted away from attention to the forces of assimilation to those of cultural persistence. Many studies have shown that within a common religion of Catholicism, the church actually helped to reinforce ethnicity for diverse ethnic groups (e.g., Dolan 1972; Abramson 1973). It may seem puzzling to see that a universalistic religion would help to uphold ethnicity for various ethnic groups. However, the key to understanding this perplexing phenomenon lies in the local church, where face-to-face interaction of people happens frequently.

The establishment of ethnic churches, very often lay-initiated and controlled, served the purposes of cultural defense and religious adjustment. The ethnic parish, in contrast to the territorial parish, not only satisfied religious needs but also reinforced ethnic group consciousness and helped to preserve traditional culture (Dolan 1975). At the local church, the old dialects and language, religion, traditions, and customs were preserved to protect the immigrant group from social disorganization and the shock of adjustment to the new culture. The ethnic congregation contributes to ethnic attachment by increasing social interactions among co-ethnic members and by providing a social space for comfort, fellowship, and a sense of belonging. Many recent studies of new immigrant religions also highlight the ethnicity function of transplanted religious organizations (e.g., Williams 1988; B. Y. Choy 1979; Kim 1981; Hurh and Kim 1990; Min 1992).

During the process of adjustment to American life, the public education system offers both an opportunity to immigrants for future progress and a danger to valued traditions. Immigrants "reacted in various ways, ranging from the formation of separate educational initiatives that sought to maintain cherished values to the avoidance of formal educational institutions altogether" (Pozzetta 1991, ix). Very often European immigrant churches established their own parochial schools. A study (Mohl and Betten 1981) shows that the Catholic, Orthodox, Lutheran, and Jewish immigrant churches in Gary, Indiana, all had their own parochial schools. These parochial schools played an important role in preserving ethnic identity and culture by passing on the original language, customs, and cherished values to their children's generations.

The Chinese church under study has been a nondenominational independent church; therefore, the mechanism of assimilation through denominational hierarchy does not exist. However, because the majority of church members are converts to Christianity whose symbols are commonly shared in American culture, the church may still help to assimilate its members into the American culture. To understand the dramatic changes in their religious conversion, Americanization, and reconstruction of Chinese identity, in the following chapter, we will briefly review the history of Chinese immigration to the United States and Chinese cultural traditions.

2

Chinese Immigrants, Cultural Traditions, and Changing Identities

Chinese immigration to the United States has a history of about one and a half centuries. Until World War II, Chinese were unwelcome immigrants and were deprived of the right to become American citizens. Since the 1960s, however, Chinese immigrants have come in large numbers from diverse societies, including Taiwan, Hong Kong, the People's Republic of China, and Southeast Asian countries. Meanwhile, the American public has come to perceive Chinese-Americans as a successful or "model minority."

In the same period of the last one and a half centuries, China has been full of wars, revolutions, social turmoil, and natural disasters, which have pushed many people to emigrate. Chinese cultural traditions have received devastating attacks by Chinese intellectuals and political elites for the sake of modernizing China. Consequently, the meaning of Chineseness has significantly changed.

Within these social, cultural, and historical contexts, Chinese immigrants struggle to construct and reconstruct their identities. To understand the identity construction of Chinese Christians in America, this chapter provides a brief review of Chinese immigration and ethnic Chinese organizations, Chinese cultural traditions and their predicaments in modern times, and changing identities among Chinese in the diaspora.

Chinese Immigrants

Chinese immigrants began to arrive in the United States in large numbers in the late 1840s, but the Chinese-American population began to grow significantly only after the 1960s. According to the U.S. census, the Chinese constitute the largest Asian-American population, numbering 1,654,472 in 1990 (see Table 3).[1]

During the years of the Chinese Exclusion Acts (1882–1943), which barred Chinese immigration and naturalization, the Chinese population in the United States first decreased, then slowly grew. Legal Chinese immigration resumed in 1943 when the exclusion acts were repealed, albeit with a meager quota of 105 persons per year. Between 1945 and 1965, tens of thousands of Chinese came as refugees, war brides, and international students (Chinn 1969).[2] The Immigration and Nationality Act Amendments of 1965 established an annual quota of a maximum of 20,000 immigrants per country in the Eastern Hemisphere and allowed some immediate family members of U.S. citizens to immigrate without quota limits. Since then, Chinese immigrants have come continuously in large numbers.

Several special acts have contributed to the accelerating increase of Chinese immigrants, including the Indochina Migration and Refugee Assistant Act of 1975 (many Indochinese refugees were ethnic Chinese); the Taiwan Relations Act of 1979 (which treats Taiwan as a chargeable country with an annual quota of 20,000); the Immigration Reform and Control Act of 1986 (13,752 Chinese in the United States were granted legalization); the

Table 3. Chinese Population in the United States and the Washington, D.C., Area, 1860–1990

Year	Total in U.S.	Total in Washington Area
1860	34,933	—
1870	63,199	—
1880	105,613	—
1890	107,488	91
1900	89,863 (118,746)[a]	455
1910	71,531 (94,414)	369
1920	61,639 (85,202)	461
1930	74,954 (102,159)	398
1940	77,504 (106,334)	656
1950	117,629 (150,005)	1,825
1960	198,958 (237,292)	3,925[b]
1970	383,023 (431,583)	8,298
1980	806,042 (812,178)	18,250
1990	1,645,472	39,034

[a] The numbers in parentheses are probably adjusted numbers including Hawaii and Alaska (see note 2).
[b] The Metropolitan Washington, D.C., area (DC-MD-VA MSA) became a unit after the 1960 U.S. Census. Before that the numbers are those in the District of Columbia only.

Immigration Act of 1990 (which raises the quota for Hong Kong from 5,000 to 10,000 per year); and the Chinese Students Protection Act of 1992 (52,425 mainland Chinese in the United States adjusted to immigrant status). The rapid growth of Chinese immigrants continues in the 1990s.

In the first hundred years of Chinese immigration to the United States, most people came as laborers from the surrounding rural areas of Guang-zhou (Canton) in the Southern province of Guangdong. The Chinese community usually refers to them as *laoqiao* (earlier immigrants), whereas people who have come since the 1960s are referred to as *xinqiao* (new immigrants).

Earlier Chinese Immigrants and Chinatown Organizations

Earlier Chinese immigrants were also called "sojourners" because they commonly wanted to retire to China after making a fortune in America. In the nineteenth century Chinese laborers first worked in the gold mines along the West Coast, then in cross-continental railroad construction. However, anti-Chinese violence and discrimination laws in the western coastal states, and the Chinese Exclusion Act passed in 1882 by the U.S. Congress drove many Chinese back to China or to other countries. Some escaped from the hostile West Coast and moved eastward to Chicago, New York, Boston, and Washington, D.C. (Sung 1967; Daniels 1988). The first group of Chinese arrived in the U.S. capital by 1890.

Responding to the hostile climate and racist violence, Chinese immigrants retreated into Chinatowns in the big cities. These urban ghettos, to a certain extent, shielded these people from outside dangers, forged a sense of community solidarity, and constructed a familiar cultural environment. Economically, Chinese immigrants depended on laundries, restaurants, gift shops, and domestic services. Politically, they were deprived of the right of naturalization, which reinforced their national allegiance to China. Although they wished to return to their ancestral homeland to retire, many either failed to achieve the necessary wealth or decided to make their homes in this land. Until the 1960s, Chinatown was very much a "bachelor society" crowded by men (Nee and Nee 1973). These male "sojourners" either failed to marry or were unable to bring their wives to the United States because of immigration restrictions. The sex ratio was extremely unbalanced for many decades, with 26.8 Chinese males for every female in 1890. The ratio gradually declined to 2.9 by 1940. Meanwhile, American-born Chinese slowly increased, and for the first time outnumbered the foreign-born Chinese by 1940 (Sung 1967; M. G. Wong 1995).

World War II was a turning point for the Chinese. The great demand for manpower during the war opened doors for Chinese Americans to engineering and professional jobs. The alliance of the United States and China during the war prompted repeal of the Chinese Exclusion Acts in 1943. Legal immigration resumed. Longtime residents who had been barred from naturalization began to achieve citizenship. Thanks to several war-related acts, large numbers of Chinese women immigrated to the United States. By 1960 the ratio of Chinese men to Chinese women declined to 1.4, and the American-born Chinese comprised nearly 60 percent of the Chinese-American population (see M. G. Wong 1995). Many Chinese experienced upward mobility in socioeconomic status.

In traditional Chinatowns, the dominant ethnic organizations were *huiguan* and *tang* (Lyman 1974). *Huiguan* were based on primordial sentiments, including home-district associations and clan (or same-surname) associations. For those who were unable to join a *huiguan,* there were *tang* (triads or secret societies), which were based on fraternal principles (Pan 1994; Wickberg 1994). Membership in these associations was not voluntary but was often ascribed or forced upon persons.

Above these separate and competing *huiguan* and *tang* was the umbrella Chinese Consolidated Benevolent Association (CCBA). The CCBA coordinated and mediated among its member associations and represented the Chinese community to the larger society. These ethnic organizations provided many services to Chinatown Chinese, including housing and employment, social support and protection, credit union and financial help, medical clinics and evacuation service in case of death, and mediation service in case of disputes. These organizations also mobilized Chinese immigrants to support China's "Xinhai Revolution" (1911), which overthrew the Qing Empire and established the Republic of China, and the Anti-Japanese War (1937–45). Since the 1950s, when the anti-Communist McCarthyism was strong, the CCBA and most Chinatown organizations have sided with the Guomindang (Kuomintang) government in Taiwan (the Republic of China) and expressed opposition to the Chinese Communists in the mainland (the People's Republic of China).[3]

Formal religious institutions were almost absent in early Chinatowns. Some "joss houses" (halls of gods) provided a space for worshiping a variety of gods and spirits, some from Buddhism and Daoism (Taoism) and some only known to a particular Chinese village or district.[4] A joss house was primarily for individual rituals, not for congregating with fellow believers. Many families and businesses, such as restaurants, had private in-house shrines for ancestors and/or a mixture of gods and spirits. *Huiguan* and *tang* also had some religious dimensions in their organization and activities (B. P. Wong 1982, 17–21; Tsai 1986, 48–49). The same-district associations often kept shrines to their own local heroes and tutelary deities. The clan associations always performed rituals of venerating common ancestors, real or imagined. The triads commonly held cultic practices. Organized Chinese Buddhist and Daoist groups and temples began to appear in the United States only after the 1960s (Yu 1996).

As noted in the Introduction, Christian missions to Chinese immigrants began in the 1850s. However, amid persisting anti-Chinese social sentiments, some early Christian missions were closed, while others tenaciously survived in or near Chinatowns. These mission churches had only limited success in terms of converting the Chinese in part because of the anti-Chinese social environments and in part because of missionaries' racist, nativist, and paternalistic attitudes toward the Chinese (Woo 1983; Fung 1989; Tseng 1994). Nonetheless, these churches provided a place for Chinese immigrants to learn English, to learn American values and lifestyles, to receive social services, and to meet non-Chinese Americans (Loewen 1971; Weiss 1974; Pan 1994; Wickberg 1994).

During the Civil Rights movement in the 1960s and 1970s, some new forms of Chinese ethnic organizations arose in Chinatowns, including community service agencies, political organizations, and recreational clubs (Weiss 1974; B. P. Wong 1982). These new organizations promoted the interaction between ethnic Chinese and the larger society. Some brought in money with governmental financial programs to improve social and economic situations of the Chinatown community. The Organization of Chinese Americans (OCA), which was established in the 1970s, has mobilized Chinese American citizens to participate in American politics and society, and lobbied the United States Congress and the administration on behalf of Chinese Americans. The OCA has headquarters in Washington, D.C., and branches in every metropolitan area where there is a sizable Chinese population.

The Chinatown in Washington, D.C., has a short history. It was not until the 1930s that Chinese immigrants in the District of Columbia consolidated their collectivity in the Chinatown between 6th and 7th Streets on H Street, Northwest. Because of this short history, traditional Chinatown organizations had a limited influence. The Chinese Consolidated Benevolent Association (CCBA) was formed only in 1955. Interestingly, the founding organizations of the CCBA included the Chinese Community Church, which was formed in 1935. A Chinese Christian church so integral in the Chinatown community was not common in traditional Chinatowns.[5]

New Chinese Immigrants and New Ethnic Associations

Chinese immigrants since the 1960s, like other Asian immigrants but in contrast with early Chinese immigrants, are characterized by their urban background, high educational attainment, and professional occupations before immigration (B. P. Wong 1982; Min 1995). This is due to the new immigration laws that established a preference system favoring skilled workers. Many Chinese came first as students and then adjusted to permanent resident status upon achieving graduate degrees and finding employment. Hence, most people work as professionals in nonethnic companies or as technocrats in government agencies. The ethnic economies have changed too: Chinese restaurants have boomed, hand-wash laundries have disappeared, travel agencies with service specialties for trans-Pacific air routes have arisen, and real estate and insurance companies have Chinese agents for the growing market among Chinese residents. Most new Chinese immigrants have bypassed the urban ghetto Chinatown and settled in ethnically mixed suburbs. For these new immigrants, the ethnic community is no longer a geographically separate enclave, but is a community scattered in the metropolis. Because they came during and after the Civil Rights movement, they usually suffer less discrimination than their predecessors.

Meanwhile, the Chinese population has become very diverse in many respects. First, a significant division exists between *laoqiao* (earlier immigrants) and *xinqiao* (new immigrants). The new immigrants "consider themselves more genteel, more literate, and more modern as most of them have lived in urban areas of China or Hong Kong. They feel that the [earlier] settlers who came from rural areas of the old country are bumpkins with unrefined manners" (B. P. Wong 1994, 237). Second, linguistic diversity has become very apparent. Taishanese, commonly spoken by people from the Taishan district of Guangdong, was once the lingua franca in American Chinatowns; then it was replaced by the standard Cantonese as spoken in the cities of Hong Kong, Macau, and Canton. Mandarin has become increasingly common in and outside Chinatowns. Mandarin is the official dialect of China (*guoyu* or *putonghua*) that every educated Chinese is supposed to be able to speak, no matter what his or her mother tongue is. However, some people from Taiwan cling to Taiwanese, which is a variation of Minnanese or Fujianese. Many Cantonese-speaking Hong Kong immigrants know little or no Mandarin. Moreover, many ethnic Chinese from Southeast Asia speak none of the Chinese dialects but instead speak Vietnamese, Malaysian, Tagalog, or English.

Third and more important, the sociopolitical background of new Chinese immigrants is very complex. In the 1950s to 1970s, many Chinese immigrants were the uprooted and rootless people. They were born in the mainland under the rule of Guomindang's Republic of China, escaped from wars or fled the Communist mainland, then wandered around in several places—Taiwan, Hong Kong, or Southeast Asia—before coming to the United States. Socially and politically, they often have connections with the Republic of China in Taiwan. Meanwhile, many also have strong attachments to their birthplace in mainland China and hold a vision of a united and strong Chinese nation. Also from Taiwan and Hong Kong are these people's sons and daughters. Growing up during the economic boom in Taiwan or Hong Kong, this generation generally has less attachment to mainland China than their parents' generation, although their Chinese national identity can be similarly strong. Some Taiwan natives, whose families have lived in Taiwan for three or more generations, have become sympathizers or supporters of the Taiwan independence movement.

Beginning in the early 1980s, tens of thousands of students and scholars from the People's Republic of China came to the United States. Some of them adjusted to immigrant status upon finding employment. After the Tiananmen Square incident in 1989, when the student-led democracy movement in Beijing was violently suppressed by the Chinese Communist government, the U.S. Congress passed the Chinese Student Protection Act in 1992. Under this act 52,425 Chinese nationals in the United States achieved permanent residence (INS 1996). These mainland Chinese commonly have great concern for China's economic modernization and political democratization and for the unification of Taiwan and mainland China. In addition, many ethnic Chinese have come as refugees from Indo-Chinese countries since the mid-1970s. They had suffered doubly—first as Chinese minorities in the hostile societies, then banished by the Communists in those countries. Ethnic Chinese from Malaysia, Indonesia, the Philippines, and other countries also experienced ethnic discrimination or political persecution.

All of the aforementioned linguistic and sociopolitical groups share similar challenges from yet another group—the American-born Chinese (ABC) and the American-raised Chinese (ARC). These second-generation or "1.5-generation" children of immigrants speak English as their first language or as the only language they can speak. Compared with their immigrant parents, ABCs and ARCs usually have greater concern for the social and political issues of the United States. In addition there are, of course, people of third- and fourth-generation Chinese descent. With such diversity, Chinese identity becomes extremely complicated in contemporary American society.

The growing Chinese population and increasing heterogeneity have been accompanied by the burgeoning growth of various Chinese associations in the last three decades (B. P. Wong 1982). Many *tongxianghui* (same-district associations) have emerged, but with expanded boundaries to the province or a cluster of provinces. In the Greater Washington area, there are provincial *tongxianghui* of Beijing, Fujian, Henan, Shandong, and Shanghai as well as associations across provinces or even countries, including the *Dongbei* (the three provinces of Northeast China), the *Jiangzhehu* (the provinces of Jiangsu and Zhejiang and the city of Shanghai), and the *Indochinese Association* (Chinese from Vietnam, Cambodia and Laos). Compared with the old same-district associations (*huiguan*) in Chinatown, these new *tongxianghui* are more voluntary than ascribed in membership, and serve mostly for networking and socials. Because people live scattered in suburbs, interactions among association members are not as frequent and intense as in the Chinatown organizations.

An entirely new type of Chinese organization is alumni associations of Chinese universities. In the Greater Washington area, there are more than thirty alumni associations of the major universities in Taiwan and mainland China. This reflects the social status or educational achievement of many new Chinese immigrants. These alumni associations hold frequent activities of lectures, forums, karaoke dancing, and so on.

Meanwhile, the number of Chinese weekend language schools (*zhongwen xuexiao*) has rapidly increased. Currently in the Washington metropolitan area, more than thirty Chinese schools are teaching Chinese language and cultural customs at levels from kindergarten to high school. These schools are not only for children, but also function as a weekly social occasion for their parents. Some schools provide *qigong* or *taiji* classes for the parents. The content of teaching at these Chinese schools is politically and culturally diverse. Most Chinese schools teach Mandarin, although a few teach Cantonese or Taiwanese. Most schools use textbooks imported from Taiwan, teach traditional Chinese characters, and adopt the traditional *bopomofo* spelling system. Recently mainland Chinese have established Chinese schools for their children, which teach simplified Chinese characters used in the People's Republic of China (PRC) and adopt the spelling system of *hanyu pinyin*. These pedagogical differences often have political implications—pro-PRC, pro-ROC, or pro-Taiwan independence.

The establishment of diplomatic relations between the United States and the PRC in 1979 caused some angry protests by those Chinese loyal to Guomindang. Today the political stands of Chinese Americans toward China are much more diverse. The Guomindang supporters split before the first direct presidential election in Taiwan in March 1996, with one camp pro–Lee Teng-hui and the other pro–Lin Yang-kang. The central controversy was about the unification of Taiwan with mainland China. The pro–Lin Yang-kang camp, which appeared to be a larger group, worried that incumbent Lee Teng-hui's ambiguous stands on unification could draw Taiwan and mainland China into a disastrous war. Besides these, the "Taiwan *tongxianghui*" rallied open sympathizers for the Taiwan independence movement. Since the late 1980s, many mainland Chinese have formed their own associations, but they are either apolitical or parts of anti-Communist democracy movements.

In spite of these political fractions, the ethnic media seem to have significant influence in forging a sense of Chinese community. Several Chinese language newspapers and monthly magazines are widely circulated in the greater Washington area. Some are nationally or even internationally syndicated, reporting current events in Asia as well as local events of concern to Chinese people.

Chinese religious groups have increased too. Buddhism is the most prominent traditional religion among Chinese Americans, with about 150 temples and local associations in the United States (Yu 1996). Two sects or denominations have many branch temples in major metropolitan areas. One is the International Buddhist Progress Society, headquartered at the Hsi Lai Temple in the Los Angeles area. The Hsi Lai Temple, built in 1988, is the largest overseas branch of the Fo Kuang Shan (Buddha Light Mountain) in Taiwan, which was founded in 1967 by Hsing-yun, a mainland-born monk in the Chan Buddhist tradition (I. Lin 1996). Another Chinese Buddhist sect is the True Buddha Sect (*zhenfo zong*), which was founded in the mid-1980s in Seattle, Washington, by Lu Shengyan, an immigrant from Taiwan. The True Buddha Sect is more of a syncretic type in the Vajrayana (Tibetan Buddhist) tradition. There are also many independent Chinese Buddhist temples and groups in major metropolises of the United States.

In the greater Washington area, two Buddhist centers and a syncretic Tianhou temple have been established in the last decade or so. Most participants in the Buddhist centers are immigrants from Taiwan and Hong Kong, whereas the Tianhou temple is mostly for ethnic Chinese from Indochina. Meanwhile, many nontraditional Chinese religions are working to recruit Chinese immigrants. In the Washington area, there are a Chinese Mormon Ward, two Catholic churches, and more than twenty Chinese Protestant churches. Obviously, Protestant churches are the most numerous religious institutions among Chinese Americans. Nationally, there were at least 700 Protestant churches in 1994, and given the rapid rate of establishing new churches in the last four years, the number has probably reached 900 in 1998. Chinese churches usually begin as monolingual churches, either Mandarin, Cantonese, or Taiwanese. Before long, however, many become trilingual in English, Mandarin, and one other Chinese dialect.

In brief, Chinese associations and organizations are numerous, diverse, and often unrelated to each other. Chinese people are divided by political stands, cultural orientations, and socioeconomic status in American society. Ethnic associations help to maintain Chinese identity one way or another; however, sociopolitical tensions and frictions among these ethnic associations have fragmented the Chinese community. Nevertheless, the fragmented Chinese community shares common cultural traditions.

Chinese Cultural Traditions

The Chinese claim an uninterrupted culture of five thousand years with rich religious and cultural traditions. Confucianism, Daoism (Taoism), and Buddhism were the major traditions, accompanied by a great variety of popular religions or cultic practices developed in relation to these three traditions (C. K. Yang 1961; Thompson 1989; Ching 1993). In the last two centuries, however, Chinese traditions have faced great challenges from the West, including the challenge of Christianity. Responding to the modern or modernization forces, "iconoclastic nationalism" arose in the early decades of the twentieth century. Chinese cultural traditions and their modern transformation provide both resources and burdens for Chinese Christians in America in their identity construction.

Chinese Orthodoxy and Heterodoxies

In traditional China, Confucianism was the orthodoxy, while Daoism and Buddhism had profound influences. In fact, Confucian tradition is often seen as synonymous with Chinese culture (de Bary 1981; Tu 1985, 1991). Strictly speaking, however, the term *Confucianism* is a misnomer coined by Jesuit missionaries in the seventeenth century and has no Chinese equivalent. The Chinese term for Confucianism is *rujia* (the "scholarly tradition"). Confucius (*kong fu zi*, 552?–479 B.C.) is commonly recognized as the founder of this tradition, but many Confucian notions were embedded in the ancient classics before the time of Confucius.[6]

The fundamental concern of Confucianism is the person and human relationships in this world. It sanctifies human institutions—families, schools, societies, and states. The Confucian humanist concern for personal well-being, family harmony, social solidarity, political stability, and universal peace has become a defining characteristic of the Chinese view of the good life (Tu 1991). A core concept of Confucianism is *ren* (also as *jen*, or humanity, benevolence, and love; see Chan 1967). *Ren* means an attitude of harmony and goodness that is to prevail between two persons. It is the foundation of all virtues. "In essence, *jen* involves love for all and at the same time specific virtues in one's various social relations. In other words, in its oneness it is universal love for all, while in its multiplicity it operates as filial piety, brotherly respect, and so forth in various human relations" (Chan 1967, xxii).

The primary virtue in Confucian ethics is *xiao* (also as *hsiao*, or filial piety). It puts the family in the center of human society and regards filial piety as the basis of proper human relations. Among the "five basic relationships" (*wulun*)—ruler-minister, father-son, husband-wife, elder-younger brothers, and friend-friend—three are family relationships, while the other two are usually conceived in terms of the family models. The ruler-minister relationship resembles the father-son, and friendship resembles brotherliness.

Confucianism was not merely a system of ethics or a philosophy of life. It also had a ritual aspect, including the cult of Heaven, the cult of ancestors, and the cult of Confucius. The ritual system was hierarchical: the worship of Heaven was performed as a prerogative by the emperor, the worship of Confucius was mandated by edict for all government officials and would-be officials, and the worship of ancestors was practiced by all people (Ching 1993).

Confucian orthodoxy was enforced by the imperial state, especially through the imperial examination system (*keju zhidu*). This examination system was the mechanism for selecting imperial bureaucrats, and individuals of all social strata who had a Confucian education could pass the exams and become qualified for government offices. Consequently, education was the key means for upward social mobility in traditional China. This emphasis on education has continual influence among the Chinese. Another institutional pillar of Confucianism was the family and clan structure. The traditional patriarchal kinship structure and the Confucian emphasis on filial piety and obedience to the elders (*xiao shun*) mutually reinforced each other. In the process of modernization, however, the imperial pillar was broken off; and the foundation of the other pillar, the family, has been significantly eroded. The transmission of Confucian values thus fell into deep crisis. I will return to this later in this chapter.

Daoism is another indigenous Chinese tradition. Its origins can be traced back to the same ancient classics used by Confucianism, but the key text is the *Dao De Jing* (*Tao-Te Ching*), which is ascribed to Laozi (Lao-tzu), a contemporary of Confucius. The central principle of Daoism is the Dao (Tao), the concept that has given this tradition its name. "Dao" is a commonly used term, meaning road, way, method, principle, truth, or words. However, in *Dao De Jing* it is a mystical force. *Dao De Jing* begins with this verse:

> The Dao which can be told is not the constant Dao.
> The name which can be named is not the constant name.

Chapter XXV of *Dao De Jing* explains some attributes of the Dao:

> There is an integral being, born before heaven and earth.
> Silent! Void! Self-independent and unchanging, ever moving
>   and unwearying.
> It can be called the mother of the heaven and the earth.
> I know not its name, reluctantly call it the "Dao," hesitantly
>   name it as the "Great."
> . . . .
> The person models on earth, earth on heaven, heaven on
>   the Dao, and the Dao on itself.

Many philosophers and religionists have tried to interpret the mystic Dao in *Dao De Jing*, but disagreements have been myriad. Today, some Chinese Christians are offering a new interpretation, which I will discuss in Chapter 5.

The development of Daoism took two divergent paths: one is philosophical Daoism (*Dao jia*); the other is religious Daoism (*Dao jiao*). Philosophical Daoism acted like the yin to the Confucian yang. For centuries, the ruling class of the literati read both Confucian and Daoist classics. A man would be a Confucian in office and a Daoist out of office. In office, he would carry out Confucian ideals of governing the society and maintaining the order and peace. Out of office, he would become a Daoist, pursuing personal spiritual cultivation. At its extreme, Daoist philosophy shows a completely eremitical distaste for politics and makes an ardent plea for spiritual freedom both from ethical restraints and from limitations of one's own mind. Such freedom can only be discovered in embracing the Dao and nature. Meanwhile, religious Daoism developed into a mixture of some notions of Daoist philosophy, ancient animist beliefs, and various shamanistic practices. Religious Daoism also established monastic and hereditary systems, developed elaborate rituals, and formed a hierarchical pantheon composed of the supreme God, many gods, spirits, and ghosts, in which Laozi was deified as well. The Daoist religion was also diffused through numerous eclectic popular religions.

Daoism and Confucianism share many terminologies, such as Dao (Tao) and yin and yang, and indeed share a great deal in their cosmology and ontology. Compared with the Confucian focus on human relations, Daoism is more articulate in cosmology, ontology, and personal spirituality. Confucianism emphasizes the importance of human action and this-worldly asceticism, whereas Daoism proclaims "inaction" (*wuwei*) and "spontaneity" (*ziran*). Since the Han Dynasty (206 B.C. to A.D. 220), Confucianism became the state orthodoxy, whereas Daoism functioned as a major heterodoxy.

At about the time when Daoist religion was in creation, Buddhism was introduced to China and soon attracted enthusiastic response from many people. While Confucianism and Daoist philosophy continued to dominate among the ruling elites, Buddhism and Daoist religion had particular appeal to the populace. Buddhism brought in many notions and values radically alien to the orthodox Confucianism and the indigenous Daoist religions. The confrontation and conflict between Buddhism on the one hand and Confucianism and Daoism on the other hand sometimes became fierce and violent, as shown in the bloody suppressions of Buddhism by the dynastic state. Eventually, Buddhism accepted the orthodox position of Confucianism, adjusted its teachings to the Confucian ethics, and became Sinicized (*hanhua*) in form. Subsequently, Buddhism took root in China and became an integral element of Chinese culture. "Buddhism is of foreign origin, but it has been so assimilated into Chinese culture that the untutored common man in China is no longer aware that it was introduced from India" (C. K. Yang 1961, 21).

Buddhism provides an explanation about the sufferings of life—from birth to aging, illness, and death. It proclaims the illusiveness of worldly life and suggests paths to the blissful nirvana. Chinese Buddhism inherited the basic Buddhist teachings and developed into many indigenous sects or denominations. The most popular ones were Chan (Ch'an or Zen) among the literati and the Pure Land among the populace. Chan Buddhism emphasizes that enlightenment has to be achieved through one's own efforts, while Pure Land Buddhism believes that escaping the "soul transmigration," or being reborn into the blissful "Pure Land," must rely on faith in "other-power." Chan meditation halls often show a preference for simplicity, with little religious ornamentation, and reflect a history of iconoclasm. Pure Land temples, on the other hand, manifest a baroque-like exuberance with a multiplicity of Buddhas, Bodhisattvas, and Lohans. Similar to religious Daoism, Buddhism was diffused through many eclectic popular religions.

Confucian orthodoxy in dynastic times allowed religious pluralism, including Daoism, Buddhism, and many other religions. An important question to this study, therefore, is: Is Confucianism a religion? This question has been subject to debate in modern times. Generally speaking, most Chinese people do not see Confucianism as a religion, whereas Western scholars of comparative religion often treat it as one of the religions. The controversy over the religious nature of Confucianism is partly due to an etymological problem. The English word *religion*, or the Latin *religio*, had no matching word in traditional Chinese language. In traditional China Confucianism was called one of the three *jiao*—teachings or doctrines. The Chinese term *zongjiao* (religion) came to exist only in the late nineteenth century when Western writings were translated into Chinese. The word *zongjiao* is composed of the character *zong* (clan lineage) and the character *jiao* (teaching). In the modern debates about whether Confucianism is a religion, people who *honor* Confucianism as a religion argue for the religious nature of certain Confucian doctrines, such as transcendence and self-perfection; whereas those who *stigmatize* Confucianism as a religion often highlight the ritualistic dimension of Confucianism as *lijiao* (religion of rites and propriety). This Confucian *lijiao* has received fierce attacks since the May Fourth Movement (1919) and has been mostly abolished in modern China, as we will see below.

Responding mainly to Western scholarship, some Chinese scholars argue for the "religious dimension" of Confucianism (e.g., Tu 1989) or regard Confucianism as a "diffused religion" (e.g., C. K. Yang 1961). However, these scholars also acknowledge that Confucianism is substantially different; it is not an organized religion comparable to other world religions. Most scholars agree that Confucianism is essentially a form of humanism, a system of ethics or moral values. Some insist that Confucian humanism is "religious humanism" or one that is open to religious notions (Tu 1989, 97; Ching 1993, 52). In this regard, the "unity of humanity and Heaven" (*tianren heyi*) as the highest Confucian ideal of the self-realization may open the possibility of talking about the transcendent or Heaven (*Tian*). However, "Heaven" in Confucianism is ambiguous and feeble. Tu Wei-ming, an eminent contemporary interpreter of Confucianism, acknowledges, "Certainly the idea of theistic God, not to mention the 'wholly other,' is totally absent from the symbolic resources of the Confucian tradition" (1989, 116). Confucius himself and most ancient Confucian scholars have no clear teaching about life beyond this world. Confucianism exclusively focuses on things in this world, regarding "the secular as the sacred" (Fingarette 1972).

In traditional China, there were tensions and periodic conflicts between Confucianism on the one hand and religious Daoism and Buddhism on the other. However, the three great teachings (*san jiao*) generally did not compete on the same level. What Confucians insisted on were moral values and political allegiance. As long as the essential Confucian values were not seriously challenged and the orthodox position not jeopardized, orthodox Confucianism made peace with all religions. Confucian orthodoxy defined Chineseness, or more accurately, "civilizedness," and all religions had to accommodate the basic Confucian ethics in order to be accepted as Chinese. However, it left the religious space of supernatural and superhuman matters open to competition by all religions. In this sense, I agree that Confucianism is not a religion, but a system of ethics. This nonreligious nature of Confucianism makes it possible for Chinese Christians to claim their Chinese identity while adopting a nontraditional Chinese religion.

Chinese Orthopraxy: Rituals, Symbols, and the Language

Contrary to the "orthodoxy" claims, some anthropologists believe that it was Chinese orthopraxy that united Chinese culture in religious pluralism, across the vast land, and over centuries. Orthopraxy (correct practice) reigned over orthodoxy (correct belief) as the principal means of attaining and maintaining cultural unity. "From the perspective of ordinary people, to be Chinese was to understand and accept the view that there was a correct way to perform key rituals associated with the life cycle, namely, the rites of birth, marriage, death, and ancestorhood" (Watson 1993, 87). "A key element in China's unified culture was acceptance of particular standardized rituals. Through participation in such rituals one was Chinese, and one was civilized. The use of ritual to validate cultural status is indicative of the Chinese focus on proper behavior rather than on proper ideas, on orthopraxy rather than orthodoxy" (Cohen 1994, 92). The arguments for Chinese orthopraxy over orthodoxy may have anthropologists' penchant, but they do suggest an important dimension of cultural identity among all people, whether elites or ordinary people. This is the symbolic dimension of Chinese identity.

Anthropologists have done extensive research on death rituals in various areas of China and found a surprising degree of consistency of ritual patterns (see Watson and Rawski 1988).[7] However, anthropological studies so far have focused mostly on a limited set of rituals—funerals, weddings, and ancestral worship—which often have obvious religious meanings. But there are also many important secular festivals. For instance, the Chinese New Year's Day is not a religious holy day of Confucianism, of Daoism, or of

Buddhism. Nonetheless, it is a very important day that all Chinese celebrate. Participation in the festival celebration creates and fortifies a sense of being united with other participants, a sense of shared tradition, and a ritualistic sense of being part of a great community. Different people may attach very different meanings to the festivity, religious or secular, but the New Year's Day itself is not a religious holiday. Besides rituals, there are also various cultural symbols that are characteristically Chinese, such as those commonly seen in Chinese paintings and sculptures. These are important things that Chinese Christians have to deal with in their reconstruction of the Chinese identity.

Language has a special position in the symbolic system. The Chinese language is quite unique among languages in the world. The ideographic (nonphonetic) script cuts across numerous speaking dialects. Many Chinese dialects are mutually unintelligible, but the written characters and grammar are very much the same. Thus written Chinese language provides an uninterrupted, rich resource of literature spanning several millennia. Both the universality of the Chinese script and the continuity of the voluminous heritage in this language are grounds on which Chinese may build their national or ethnic pride. The historical consciousness informed by this literature is powerful:

> The collective memory of the educated Chinese is such that when they talk about Tu Fu's (712–770) poetry, Sima Qian's (died c. 85 B.C.) *Historical Records*, or Confucius's *Analects*, they refer to a cumulative tradition preserved in Chinese characters, a script separable from and thus unaffected by phonological transmutations. An encounter with Tu Fu, Sima Qian, or Confucius through ideographic symbols evokes a sensation of reality as if their presence was forever inscribed in the script. (Tu 1994, 3–4)

Many scholars agree that the Chinese language is a strong factor upholding Chinese cultural unity. "In addition to consciousness of history, the Chinese language itself provides another, even more constant, reinforcement of deeply-embedded notions of propriety, dignity, and Chineseness" (Link 1994, 195; also see Watson 1993, 81; Cohen 1994, 89–92).

Iconoclastic Nationalism

Modern Chinese history began with humiliation when British gunboats knocked down the door of the Qing Empire in the Opium War (1840–42).

This was followed by numerous domestic troubles and foreign aggressions that put the Chinese nation in danger of devastation and Chinese culture in danger of demolition. Chinese identity thus fell into deep crisis. Tu Wei-ming aptly recapitulates China's turbulent modern history and the troubles of being Chinese today:

> The untold suffering of the Chinese people—caused by Western imperialism, the Taiping Rebellion, the collapse of the Manchu dynasty, the internecine struggle of the warlords, Japanese aggression, the conflict between the Nationalists and the Communists, and the misguided policies of the People's Republic of China—contextualized the meaning of Chineseness in a new symbolic structure. Marginality, rootlessness, amnesia, anger, frustration, alienation, and helplessness have gained much salience in characterizing the collective psyche of the modern Chinese. (Tu 1994b, vii)

Since the mid–nineteenth century, various imported or invented "isms" have been advocated, but each social experimentation ended with further and deeper frustration. At the beginning, under the banner of *zhongti xiyong* (Chinese substance and Western appliance), the Chinese tried to adopt Western technology while refusing Western culture. They insisted on the superiority of Chinese culture over Western barbarian imperialism. However, this did not enable the Chinese to defend their country against imperialist aggressions. Then, under the banner of "Mr. De and Mr. Sai" (democracy and science), they tried to adopt the prevalent modern Western political philosophies, including pragmatism, realism, liberalism, and social Darwinism, but rejected the "outmoded" Christian religion. Chinese traditional culture was also denounced as part of the backward feudalism. Eventually, Marxism-Leninism, the revolutionary doctrines invented in Europe and developed in Russia, achieved the new orthodox position on mainland China.

In this process, traditional Chinese culture received repeated attacks. When the imperial examination system was abolished in 1905, the orthodoxy of Confucianism immediately collapsed. The May Fourth Movement in 1919 initiated an iconoclastic nationalism with radical antitradition sentiments—saving the Chinese nation through radically rejecting Chinese traditional culture (Y. Lin 1979; Tu 1987). A slogan of the movement was "Down with the Confucian temples" (*dadao kongjiadian*). Iconoclastic nationalism affirms one kind of Chinese identity—racial or biological, but it disputes the cultural identity. Both Confucian ethics and Confucian *lijiao* (the religion of rituals and proprieties) were seriously criticized, senselessly ridiculed, and resolutely rejected. Attacks on Confucianism have continued ever since then, climaxing in complete destruction of anything traditional during the "Great Cultural Revolution" (1966 to 1976) in the People's Republic of China.

After the century-long radical antitradition movements, however, Confucianism began to show its resiliency and tenacity in the 1990s, as witnessed in the growing interest among Chinese in their search for cultural roots (Tu 1991). Several factors may account for this renewed interest in traditional culture, including the economic rise of East and Southeast Asian countries within the so-called "Confucian civilization" or "Sinic world," the 1989 Democracy Movement in Beijing that finally disavowed the orthodoxy of Marxism-Leninism-Maoism, and the growing presence and consciousness of Chinese in the diaspora. "For the first time, Chinese intellectuals worldwide developed a truly new, communal, critical self-consciousness, in which the agenda of iconoclasm and nationalism is reversed; a search for cultural roots and a commitment to a form of depoliticized humanism became a strong voice in the discourse of cultural China" (Tu 1994, 30).

However, the destruction of traditional culture in the process of modernization, especially under the Communist dictatorship, may have been fatal. For the generations growing up in the People's Republic of China and in many other parts of the world, Confucianism has become a history belonging to the distant past. Traditional wedding and funeral rites, and other rituals as well, the defining orthopraxy of the Chinese according to some anthropologists, were denounced as backward and obscure superstitions. The cultural identity of the Chinese has largely been discontinued: "Those who today identify themselves as Chinese do so without the cultural support provided by tradition" (Cohen 1994, 88). There is, nonetheless, a continual influence of certain ethical values as "habits of the heart" among ordinary people.

The institutional pillars of Confucianism—the state and the family—have had irreversible structural changes, yet fragments of this system of ethics continue to influence the everyday life of most people. Moreover, some Neo-Confucian scholars are making tremendous efforts to revive Confucianism in China and the rest of East Asia. From a sociological perspective, it is apparent that the revival of Confucianism will not be possible without a tangible institutional base. Neo-Confucian scholars are still struggling to find such a base. In this regard, this study finds an interesting integration of Confucianism and Christianity. I will argue that the Chinese Christian church has become an institutional base for passing on transformed Confucian values to younger generations. However, this integration has come only after many clashes between Christianity and Confucianism, or Chineseness in general, in modern times.

Chinese and Christian: Tensions and Conflicts

Christianity is not a traditional Chinese religion. Its introduction to the Chinese has met many cultural, social, and political obstacles. The first presence of Christianity in China can be traced to the seventh century when the Nestorians arrived. But the first significant impact of Christianity on China was not felt until the sixteenth century when Jesuit missionaries had substantial success in the late Ming and early Qing dynasties.

Chinese converts to Catholicism once reached several thousands, including some prominent members of the royal family and the elite gentry. However, the "rites controversy" and the "terms controversy" soon halted its spread. The "rites controversy" was about the nature of Chinese traditional rituals: "Should Christian converts be permitted to continue the practice of the ancestral cult, so central to the entire family and clan system, as well as the veneration of Confucius, in those temples dedicated to his name which were attached to every school in the country?" (Ching 1993, 192). Matteo Ricci and his fellow Jesuits considered these rites nonreligious, so they favored cultural accommodation. But Franciscans and Dominicans perceived these rites as integral parts of pagan religions so they opposed them. The "terms controversy" was a linguistic disagreement with deep cultural implications. Jesuit missionaries favored translating the word *God* to existing Chinese terms such as *Tian* (Heaven) or *Shangdi* (literally, Supreme Emperor). Their opponents considered these Chinese terms pantheistic, and after experimenting with a transliteration of the Latin word *Deu*, they coined a new name: *Tianzhu* (Lord of Heaven). Eventually, the Pope banned the Chinese rites with a decree *Ex quo singulari* and officially adopted *Tianzhu* for God. "As a result of the papal decision, Chinese converts could no longer attend Confucian schools, and their religion became known as the Religion of the Lord of Heaven. . . . Basically, it meant that one had to choose between 'being Chinese' and 'being Catholic'" (Ching 1993, 194). In response, the Qing emperor became very upset about what he saw as foreigners making presumptuous resolutions concerning "Chinese" affairs, and he subsequently issued an imperial edict in 1724 to completely ban Christianity in China. Catholic missionaries were expelled, and the practice of *Tianzhu Jiao* by the Chinese was punished. These cultural conflicts left a legacy with continuing influence on Christian evangelism among the Chinese, although Chinese culture has undergone great changes (see Covell 1986).[8]

Protestant missions in China began in the early nineteenth century. In 1807 Robert Morrison, the first Protestant missionary sent by the London Missionary Society, arrived in Guangzhou (Canton). Upon arriving, Morrison found that staying in China as a missionary was impossible because the Qing Dynasty had set up a closed-door policy. He managed to stay as an employee of the East Indian Company, which later became notorious for its opium trade and its vicious role in the Opium War (1840).

Beginning with the Opium War, all Western imperialist powers went to China with aggressive demands. The once-closed door was smashed by the imperialist gunboats. As more ports were forced to open to "free trade" under the "unequal treaties," Christian missionaries took opportunities to advance their evangelism missions. However, their close relationship and simultaneous arrival with imperialists and opium traders caused great resentment from Chinese people. In the rising consciousness of nationalism, Christianity became stigmatized as the "alien" religion—a spiritual poison colluding with the poisonous opium in a conspiracy to seduce and conquer the Chinese nation. Chinese converts to Christianity were treated as traitors to the nation. "One more Christian, one less Chinese" was a common sarcasm. For most Chinese, both elites and ordinary people, Christianity and Chineseness became incompatible, both culturally and politically.

Political conflicts with Christianity worsened under the rule of the Chinese Communist Party. Added to the conflict of nationalism and imperialism was an ideological confrontation between the atheism of Marxist orthodoxy and the Christian religion. Not long after the establishment of the People's Republic of China in 1949, all foreign missionaries were expelled, and the practice of Christianity was restricted, and even completely banned, for many years. Although the Chinese government has generally and significantly relaxed the control over religions in the last two decades, the authorities are still more suspicious of Christianity than of other religions.

Besides cultural and political conflicts, the Christian religion was also opposed as a premodern relic. The Chinese did not reject everything foreign. Actually, since the late nineteenth century, they have been eager to learn and adopt many Western things. In addition to modern technology, most schools of Western philosophy and political ideology were introduced into China, and every school had enthusiastic Chinese followers. Eventually Marxism-Leninism prevailed and became the new orthodoxy in the People's Republic of China. Therefore, the rejection of Christian religion should not be simplistically viewed as Chinese xenophobia.

Two considerations have been important for the Chinese in their selective acceptance of non-Chinese things in modern times. One is whether it is perceived as modern; the other is whether it is useful for strengthening China against imperialist aggression. The collision with the modernized West made the Chinese awaken from the dream of self-satisfaction in the old immortal ways. The elite came to realize China's backwardness and consequently became eager to modernize the beloved "Central Country." In the modern West, Christianity was rejected by the dominant thinkers exemplified by Karl Marx, Bertrand Russell, and John Dewey (both of the latter made significant impacts among Chinese intellectuals during the May Fourth Movement). The Christian religion and all religions were seen as outmoded relics of ancient times bound to die out in the modernization process. If the West is in the process of discarding Christianity, the reasoning goes, why should we Chinese accept it?

A more important consideration was that the integrity of the Chinese nation was threatened by the imperialist aggressions. In that situation, only social Darwinism seemed to make sense of the reality. The most urgent need was to save the nation from physical extinction (*jiuguo*). Christian missions may have contributed to some social reforms. Christian moral ideals may be admirable. But, according to revolutionary theories, Christianity was useless and reactionary to social progress. Therefore, in their striving to modernize the society and strengthen the nation, it was quite natural for the Chinese to reject Christian and other religions. The modernist opposition to Christianity and all religions became stronger along with the increasing spread of modern education. Science and scientism became the standard and norm. Darwin's evolutionism became *the* scientific truth. Consequently, educated people saw Christian creationism as an unscientific mythological tale at the best. In this regard, Chinese rejection of Christian religion is also part of a universal modern phenomenon, not a particularly Chinese rejection.

Changing Identities Among Chinese in the Diaspora

Chinese emigration has a long history. Today there are about 36 million Chinese scattered in many countries outside mainland China, Taiwan, Hong Kong, and Macau. For these Chinese people living as a minority among non-Chinese peoples, identity problems are acute. Being among non-Chinese often forces them to become more conscious of their Chineseness. To look different, to speak differently, to be regarded as Chinese by others leads naturally to a greater awareness of what is or is not Chinese. "Being Chinese in China is in itself a complex problem, but being Chinese outside China has several additional complicating features. It can mean the effort to reproduce what is remembered of Chinese ways and then transmitting them, however imperfectly, to descendants. It can mean straining to keep up with developments in China through relatives at home, or by reading news of the fortunes of the empire or the republic" (G. Wang 1994, 128). A foremost question for Chinese outside China is political loyalty. Chinese nationals (*Zhongguoren*) living outside China are called *huaqiao* (sojourners). Whether having achieved citizenship in the host society or not, they are often referred to by the political authorities in Beijing and Taipei as *huaqiao* and are targets for contributions to their ancestral country (*zuguo*). In the meantime, discrimination policies and anti-Chinese violence in the host society often give ethnic Chinese no choice but to identify with China. Their perception that their fate abroad is bound with the national strength of China enforces their political or nationalistic attachment to China. The push of the host society and the pull of the homeland both fortify this identification, resulting in a "sojourner mentality" (Siu 1952)—a plan to return to the ancestral homeland to retire (*luoye guigen*).[9]

Since World War II, however, the idea of being Chinese sojourners has been challenged (Wang 1981, 1991). Many have come to "define themselves as members of the Chinese 'diaspora,' meaning those who have settled in scattered communities of Chinese far from their ancestral homeland" (Tu 1994a, 13). As diaspora Chinese, their political loyalty or nationalistic attachment to the Chinese nation-state weakens. Their Chinese identity is shifting toward "cultural China." Rhetorically, their identity shifted from *huaqiao* (Chinese sojourners) to *huaren* (Chinese in the diaspora or Chinese Americans) (Lai 1992).

Anthropologist Bernard Wong observed in the early 1980s that even the "sojourners" in New York Chinatown, although still maintaining close ties with the Nationalist Government in Taiwan, had "no intention of returning to China. They identify principally with Chinese culture rather than Chinese politics" (1982, 75). Similarly, he observed that post-1965 new immigrants "have no sympathy for communism, nor do they like Taiwan: They are apolitical" as far as China is concerned (83). Some people are moving further away from Chinese culture and reducing their Chinese identity to a merely biological meaning as Chinese descent (*huayi*). Some even undergo a process of *Peranakanization*, a term adopted from Malaysian, meaning becoming non-Chinese by completely assimilating into the native society and culture (Wu 1994, 161).[10]

A very interesting and significant phenomenon is that many ethnic Chinese in Southeast Asia have been remigrating to Western countries with the explicit intention of better preserving their Chinese identity:

> These financially secure Malaysian, Indonesian, Filipino, and Vietnamese Chinese have ostensibly emigrated from their adopted homelands of several generations to escape from anti-Chinese discrimination. In other words, to escape the pressure to assimilate imposed by the new nation-states of Southeast Asia and to preserve a measure of Chineseness for their descendants, they have opted to emigrate to modern Western-style nations with strong democratic traditions of human rights, freedom of speech, thought, religion, and assembly, and due process of law. By disappearing into a big country, the reasoning goes, they can avoid becoming targets of discrimination, and they and their children will have a better chance of making a decent living and of keeping their Chineseness. (Tu 1994, 24)

It might seem puzzling to see that in order to preserve their Chinese identity these overseas Chinese do not return to their ancestral homeland but move farther away from China. However, more perplexing is the "exodus" from mainland China, Taiwan, and Hong Kong. Driven out of China by civil wars or social-political turmoil, or afraid of an unpredictable fate under authoritarian governments, millions have left and continue to leave China. This can be seen as a self-exiling movement from the ancestral homeland. Many of these people consciously give up their political or nationalistic allegiance to the state; however, they may not give up their cultural identification with China and the Chinese people. How do these contemporary Chinese emigrants reconstruct their identity? Little empirical research has been done.

In short, there have been important changes in the meaning of Chinese identity in modern times. The Chinese have a rich cultural heritage and a difficult modern history. These can be both resources and heavy burdens in their identity construction. Chinese in the diaspora face even greater challenges as a minority in the changing host society.

3

Becoming Christian

Sociological and social historical studies of immigrant churches commonly focus on their social and psychological functions. However, a church is first of all a religious organization, the sacred place for Christian believers to conduct religious rituals and activities, express religious feelings and ideas, and collectively create and maintain a religious meaning system. The religious dimension of Chinese immigrant churches especially deserves attention because most Chinese churches are conservative in theology and a majority of church members are adult converts from non-Christian backgrounds. In contemporary American society, which has become increasingly pluralistic and postmodern, why do so many immigrants convert to conservative Christianity? Existing theories of religious conversion cannot adequately explain the phenomenon of immigrant conversions. We must go beyond the factors of individual psychology, personal bonds, and institutional strictness that have been dominant in the scholarship of religious conversion. We need to understand the social and cultural changes that these immigrants have experienced in their original country as well as in the United States.

This chapter focuses on how people at the Chinese Christian Church (CCC) of Greater Washington, D.C., construct their Christian identity. The CCC is an evangelical church. Its rituals exhibit simplicity in the Reformed tradition; its leaders and members have conservative Christian backgrounds; and its ministry has an exclusive focus on evangelistic missions. The CCC is also a nondenominational church. Within the boundaries of evangelicalism, the church shows significant diversity in denominational background and theological orientation among its members. This average Chinese American church has converted many people. Indeed, most of its immigrant members are adult converts from non-Christian backgrounds. As a convert group, their construction of Christian identity is an ongoing process and a challenging task.

Collective Rituals

Religious rituals are full of symbolic meanings reflecting collectively shared religious feelings and ideas (Durkheim 1947). At this Protestant church, regular rituals are worship services every Sunday, Holy Communion every month, and baptism throughout the year.

On most Sundays, two worship services are held, one in Chinese and one in English (see also the Introduction). The Chinese service is bi-dialectal in Mandarin and Cantonese and is held in the main sanctuary. Most participants are first generation immigrants. The English service, held in the fellowship hall of another building, is attended by young American-born Chinese (ABC) and American-raised Chinese (ARC). Most people in the English congregation are children of the immigrant members who attend the Chinese service. These two services have a common feature of simplicity: there are no recitation of creeds and no prearranged responses between the preacher and the congregation. Singing and preaching take most of the time. This lack of liturgical formality is common in evangelical and fundamentalist churches of the Reformed tradition.

The two services differ slightly in style and format. The Chinese service is more formal: participants are more likely to dress up with suits and ties; they sing classical hymns and the doxology; and the service starts and ends with formal calls and a prelude and a postlude. Sometimes the song leader asks people to stand up while singing or to hold up their arms or clap their hands. All stand up when asked, but few stretch out their arms or clap their hands. Most people are rather reserved. In contrast, the young people at the English service wear jeans and T-shirts; they like clapping hands and raising up their arms; and the singing usually takes more than thirty minutes without interruption while the congregation remains standing.

The singing in the Chinese service, accompanied by piano and organ, tends to express the need for comfort, as reflected in one of the favorite short songs, "Abba Father":

> Abba Father, Abba Father
> Deep within my heart I cry

Abba Father, Abba Father
I will never cease to love you

This and similar gospel songs call for a close relationship with God, who is praised for his protection, comfort, and assurance to the believers. In the English service, on the other hand, the singing often starts with an assortment of fast rhythms accompanied by tambourines, guitars, and electronic keyboard, then gradually moves to slow and devotional ones. The fast rhythms are to draw the attention of the young people into the worship, whereas the slow rhythms lead to "a direct conversation with God," as the pastor put it. One example of the latter kind is "I Love You, Oh Lord":

> I love you oh Lord,
> my strength, my fortress, my stronghold forever.
> The Rock of salvation,
> my only foundation,
> when the world all around me moves on.
> I love you oh Lord,
> my strength, my fortress, my stronghold forever.
> The Rock of salvation,
> my only foundation,
> I trust in your holy name oh Lord,
> I trust in your holy name.
> I love you, oh Lord.
> I love you Lord, oh Lord.

In the English service, skits are sometimes performed before the sermon; the preaching is often expository of biblical doctrines. In comparison, preaching often takes the largest block of time in the Chinese service and rational discourses are preferred to symbolic rituals. The immigrants, especially immigrant converts, rely on the preacher to explain Christian beliefs, to provide a reasonable worldview, and to make sense of their experiences as immigrants in this strange land. They want the preacher to suggest the wisdom of life, ease their anxieties, comfort their hearts, and assure their identity in American society. Preaching is thus a very demanding task for the Chinese pastor. The over-requirement for the pastorship has been one of the reasons leading to tensions and conflicts between the Chinese pastor and the members in this and other Chinese immigrant churches. The differences between the Chinese service and the English service reflect the different needs of the immigrants and their American-educated children growing up in a church.

The monthly communion service is held on the first Sunday of each month, when the Chinese and English congregations join in a combined worship service in the main sanctuary. The combined service is intended to symbolize the unity of the whole church. It normally follows the Chinese service format, but the singing, announcing, and preaching are all bilingual, with sentence-by-sentence interpretation between Mandarin and English.

Holy Communion is celebrated as commemoration. After the sermon and a hymn the pastor, standing behind the communion table and facing the congregation, explains the meaning of the bread and the cup as symbolizing the body and the blood of Jesus who died for our sins. He asks every Christian to have a silent prayer of confession and be reconciled with Christ before taking the bread and the cup. No public confession and reconciliation are required. The pastor then calls four or five deacons to walk to the front, receive the plates from the pastor, and pass them to every person row by row. Each person takes a piece of small bread, holds it, and waits until the plates are passed through the whole congregation. The pastor then calls the congregation to rise, says a prayer, and the congregation eats the bread as one. Plates holding small cups of grape juice are similarly passed out, and the congregation rises again to take the cup.

Baptism is another important ordinance in this church. It is always an event of the whole church, held as part of a Sunday worship service in the main sanctuary. The person to be baptized is required to take one or two preparation classes and to fill out an application form on which he or she needs to write down his or her salvation and born-again experience. During the Sunday service, the candidates for baptism line up in the order of females before males and the younger behind the older. This manifests accommodation to the modern American principle of "ladies first" and yet maintains the traditional Chinese principle of "seniors first." One at a time, persons walk down to the baptismal pool behind the altar. The pastor asks each person, "Do you accept Jesus Christ as your personal savior?" Upon hearing an affirmative answer, the pastor proclaims, "In the name of the Father, and the name of the Son, and the name of the Holy Spirit, I baptize you," and dips the person in the water with face up.

Baptism is conducted only for adults and youth. During the time of my field work, CCC did not have infant baptism, although church records show that they did it in the 1970s. In the 1990s an infant dedication ceremony, a Baptist substitute for infant baptism, is sometimes performed upon parents' request. Baptism by immersion is always preferred at this church unless the candidate is too ill or too old. The insistence on adult baptism through total immersion, however, applies only to those receiving baptism at this church. As a nondenominational independent church, the CCC has received many Christians from diverse denominational backgrounds. For the transferees, no immersion is required to join this church. Overall, the public rituals at this ethnic Chinese church manifest strong influences of the Reformed tradition with a Baptist tone.

Evangelical Unity and Denominational Diversity

Although this independent church opens its doors to Christians of diverse denominational backgrounds, in general, it is evangelical, as reflected in the denominational backgrounds of church members and the conservative orientations of the pastors. Baptists and Presbyterians have been the most numerous among the transferred members (see Table 4). Table 4 shows that over the years the proportion of converts who were baptized at this church has increased from 33 percent in 1976 to 58 percent in 1995. But the number of transferred members remains large, and their denominational backgrounds differ remarkably.

Many lay leaders have had Presbyterian or Baptist backgrounds. Mr. Theodore Choy, the evangelist of International Students, Incorporated who initiated the Bible study group preceding the CCC, was born into a Christian family in Chaozhou (Swato), Guangdong. He received his theological training at the Evangelical Free Church Seminary in Chicago (now Trinity Evangelical Divinity School in Deerfield, Illinois) and Wheaton College near Chicago, Illinois. His wife Leona, born into a Czech family, was also a graduate of Wheaton College. Both were members of a Presbyterian church in Maryland before the start of the CCC.[1] The twin brothers Colin and Parker Meng played very important leadership roles at this church from the beginning until the schism in 1976. They were continuously elected as deacons for many years, and Colin became one of the first two elders in 1971. The Meng brothers were born in Guangzhou of a Baptist family and attended Baptist missionary schools.

The influence of the Reformed traditions at this church is in part because of the greater success of Baptist and Presbyterian missions in Southern China and among Chinese in Southeast Asia. After the 1930s, as liberal churches shifted their resources to programs of social gospel and social reforms, conservative missionaries labored extensively in the inland and

Table 4. Denominational Backgrounds of Members of the Chinese Christian Church of Greater Washington, D.C., 1976 and 1995

Denominational Background	1976		1995	
	N	Percent	N	Percent
Baptized at this church	145	33	170	58
Transferred members	300	67	121	42
Total members	445	100	291	100
Among transferred members:				
Baptists	58	19	24	20
Presbyterians	35	12	11	9
Lingliang Tang	18	6	2	2
Episcopalians/Anglicans	17	6	8	7
Methodists	15	5	7	6
Lutherans	15	5	8	7
Little Flock	13	4	6	5
Other[a]	62	21	24	20
Unknown	67	22	31	26
Total transferred	300	100	121	102

NOTE: Members in 1976 include all those who joined the church by 1976. Some had left by 1976, but there was no systematic pattern among them. Members in 1995 include all those who were marked as current members in the 1996 Church Directory. Twenty-one names had no membership record, but I found no systematic pattern among them.

[a] Other denominations include the Adventist, Assemblies of God, Catholic, Christian and Missionary Alliance, Church of Christ in China (Zhonghua Jidu Jiaohui), Congregationalist, Church of the Nazarene, Free Evangelical Church, Reformed, United Church of Christ, and some independent Chinese churches or protodenominations.

cities of China.[2] The anti-Japanese War (1937–45), the civil war (1945–49), and the founding of the People's Republic of China became harvesting times of Christian evangelism in mainland China, Hong Kong, and Taiwan. Conservative missionaries extended their influence to America through the immigration of converts or children of converts whom they nurtured. Many older CCC members have conversion stories related to some conservative missionaries, as we will see later in this chapter.

Table 4 also shows that there are some people from other Western denominations and from Lingliang Tang and Little Flock churches. Lingliang Tang had Presbyterian roots. Little Flock was influenced by the Plymouth Brethren tradition. Both are conservative indigenous Chinese churches. Watchman Nee, the founder of the Little Flock, was martyred by the Chinese Communists in the 1970s. He has had enormous influence among Chinese Christians in America through the wide circulation of writings by and about him.

Denominational backgrounds are usually downplayed in this independent church. CCC leaders often proclaim that the real difference among Christians today is not between denominations, but between evangelicals and liberals. This view is shared by many Chinese Christian leaders in the United States. In 1986 some Chinese Christian leaders in the United States embarked on a debate about denominationalism.[3] Some well-known Chinese Christian leaders criticized misconceptions that Chinese Christians held on denominationalism. They urged Chinese churches to join American denominations in order to avoid unsettling experimentation in church polity as well as to achieve assistance in personnel and material resources. However, most responding articles rejected denominationalism, contending that the theological, liturgical, and organizational differences of various denominations confused more than attracted people. Some articles blamed denominational competition for the failure of Christian missions in China.[4] They saw no need for Chinese Christians to rely on American denominations for assistance in material and personnel resources and insisted that Chinese Christians should take up the responsibility for supporting and nurturing their own churches. More importantly, some stated that the only meaningful distinction today was between liberalism and evangelicalism. "Evangelical Presbyterians are closer to evangelical Baptists than to liberal Presbyterians," as one wrote. Moreover, they saw denominationalism as unbiblical and as contradictory to unity in Christ.

However, when forming opinions is necessary at this nondenominational Chinese church, the latent denominational differences of some members can become crucial. This has manifested, among other things, in the frequent disagreements over the form of church polity. Baptists and Little Flock people generally favor a democratic congregationalist polity and emphasize the equality of all members. In contrast, Presbyterians and some people of other denominations tend to ascribe more authority to ordained elders and pastors. A member with an Episcopal background published an article in the church magazine calling for "saluting to the uniform" of pastorship no matter whether the pastor was capable or not.

Because of continuous disagreements, the church polity of CCC has had twisting changes in its forty-year history. Growing out of a fellowship group, the CCC at the beginning followed a congregationalist form of church governance. The congregational meeting had the highest authority and was the decision-making body. Democratically elected lay deacons formed the Deacons Board to govern the everyday operation of the church. When the church grew in size, deacons gained greater power in decision making. Nevertheless, deacons were elected annually, and no one could hold a position for more than two consecutive years. Under Pastor Frank Chao (1969–76), however, the CCC ordained three elders in the early 1970s. Elders were supposed to be permanent, and the Elders Board, chaired by the pastor, claimed greater power than the Deacons Board in decision making.

Church polity became one of the foci of conflicts leading to the 1976 schism. Eventually, Rev. Chao resigned, and his hand-picked assistant pastor led about half of the church members to establish another nondenominational church. That church, the nondenominational Chinese Bible Church of Maryland, has maintained a Presbyterian polity that grants great authority to ordained permanent elders and pastors. After the split, the CCC restored the congregational democracy, and the one remaining elder became ineffective. The church constitution also imposed a two-year term of the pastorship: the tenure of a pastor must be renewed every two years by the congregational meeting with two-thirds of votes positive. Although the "eldership" clause is still kept in the church constitution, there has been no elder in the last two decades. Every once in a while, some members and pastors try to elect or select new elders; however, all the attempts have failed so far. In 1994 the church formed a special committee to study how to select elders, but by mid-1998, no elder had been installed.

Three pastors who served CCC for long periods and made lasting imprints on the church were conservative in theological training and orientation. The first pastor was Moses Chow, who served from 1962 to 1968.[5] Rev. Chow had been a missionary to Indonesia (1949–56) sent by the Chinese indigenous church of Lingliang Tang in Shanghai. From 1956 to 1959 he studied theology in the United States, first at a Bible school of a small denomination that split off from the Mennonite Brethren in Christ, then at the Columbia Biblical Seminary in South Carolina. During that period, Rev. Chow attended a missions convention at Urbana, Illinois, sponsored by InterVarsity Christian Fellowship. He also became involved in student ministries of International Students, Incorporated. He then spent more than two years (1959–61) in Japan as a missionary pastor at a Chinese church.

After he became CCC's first pastor, Rev. Chow helped to formalize the leadership structure of the church, organized two fellowship groups, one for men and one for women, initiated evangelism meetings, and started outreach programs to actively evangelize Chinese residents in the Washington area. During his time the church grew steadily from a dozen people to about a hundred members. He and Mr. Theodore Choy also co-founded Ambassadors for Christ, Incorporated (AFC) in 1963. AFC became an influential Chinese evangelical Christian organization on university campuses. It helped to organize and nurture campus Bible study groups through itinerant preaching, camp meetings, and publishing books and the *Ambassadors* magazine. It also helped many Bible study groups to evolve into churches. In 1968 Rev. Chow resigned from the church to concentrate on the growing ministry of AFC.

The second pastor was Frank Chao[6] from Hong Kong, who served from 1969 to 1976. He had a Presbyterian background and had studied at Covenant Theological Seminary in St. Louis, Missouri, which belongs to the conservative wing of the Presbyterian Church in America. He had a great concern for evangelistic missions and claimed that "the most important thing for a church is to save souls—spreading the gospel." He led a team to draft the "Missions Department Working Principles," which stated:

> We must realize the urgency of saving the lost: The world is lost in sins, and having no hope and without God (Eph. 2:12). Tens of thousands perish every day. The work of the Gospel is urgent. We must by all means save some (I Cor. 9:22; II Tim. 4:1–2), we must redeem the time to save souls with all efforts.

Rev. Chao pushed the church to start missions' programs, raise missions funds, and train members to go to overseas mission fields. Under his leadership the CCC became one of about a dozen pioneering Chinese American churches that started missions programs. Rev. Chao was also actively involved in the formation and leadership of the North American Congress of Chinese Evangelicals (NACOCE), an association of evangelical Chinese churches. The National Conference of Chinese Churches (CONFAB) had been formed in 1955 under the National Council of Churches for Chinese churches in mainline denominations, but new churches established by Chinese immigrants were reluctant to join CONFAB. The NACOCE held its first convention in 1972, which then became a triennial event that continues today. The NACOCE allied Chinese American churches with evangelical concerns and promoted evangelism among the Chinese all over the world. It later expanded to become the Chinese Congress for World Evangelism (CCOWE). The CCOWE established its headquarters in Hong Kong and has many regional branch offices in Southeast Asia, North America, South America, Australia, and Europe. Rev. Frank Chao resigned in 1976 amid complex and interlocking conflicts within the CCC.

Philip Hung, the fourth pastor, served from 1982 to 1990. Before him, a pastor of Baptist background served the church for one year but left without making much contribution to the church. Rev. Hung received his seminary education in Hong Kong. Upon arriving at the CCC, he requested that no woman should be a worship leader in the Sunday service. He always had a sermon of "year-end proclamation" in which he reviewed the past year as a chaotic and deteriorating world, condemned worldly life, and called for saving souls and living a holy Christian life. Church records show that Pastor Hung attended several pastors' conferences organized by the Moody Bible Institute, a very conservative Christian organization. He also kept up with the NACOCE conferences. In 1990 Rev. Hung resigned and moved to a Southern state to minister to a Chinese church. He later returned to Hong Kong.

These three pastors made a significant impact on many longtime members through many years of nurturing and teaching. As a result, church members continue in the conservative track. The different fates of two recent pastors reflect the conservative orientation of the CCC members. In 1989 Allan Houston became the assistant pastor to minister to the English-speaking people. Rev. Houston and his wife were white Americans from Arkansas and Kansas. He was a graduate of Capital Bible College in Maryland, a small conservative seminary. He also attended Dallas Theological Seminary, an influential conservative seminary. Rev. Houston described himself as "a conservative evangelical" and stated that he was "sympathetic with a premillenial, pretribulational view." He believed that, according to the inerrant Bible, women should not serve as spiritual leaders—pastors and elders, and probably deacons as well. After Rev. Philip Hung left in 1990, Rev. Houston took greater responsibility for the whole church. He opposed having women deacons serving on the Official Board. Together with some fundamentalist lay leaders, he successfully managed to form an Official Board without a female for a year. Because his conservativeness matched well with the general orientation of the church, he safely passed four biennial votes of the congregation to renew his pastoral term.

In 1991 the church hired Daniel Tang as the senior pastor. Rev. Tang could be regarded as an evangelical, but his theological positions leaned toward liberal evangelicalism. Rev. Tang was a graduate of the Trinity Evangelical Divinity School in Illinois (the Evangelical Free Church of America) and Fuller Theological Seminary in California. He was ordained by the American Baptist Churches in the U.S.A. and served a United Methodist church in California. Soon after he became the senior pastor, some lay leaders openly criticized him for holding unorthodox views. Rev. Tang said on various occasions that women could be deaconesses, elders, and pastors. In 1994 Rev. Tang received an invitation to attend a conference in the People's Republic of China organized by the government-sanctioned "Three Self" churches. Most Chinese Christians in America perceived the "Three Self" churches as the accomplice of the Communist government to suppress Christianity.[7] When Rev. Tang made a request for traveling funds to attend the meeting in China, it caused antagonism from several lay leaders. Eventually, Rev. Tang was voted out by the congregation in 1995. Among many factors leading to this result, theological disagreements between more conservative members and the not-so-conservative senior pastor were important.

Evangelism: *The* Mission

Since its very beginning the CCC has been active in evangelism. The high proportion of adult converts being baptized at this church is the evidence of its effectiveness. Indeed, evangelism has been *the* mission of this Chinese church, and all programs are centered around it.

Student ministry has been the emphasis of local evangelism. A majority of the early church members were graduate students themselves. They organized Bible study groups on various campuses in this area. These Bible study groups provided fellowship opportunities for the lonely Chinese students and became effective means of converting fellow Chinese students. Bible study groups on university campuses have been continually organized since the 1950s.

In 1990 CCC further established an evangelistic ministry, the Ark Fellowship, targeting mainland Chinese students and scholars. Since its early years, the church has regularly prayed for their compatriots behind the bamboo curtain in Communist China. Many members and leaders have expressed their unfulfilled wish to evangelize in China. When they saw the opening of the door of the People's Republic of China and the coming of tens of thousands of students and scholars to the United States in the 1980s, they believed that God had answered their prayers. They seized the opportunity to evangelize this group of people. In the Ark Fellowship they organized lectures, picnics, festival celebrations, and camp meetings. These activities often attracted more than two hundred enquirers. Disillusioned with the Communist utopia and trying to make sense of life in this new and strange land, many mainland Chinese were compelled toward a new meaning system and worldview. Christians saw this as their spiritual thirst for the living water—the Christian gospel. The enthusiastic responses of mainland Chinese to Christian evangelism excited many church members. More and more mainland Chinese have been baptized. Actually, most new converts in the 1990s have been mainland Chinese. They count about a quarter of the total CCC membership today.

The CCC is also a pioneer church in extending evangelism to overseas missions. Under the leadership of Rev. Frank Chao, the church started mission programs in the late 1960s. For two years in the early 1970s the missions fund even superseded the general fund. The church continues its support of missions today. With an average attendance of 270 people, the missions fund was $102,580 in 1995–96. The church uses this fund to support eight Christian organizations, five theological seminaries, five literature ministries, three broadcast ministries aiming at mainland China, two frontier missions, and fifteen individual missionaries in Asia (Taiwan, Hong Kong, Singapore, Macau, Thailand, Indonesia, and Japan), South America, Europe, and North America. The church also regularly sends church members overseas for short-term missions.

In contrast, the church has had little interest in community services. Early church records suggest that some members called the church to provide community services, but few plans were actually carried out. In the early 1970s some members proposed establishing a child-care center and an elderly-care center, but both failed due to the lack of support from church leaders and members. The church also refused invitations from other Chinese organizations and the D.C. Council of Churches to cosponsor programs of community services.

The only continuous work that may be regarded as a social service ministry is the Chinese School, which teaches the Chinese language and culture to children on the weekends. Established in 1971 as the first Chinese school teaching Mandarin in the Washington area, it first attracted a couple of hundred children of both church members and nonmembers. However, the Chinese School has been under constant pressure to justify its existence. Some fundamentalist members have wanted every church ministry to exist solely for direct proselytization. In documents and conversations, those people who were involved in the Chinese School have had to frequently highlight the school as an effective means of converting and recruiting members into this church. However, these justifications did not always work for all church members. The school, once boasted to be the best in the whole eastern region of the United States, was gradually surpassed by other newly established Chinese schools both in quality and in size. It even faced threats of being closed on several occasions.

Between 1974 and 1976 the CCC sponsored some Vietnamese refugees because of urging, pushing, and challenging by a white American man. Some CCC members joined the effort to mobilize human and financial resources to sponsor ethnic Chinese out of refugee camps. However, some church leaders insisted on the priority of evangelism or spiritual help over material and social help to the refugees. This work ceased to operate in the middle of 1976 when the church split.

Moreover, this conservative church has had little political involvement either in Chinese or American politics. In the early 1970s some church members were active in establishing the Organization of Chinese Americans (OCA), which became an influential national civil rights organization. At its beginning, the OCA frequently used CCC facilities to hold its meetings and activities. But some church leaders opposed it in the name of separating the church (religion) and the state (politics). Consequently, the OCA had to stop using church facilities completely. Some OCA activists who had been CCC members eventually dropped out of the church.

Overseas Chinese were known for their deep involvement in Chinese politics since the Republic Revolution (*xinhai geming*) in the beginning of this century. Chinese Christians in the United States were similarly involved in Chinese nationalism around the turn of the century (Tseng 1996). Many Chinese in America today hold anti-Communist views. However, after the Tiananmen Square Incident in 1989, when the student-led pro-democracy movement in China was brutally crushed by the government, the CCC's Official Board denied Pastor Hung's request for supporting a memorial vigil service for the killed students, which was held at the Chinese Community Church, because the activity had a "political tone." Apparently, fundamentalist members had greater influence and were responsible for the lack of political involvement. Meanwhile, however, this Chinese church followed some political campaigns of the *Moody Monthly,* a very conservative Christian magazine. Church leaders mobilized people to write letters to support the astronauts reading biblical verses in the space craft as they orbited the moon in 1968, to oppose a congressional act for legal equality of men and women in 1974, and to participate in anti-abortion campaigns in the 1990s.

This lack of social services and political involvement is not rare among Chinese churches in the United States today. Many post-1965 new immigrant churches have an exclusive focus on evangelism in their ministry. These churches may provide some charity donations to help the homeless and emergency funds to help people in unexpected crises. However, they generally do not have consistent programs of social services, and the charity fund is often very small in terms of the overall budget. The Chinese Bible Church of Maryland, which split off from the CCC in 1976, has been more conservative than the CCC. For a long time it was even reluctant to open a Chinese weekend school. Moreover, several Chinese pastors objected to my reference to the Chinese church as an ethnic social organization. They insisted that the church was the body of Christ for the sole purpose of Christian life and evangelism.

The exclusive focus on evangelism might help these churches to centralize their resources for proselytization, but probably also limits their ability to reach out. Either voluntarily or involuntarily, Chinese churches are often excluded from cooperative activities in the Chinese community. Thus, Chinese churches have had little influence in the larger ethnic Chinese community.[8] Of course, a few Chinese churches, especially Chinatown churches, do participate in community services and American politics. In this regard, the Chinese Community Church in Washington, D.C., is a good example. That church became one of the founding members of the Chinese Consolidated Benevolent Association in Washington, D.C., when it was formed in 1955. The church has continuously provided social services to the Chinatown community, frequently expressed concerns about the welfare of the whole ethnic Chinese community, and sometimes participated in political actions cooperatively organized by inner-city churches.

A Church of Converts

More than half of current members at the CCC are adult converts from non-Christian backgrounds. What attracted these Chinese people into conservative Christianity? What experiences led to their conversion? I have found that the influence of pre-immigration experiences, post-immigration experiences, and Christian socialization have had different significance for people in different social groups. Considering this convert group together, however, the dramatic changes in social and cultural contexts in China are evidently the most important factor for Chinese conversion to evangelical Protestantism.

The Meaning of Conversion

The meaning of religious conversion varies widely for different people and in different disciplines (see Snow and Machalek 1984; Malony and Southard 1992). At the CCC the common understanding of "conversion" is that a person has had the experience of being "born again and saved" (*chongsheng dejiu*), or has accepted Jesus Christ as his or her personal savior and lord.

A convert needs to be baptized. They do not say that baptism is necessary for salvation, because they proclaim "justification through faith only"; but they say that a true convert must be baptized in order to publicly witness for the Lord. Anyone who wants to join the church fills out an application form, either for baptism at this church or for transferring membership from another church. This form provides some basic biographical information and, more importantly, a testimonial of born-again and salvation experiences (*chongsheng dejiu jingli*). Church members expect every new convert to give public testimonies about how God has changed his or her life. Transferees are also expected to tell their conversion story or other Christian experiences before becoming fully accepted by other members. Therefore, I use the word "conversion" in this book to mean a change from other religions or no religion to Christianity.

An observable act of Christian conversion is receiving baptism. A few people have received baptism before they have had any significant religious experience, such as those people who were born into a Christian family and received an infant baptism. Among these people, some have had life-changing experiences that have "awakened" their Christian faith. Their intense religious experiences leading to stronger religious conviction and more participation can be regarded as "conversion" too. Their stories comprise an integral part of the conversion discourse in this evangelical church. However, I use "baptism" as my operational definition of conversion when I compare various social groups within this Chinese church.

During the time of my field work I heard many conversion stories at various gatherings and read many testimonials in the membership application forms, church magazines, and various newsletters. In total, I collected more than a hundred personal testimonials. I also conducted life-history interviews with dozens of church members, some informal and some semistructured. In addition, I read many testimonials in nationally circulated Chinese Christian magazines and heard many conversion stories in other Chinese churches and at various camp meetings.

Self-reported experiences are not always objective because converts may reorganize their biographical histories according to their newly achieved belief system (Beckford 1978; Snow and Machalek 1984). However, these materials are probably the best empirical data a researcher can expect in order to achieve an in-depth understanding of conversion. In this study, personal conversion accounts were cross-checked by participant observation in the church. Because I had an extended period of field work at the church, I observed some individuals going through the conversion process and interviewed them at various points in the process. Comparing these interviews with their written testimonials, I found a high degree of consistency. Actually, the written testimonials are often more reliable in terms of recalling personal experiences than face-to-face interviews. Applicants seemed serious and grave in filling the application form and writing down the experience leading to their conversion.

Adult Converts

Among the people who have become formal members of the CCC, about half joined it through baptism at this very church, and the other half came through membership transfers. Figure 1 compares two types of new members who joined the church every year. There were more transferees in the early years; however, since the 1980s, more people were baptized into this church (the black bars on the right side in the graph). Indeed, about 58 percent of current CCC members received baptism at this church, as shown in Table 4 above. Furthermore, many transferees are adult converts although they were baptized in another church before moving to the Washington area. This becomes evident when we examine the baptismal age of church members.

Before making further analysis, a few words about social and cultural subgroups in this church are in order. Like Chinese new immigrants overall, several distinct social and cultural groups can be distinguished: (1) the "sojourners,"[9] who were born in mainland China and fled to Taiwan or Hong Kong before coming to America; (2) their children's generation, who were born or grew up in Taiwan or Hong Kong; (3) refugees from Indo-Chinese countries; (4) mainland Chinese from the PRC; and (5) the American-born Chinese (ABC) and American-raised Chinese (ARC). At the CCC, the number of ethnic Chinese from Southeast Asian countries, including Singapore, Malaysia, Indonesia, and the Philippines, is small. Their conversion experiences seem to resemble the second group of people.

The Chinese version of the CCC membership form has an item of *jiguan*, which can be understood as the "ancestral place" (*zuji di*), "place of residence" (*huji di*), or "birthplace" (*chusheng di*). In the past these three places were often the same. However, for many contemporary Chinese immigrants to America, these three places are different. While their parents or grandparents come from one place, they were born in another place and then moved to a new place, or several different places, to live for a period of time. Therefore, their answers to this question vary widely. Depending on how the applicant understands the question, one could put either the

year

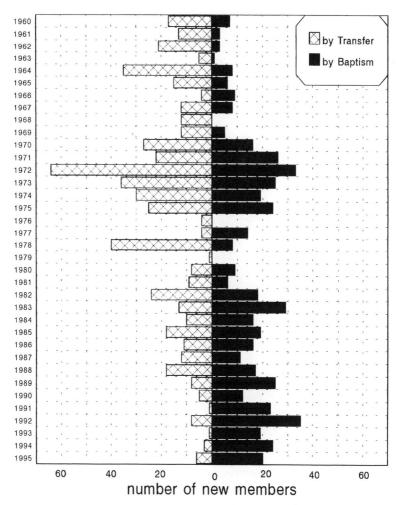

Total N=1068 (including people who have left);
Joined by baptism N=514;
1960 actually includes 1958-1960.

Fig. 1.   Members of the Chinese Christian Church of Greater Washington, D.C.,
Joining type by year, 1960–1995

ancestral home district (although they may never have lived there), or the birthplace (although they may have lived there for only a month), or the place of residence before immigration. No matter which is chosen, however, it probably reflects greater attachment to that place than to the other two. In spite of these subtleties, one can still roughly distinguish the social groups based on the answers to this item. The percentage of adult converts is high among all of these social and cultural groups except for American-born Chinese (see Table 5).

Table 5. Past and Present Members of the Chinese Christian Church of Greater Washington, D.C.: Age of Baptism by Place of Origin

Age-Group	PRC	Indochina	Non-PRC Mainland	Taiwan	Hong Kong	S. E. Asia	U.S.
			Place of Origin				
Percent children (preteen)	0	0	7	8	10	13	17
Percent youths (13 to 17)	2	17	24	30	17	14	47
Percent adults (18+)	98	83	69	62	73	73	36
Median age of baptism	34	24	22	21	21	21	16
Mean age of baptism	39	25	26	23	21	21	17
Standard deviation	15	8	14	11	8	6	6

The first row of Table 5 shows that almost no one from the PRC or Indochina was baptized as a preteen child, whereas 17 percent of ABCs received baptism before thirteen years old. The third row reports the percentage of people who were baptized at age eighteen or older. It varies between 62 and 98 percent among immigrant Chinese, whereas only one out of three ABCs was baptized as an adult. The fourth and fifth rows tell us that on average, PRC converts were baptized at an older age, in their thirties; other immigrant converts were in their twenties; whereas most ABCs were in their teens. The last row (standard deviation) shows that the difference of the baptismal age is large among PRC people, mainland-born sojourners, and people from Taiwan. Many of these people were baptized in their fifties, sixties, or even seventies.

Conversion Experiences

Experiences leading to conversion can be distinguished into three categories: (1) pre-immigration experiences, (2) post-immigration experiences, and (3) Christian socialization during childhood. Table 6 summarizes the different significance of these three kinds of experiences for different social groups.

Among the mainland-born sojourners who fled to Hong Kong or Taiwan in the 1940s and 1950s, both pre-immigration experiences in Asia and post-immigration experiences in America are important for their conversion. A few of these people were born into Christian families or received baptism as children; however, their pre-immigration and post-immigration experiences often intensified their religiosity. In comparison, among the children's generation of the sojourners who grew up in Taiwan and Hong Kong, more people had Christian socialization in their childhood. Because these people grew up in a time of social stability and economic boom in Taiwan and Hong Kong, pre-immigration experiences were usually not critical in their conversion. However, many people had life-changing experiences as foreign students or immigrants in the United States. For people from the PRC and Indochina, there was almost no Christian socialization. In mainland China under the Communist rule, for several decades Christian churches were closed, Christian believers were persecuted, and the compulsory education tightly controlled by the Chinese Communist Party indoctrinated students with materialism, scientism, and atheism. However, experiences of political catastrophes and social turmoil prepared many of them for religious conversion. Experiences in America as foreign students or immigrants further intensified their desire for a religion. In sharp contrast, for most ABCs and ARCs, Christian socialization was the single important factor for their receiving baptism. The immigration experiences of their parents, and their own experiences as racial minority people in the larger society, could have some impacts on their spiritual life. But these impacts show little importance up to their baptismal age as youth or children. How their religiosity changes in or after college still needs to be observed.

Sojourners

Among people of the sojourners generation, only 14 percent were baptized before 1950. Some pre-1950 converts were influenced by Western missionaries and missionary schools, and a few were inspired by indigenous Chinese Christian leaders. There were many missionary schools in the provinces of Guangdong, Zhejiang, Jiangsu, and cities of Shanghai and Hong Kong. These missionary schools attracted students from non-Christian families. Some CCC members graduated and became converted in those schools.

Table 6. Past and Present Members of the Chinese Christian Church of Greater Washington, D.C.: Types of Experiences Leading to Conversion by Social Background, in Major Waves of Immigration, 1950s–1970s, 1970s–1980s, 1970s, 1980s–1990s

Type of experiences	Social Background				
	Mainland China–born Sojourners, 1950s–1970s	Children of Sojourners from Taiwan and Hong Kong, 1970s–1980s	Vietnam Refugees, 1970s	PRC, 1980s–1990s	ABC/ARC[a]
Christian socialization	+	++			++
Pre-immigration experiences in Asia	++		++	++	
Immigration experiences in America	++	++	++	++	

NOTES: "+" = somewhat important; "++" = very important; blank = not important.
[a] ABC = American-born Chinese; ARC = American-raised Chinese.

One example is Mr. Chanbon Yew, who was born in 1908 to a wealthy family in Zhejiang:

> Through five years of secondary school education in an Episcopal missionary school at Suzhou Academy, Jiangsu, I finally accepted Jesus as my Savior in 1927. Staying on as a liberal Christian refusing to get baptized for five more years until 1932, then I was convinced and baptized, also confirmed by Bishop Graves of Jiangsu Diocese.

Notice that he was confirmed by a non-Chinese Episcopal bishop. His conversion was clearly influenced by Western missionaries. Mr. Yew had many children and grandchildren, and three of his daughters and their respective families are active members of the CCC.

Richard Sing, another example of the influence of missionary schools, was a Cantonese born in Shanghai in 1933. The Anti-Japanese War (1937–45) and the civil war between Chinese Communists and the Guomindang (1945–49) interrupted his schooling twice. His parents were Buddhists. His elementary school in Shanghai and secondary school in Hong Kong were all in Christian missionary schools. Richard finally was baptized in 1955 while attending a Christian college in Hong Kong.

Indigenous Chinese churches began to mature in the second quarter of the twentieth century (see Bays 1996). Several Chinese Christian leaders emerged, including Wang Mingdao (1900–1991) in Beijing; John Sung (Song Shangjie, 1901–1944) in Southeastern China and Southeast Asia; Timothy Dzao (Zhao Shiguang, dates unknown) in Shanghai; and Watchman Nee (1903–1972) in Southern China. Some indigenous churches became well established in the 1940s. Mr. Theodore Choy, the key founder of the CCC, was born to a Christian family in Chaozhou (Swato), Guangdong, in 1916. It was the famous evangelist Dr. John Sung who inspired Ted to go to seminary and become an evangelist.

To a large extent, Rev. Moses Chow, the first pastor of the CCC, was a product of the Chinese indigenization movement, although he benefited from missionary schools as well. Chow was born in 1925 in a village of Zhejiang. His father was a religious Daoist (Taoist) and his mother a staunch Buddhist. When he was attending a traditional Confucian school (*sishu*), a classmate brought him to a church. That church was run by Chinese Christians rather than foreign missionaries. He later brought home a copy of the Gospel of John in Chinese. His father got very interested in it and eventually led the family to be baptized. This resulted in expulsion by his grandparents and the patriarchal big family and a move to Shanghai. In Shanghai Moses

Chow met Rev. Timothy Dzao, the founder of the Lingliang Tang and the Lingliang Evangelist Team to Nanyang. Chow attended missionary primary and secondary schools; however, it was Rev. Dzao who inspired him to dedicate his life to full-time ministry. Later, he became a Lingliang Tang missionary to Indonesia before coming to the United States.

Most people who became Christians before 1950 converted because of life-threatening experiences in times of war or social turmoil. Simon Kiu, born in Hebei in 1921, wrote in his testimonial on the membership application form:

> The summer of 1943 was a heightened period of the Anti-Japanese War. I was working underground in a Japanese-occupied region. Then the enemy found me out and almost killed me. I had to escape all alone to the far away Great Rear. During the fugitive time I had many disastrous dangers, but with the protection of the Lord I overcame all the problems and safely arrived in Sichuan [in Southwestern China]. I had already learned about the Dao [Christian teaching] before and upon arriving in Chongqing [in Sichuan Province] I received baptism and committed myself to the Lord.

Suffering in wars, social turmoil, political campaigns, and natural disasters, many Chinese were forced into unwilling migration, both physically and spiritually. Many testimonials of sojourners recalled the difficulties of uprootedness. Paul Tang was born in Hunan in 1941. His family suffered from both the Chinese Communists and the social and cultural strangeness in Hong Kong:

> My grandparents were devout Buddhists. After the Chinese Communists swept the mainland, my father led our family to flee to Hong Kong. But we did not know the local dialect [Cantonese] and customs. After many difficult struggles and great efforts we started to hold on. However, although we settled down physically, my soul could not find anything to rest on. We were lost and did not know what could make life meaningful. Then I met a pastor who introduced the love of Christ to my heart. Only then I began to see that life was interesting and hopeful, thus I committed myself to the Lord and decided to be a pious believer forever.

Some sojourners received baptism after coming to the United States, but their sojourning experiences made a significant impact on their eventual conversion. Immigration experiences in the United States further intensified their spiritual needs. Fred Yu was very articulate about the sense of uprootedness resulting from his complex experiences in mainland China, Taiwan, and the United States. Born in Shandong in 1929, Fred was a college student when he fled to Taiwan along with the Guomindang in 1949. After completing a college education in Taiwan, he came to the United States for graduate study. He was baptized in 1959 in an American church in Minnesota. During a phone interview he said to me:

> Mainland China is our dear homeland, but going back to that home is impossible because of the horrible Communists. Taiwan is not really our home, because we are regarded as *waishengren* [a person from a "foreign province," or mainland-born people]. The Guomindang was terrible. They took flight from the mainland with little resistance to the Communists. In Taiwan they treated us who were not in the military or government as second-class citizens, whereas native Taiwanese were treated even worse. You see, we dare not go back to the mainland, and we are unwilling to go back to Taiwan. We have to seek to plant our roots in the American soil [*luodi shenggen*]. However, here we have to fight hard battles for civil rights as a racial minority. It is not all that easy.

Fred was among the earliest activists of the Organization of Chinese Americans. After the 1976 schism he dropped out of the church. When I interviewed him in 1995, he said he was still a Christian believer, but he had great concerns about civil rights and the ethnic Chinese community.

Because of the hardship of settling down anywhere in the world, most sojourners have a deep sense of homelessness, and consequently they seek permanence or eternity in the heavenly world promised by Christianity. A man I met in Boston expressed this feeling movingly. He was born in Guangdong, went to Taiwan, and came to the United States to study mathematics. While attending college he converted to Christianity, then dedicated himself to the ministry and entered a seminary. Upon graduation from a seminary he went to a Southeast Asian country to teach theology. However, he did not feel at home there, so he moved to Hong Kong. After several years in Hong Kong he still did not feel at home, so he came back to the United States and became a professor in a mainline seminary. He was longing to go to his ancestral homeland and work in mainland China. However, he realized that after so many years away from China, he probably would not be able to find the sense of home in China either. In addition, Christians are often persecuted in the PRC. "The only permanent home," he concluded with a deep breath, "is in the kingdom of God."

I heard many similar stories and expressions from these sojourners in various Chinese churches. An item on the CCC membership application form is "permanent address." Many members left it blank, and quite a number of them wrote down *Tianjia* (the heavenly home). This answer was not frivolous because many of these people truly had no permanent residence anywhere in this world. Their only hope of permanence was in the heavenly kingdom assured by Christian religion.

Church historian Timothy Smith (1978) argues that migration is a "theologizing experience" because of the uncertainty of sojourning or wandering around homeless. This is true among Chinese immigrants. Actually, the religious needs of Chinese sojourners were not only intensified, but they motivated them to make a conversion to a new religion. Ruthlessly uprooted, their dream to return to the ancestral homeland smashed by the Chinese Communist dictatorship in mainland China, the Chinese sojourners found themselves wandering around the world from one place to another without settling down. Their everyday life was filled with anxiety, despair, and the bitter experience of living in different cultures and political environments. Many found hope, peace, and comfort in the ethnic Chinese Christian church. Because the sojourners came in the first wave of Chinese new immigrants since the 1950s, because they were the founders and original members of the CCC, and because their heightened experiences led them to Christian conversion or revival of personal spirituality, they continue to dominate in the church as key leaders and active members.

People Born or Raised in Taiwan or Hong Kong

The second cohort of Chinese immigrants is the generation of the sojourners' children. They were born and/or grew up in Taiwan or Hong Kong in a peaceful social environment. Compared with the sojourner generation, few of them had dramatic experiences in Asia. Some were born into a Christian family or attended Christian schools so that Christian socialization was an important factor for their Christian faith. For those people who were born into a Christian family or whose parents converted when they were small children, Christian socialization prepared them in their Christian practice. Harry Sing, born in Taiwan in 1949 and baptized in 1960, expressed this "naturalness" very well:

I went to church for worship since I was very small. Going to church seemed like a necessary thing in my life, just like eating and sleeping every day. If someone asks me why do you spend so much time going to church, I can only answer that it is my spiritual need. This is unexplainable. In this world there is no better place than the church where I can often go. Therefore, going to church, worshiping God, and serving the Lord have become the most important part of my life. I will never abandon God for any worldly thing. I trust God will protect and guide every step of my life.

Western missionaries contributed to the Christian socialization of this generation. After the founding of the People's Republic of China, all Western missionaries were frightened away or expelled from mainland China. Many missionaries subsequently moved to Hong Kong, Taiwan, or Southeast Asian countries and continued to work among the Chinese. For example, the China Inland Mission, the largest interdenominational missionary society in China, reorganized itself to become the Overseas Missionaries Fellowship (OMF). OMF made its office in Hong Kong and worked among Chinese and other peoples in Southeast Asia. Some InterVarsity Christian Fellowship staff members engaged in the student ministry in Taiwan and Hong Kong and helped to stimulate revivals on various campuses. Some missionary schools, after being closed in mainland China, reestablished in Hong Kong or Taiwan. Non-Christian parents sent their children to missionary schools because they liked the educational quality, although most parents did not want their children to become Christians. However, Christian education was the purpose of these missionary schools. Many students faced the tension between accepting Christian beliefs learned at the missionary school and obeying their non-Christian parents. After immigrating to the United States away from parents, they finally had the freedom to be baptized. Anna Lee, born in Hong Kong in 1961, is a typical case in this regard:

I attended Christian schools in Hong Kong. At school I learned biblical stories and Christian teachings. But my parents were Buddhists and prohibited me from going to church. I came to the U.S. four years ago. I was invited to the Carmel Fellowship last Christmas and finally I found the home of the Lord.

The "theologizing experiences" of migration were important for some of these people in their conversion and intensification of religiosity. Some converted in the United States after enduring loneliness and hardship as foreign students or immigrants. For the lonely students, Bible study groups or fellowship activities were warm, intimate, and psychologically secure. At these meetings they could speak their familiar Chinese language rather than English, talk about things of common concern to fellow Chinese students, and have familiar Chinese food. Finding a sense of group belonging, many gradually converted. Sometimes former missionaries to China sought out these Chinese students and befriended them. Sara Tao lived with such a former missionary when she was attending a small university where there were no other Chinese students. Sara was born in Liaoning in 1948 and went to Taiwan with her parents when she was less than two years old. In 1970 she came to the United States:

> I came to the U.S. to study four years ago. God arranged for me to live at the home of a woman missionary. Being far away from home and alone in this strange country, and with heavy class work, I was quite depressed. However, my host gave me loving care. Her love really moved me and made me think seriously about Christ and God. After I came to the Eastern region in 1973, I attended the Winter Retreat in Pennsylvania [sponsored by the Ambassadors for Christ]. I had the opportunity to see Miss Christiana Tsai.[10] She made me sense the grace and power of God.

Vietnam Refugees

The third wave of new Chinese immigrants were Indo-Chinese refugees coming in the mid-1970s. The whole Indo-Chinese region underwent Communist revolutions in the 1960s and 1970s. The war and social turmoil changed many people's lives. Mary Chang was one of those who suffered such traumas. She was born in Vietnam in 1949, was baptized in Cambodia in 1963, and moved to Laos in 1965. Her testimonial provides no detail, but readers can easily sense the traumatic nature of her life experiences:

> I grew up in a Christian family and went to church with my mother since I was small. But back then I did not really know God, not until 1965, when our family moved from Cambodia to Laos. On the way we met many dangers and had many difficulties. However, I personally saw the wonderful work of God when we were in trouble. Just as Job says: I heard about you, but now I see you with my own eyes. God is the Lord of my life and I will walk on His way forever.

If Mary's words are too abstract, Kathy Trinh provided a story of agony in some detail. She was also born in Vietnam in 1949. Her sister became a Christian and brought her to a missionary church in 1974. In 1975 Kathy wrote this testimonial at the CCC:

> [Back in Vietnam] although I learned about Jesus, I did not go to church very often because I had to work on Sundays. Besides, I did not really know much about God, not until something happened in the Vietnam war. Because I worked at the U.S. consulate I and my family were allowed to come to the U.S. However, the war situation worsened quicker than we expected. One day I was told that my sister could not go to America because she was over 20 years old. We were very sad to hear this bad news. My mother insisted that she would not leave without my sister. Thinking of the coming dangers when the Communists come, we were all terribly worried and cried. But my sister was very calm. She said to me only three words—"Trust our Lord." The next day when I went back to the office, I was told that my whole family could go and would leave soon. After crying and worrying all night I was shocked by this good news and rejoiced. I felt the power of God. Oh my Lord, how wonderful you are! God really cares about me and my family. The Lord helped my family safely come out of Vietnam and settle down in America. When I prayed, He really listened and answered my prayers. Therefore I want to receive Jesus as my personal savior and get baptized now.

Many Chinese refugees from Vietnam experienced "miracles" before leaving Vietnam, on fragile sampans in the open sea, in refugee camps, or after arriving in the United States. Winston Ching was born in 1956 in Vietnam. He spent several years in refugee camps in Southeast Asia before coming to the United States:

> After I arrived in the U.S. in December 1979, I was introduced to this church, where I learned about Jesus Christ. Actually, after I left Vietnam and wandered in strange lands, I often felt deep in my heart that there must be a God who helped me in everything and opened doors for me. Especially during difficult times the Lord was always with me, although I was yet to know the Lord then.

These people came to America with hearts prepared for religious interpretations of their life crises and rescues. When Christian evangelists reached them, Christianity immediately filled their searching hearts. Meanwhile, the ethnic Chinese church provided a loving community to belong to. Ethnic Chinese refugees from Vietnam and other Indo-Chinese countries are few at the CCC, but their traumatic stories continue to be heard now and then.

PRC Chinese

The newest Chinese immigrant group is people from the People's Republic of China, which has been under Communist rule since 1949. Christian churches and all religious places were closed down before and during the "Cultural Revolution" (1966–76). Religious believers were treated not only as people who had wrong beliefs, but as counter-revolutionaries or reactionaries—the enemy of "the proletarian dictatorship." Active Christians were thrown into jails or labor camps. Many Christian leaders and believers suffered physical torture, mental abuse, and political persecution. Furthermore, for several decades the huge propaganda machine indoctrinated all people, young and old, into Marxism-Leninism-Maoism. Atheism was taught as the scientific truth in textbooks from kindergarten to university. In that situation, even if someone was born into a Christian family, it was hard to get Christian socialization. Many Christian parents feared that any teaching of Christian beliefs to their children might get their children and themselves into troubles. Sometimes children took action to denounce their parents for their "superstitious" beliefs. It is not surprising, therefore, that almost no mainland Chinese received baptism before 1980.

However, the social-political turmoil and the merciless "class struggles" ironically prepared many people to seek a religious interpretation and comfort. Their Christian conversion was not the result of one specific experience but often resulted from cumulative events over many years. Mr. Turan Lai, born in 1917 in Zhejiang, was a retired teacher when he immigrated to the United States. He was baptized in 1988 at the age of seventy-one. His testimony in the baptismal record was brief, but poignant:

> The love of the Lord healed the wounds in my heart. Those wounds resulted from many-years persecutions in the mainland. The love of the Lord made me see the real home and feel warmth. In front of the Lord, I am a sinner, imperfect, should repeatedly make self-reflection and self-examination [these are the exact words used by the Chinese Communists!]. . . . I believe in the Lord. I need the Lord. Only with the Lord can my heart have peace and joy.

Both pre-immigration and post-immigration experiences are significant for some mainland Chinese. Mr. Jingtang Zhang, born in 1945 in Shanghai, was not an articulate man. Although his short testimonial provides no details, clearly his conversion experiences included sufferings in China and "miracles" in America:

> I was born in a Christian family and attended Sunday school for some time before churches were closed down. From my own experiences I knew I was saved. Without God's grace I and my family could not survive the calamity of the "Cultural Revolution"; without God's grace I could not come out of China and come to the United States; and without God's grace I could not stay in the United States. It is God who opened the road for me, saved my soul, and made me born again. I want to commit all my life to the Lord.

Mr. Zhang has been working in a Chinese restaurant since the early 1980s.

Since the establishment of diplomatic relations between the United States and the PRC in 1979, tens of thousands of Chinese students and visiting scholars have come to the United States. As intellectuals in China, they were privileged on the one hand, because the percent of people with an higher education was very low. On the other hand, intellectuals were also subject to the harshest treatment by the Communist government because they as a social stratum were always suspected of lack of loyalty to the Chinese Communist Party. Like earlier PRC immigrants, many of them suffered terribly in the many political campaigns. After years of turmoil and struggles, many people longed for love, trust, and peace. These desires led many people to the church, and eventually they converted.

Moreover, many Chinese intellectuals have strong patriotic concerns. They came to the United States with a common ambition—to learn advanced sciences in order to contribute to the modernization of China, their beloved motherland. However, the Tiananmen Square Massacre in 1989, when the Chinese government crushed the pro-democracy student movement in Beijing, was the turning point for many mainlanders. It was the last stroke in shattering their hope that the Communist Party would reform itself and lead China to democracy and modernization. This incident helped to release many Chinese intellectuals from residual attachment to Communist idealism. Throughout the 1980s few mainland Chinese in the United States became Christians. In the 1990s, however, their openness toward the Christian gospel has amazed many people and stimulated the formation of evangelization organizations or ministries especially targeting this group. Pastors at the CCC have baptized more than 80 mainland Chinese since 1989.

Some prominent exiled Chinese political dissidents have also become Christians. They explicitly proclaim that Christianity is the only hope for the Chinese nation (e.g., Yuan 1992). Meanwhile, the Chinese Student Protection Act in 1992 allowed Chinese students and scholars to achieve U.S. permanent residency. More than fifty thousand people consequently received their "green cards." Many others adjusted to permanent resident status upon finding employment in the United States. However, many of these people are haunted by the guilt of forsaking their beloved motherland and giving up their original patriotic ambition. A religious interpretation of their fate and the meaning of life can be an outlet for relieving this guilt.

In the meantime, entering American society as racial minority people, competing for a career in sciences and engineering, and maintaining an intact marriage in a liberal social environment are all very challenging. Many have had to give up their dreamed-for careers in science or engineering in order to find a job and make a living. The pressure to survive and succeed in this capitalist society is often heavy to bear; consequently, many feel helpless, powerless, and meaningless. They are busy with making a living, but many are worried all the time and often feel lonely. In their need to readjust their philosophy of life, many have become religious seekers.

After years of indoctrination in atheism, scientism, and humanism, it is difficult for these rationalist intellectuals to accept supernatural interpretations of any religion. The existence of God the Creator is difficult to believe. However, a loving community has attracted many into the church. There are many examples. Jie Xiao, born in Shanghai in 1935, was a university professor. In 1990 she came to the United States as a visiting scholar at a medical research institute. She once said that she did not need any religion because she was strong. "Even if I had the need, I will never be able to believe in anything supernatural. Atheism and scientism have been deeply rooted and ingrained [*genshen digu*] in my mind. I don't think anybody, including myself, can change it." However, God, or the loving community of the church, changed her. She gave this testimony before being immersed in the baptistery in 1995:

> Since 1990 I started to visit the church on Sundays and attended activities organized by the Ark Fellowship. Since the Easter of 1994 I joined a Bible study group. During this period of more than a year, many loving brothers and sisters of the Bible study group helped

me to learn the Bible and understand the Christian faith. It was a miracle that I could change from an atheist to accept the existence of the omnipotent God. Now I believe that God created the world and rules all things. He is the Lord of all human beings. . . . In front of the perfect and absolute God I confess I am a sinner. I want to open my heart to receive the Lord Jesus as my savior. . . . I want to become a member of the church, to worship God together with brothers and sisters, and to spread the gospel of the Lord. I also hope to have peace, joy, and health.

Carol Song is a good example of younger people from the mainland. She was born in 1963 and graduated from a teacher's university in a big city. She came to join her husband who was studying as a graduate student. Her testimonial shows the importance of immigrant experiences for her conversion:

I came to the U.S. in 1990 and soon was introduced to church activities. At that time, Bible studies for me were just like hearing fiction stories. We received the atheist education since our birth. The claim that "God created man" is really in contradiction to what we learned—it was labor that created man. Moreover, we just came to the U.S. and felt the heavy pressure of life. First, I had language problems because I did not learn much English before coming to the U.S. Second, I was a teacher in China. After I came to America, I could only be a housewife. I lost my career in China and had no job in America. And no relatives around. Everyday life was boring. I was very depressed. After we joined the Bible study group I found joy and peace. At first I regarded Bible study just as listening to tales, but I very much enjoyed the friendship. Being together with people from mainland China, we could speak the familiar language, we had similar lifestyle and common concerns. After a while, I became moved by some Christians who made consistent efforts to explain the gospel to us because they expected nothing in return from us. Gradually, Bible study became interesting. I began to read the Bible on my own. I started to understand the Word of God concerning the meaning of life. Jesus Christ teaches us how to be a human being. We also heard many moving testimonies at meetings of the Bible study group and the Ark Fellowship. I started to try to pray and talk to God.

Later, when her husband "miraculously" received a job offer after a period of desperate job-search, she experienced the presence of living God:

> When I was considering getting baptized, one night I had a dream. In the dream I saw many people receiving baptism and heard many Ark Fellowship people talking. What a vivid dream. After I woke up in the morning, the dream scene was just like in front of my eyes. Then I said to the Lord, "I want to get baptized."

In another case, a miraculous coincidence finally convinced Mr. Henglu Yin about the existence of God. He was born in 1960 and graduated from a medical school in China. He followed suggestions from Christians to say prayers and ask God to enter his heart. Looking back, he was thankful to God for the miraculous guidance and for opening roads for him. However, for a long time he was unable to accept the notion of the actual existence of God. He sometimes thought that his successes could be good luck, by accident, and by his own hard work. One day, while riding in a car on the highway, he was arguing stubbornly with his Christian friend. He challenged his friend by questioning, "If God really exists, will he understand prayers in Chinese? Can you show me that God really understands Chinese?" Right then a beautiful voice came out of the car radio: "God is all-knowing and all-present. He knows every language, no matter if it is English, Chinese, or Arabic." This timely coincidence amazed Mr. Yin and frightened him as well. It seemed that God was right there reading his mind and answering his questions. Upon arriving home he immediately reached for the phone, called the church, and asked for baptism.

Many established scientists and engineers in Chinese churches present themselves as role models to answer enquiry questions from mainland Chinese students and scholars. They also use "scientific" or rational reasoning to evangelize mainland Chinese scholars and students. However, the initial attraction to these mainland Chinese is often the loving community of the church and the intimacy of its fellowship.

American-born Chinese

The CCC has not only converted many Chinese students and immigrants, but it has also been successful in socializing the second generation into Christianity. It has good Sunday school classes and fellowship activities for children from kindergarten to college. Most ABCs and ARCs who were baptized did not have any dramatic religious experiences. Christianity often "naturally" becomes part of their life. Betty Jung said this clearly in her simple testimonial. Born in Washington, D.C., in 1975, she was a middle-school student when she was baptized in 1988. At that time she wrote:

> I have been coming to church and going to Sunday school at this church since I was very little. I am not sure exactly how I became a Christian, probably because I was exposed to so much of the Scripture and teachings at a young age. I accepted Christ as my savior.

For these ABCs and ARCs, their Christian conversion is without much struggle. They may face identity problems after baptism, especially during college years and when they enter the larger society. Nevertheless, many ABCs and ARCs growing up in the CCC who were away from home to attend college did come back to visit the church during vacations. Some are active participants in various campus Christian groups, such as Campus Crusade for Christ, InterVarsity Christian Fellowship, Navigators, or some independently organized Bible study groups and prayer meetings. Indeed, Chinese American students are noticeably active on many university campuses (see Busto 1996).

Why Do Chinese Convert to Evangelical Christianity?

The high rate of adult converts is not unique to the CCC, but is a common characteristic of many Chinese immigrant churches. My interviews with Chinese church leaders in the Washington area and other places revealed that the proportion of adult converts in those churches often ranges between one-third to two-thirds of the church membership. What factors are leading to Chinese conversion to evangelical Christianity? An individualistic approach has dominated the scholarship of religious conversion. The most influential process model, that proposed by Lofland and Stark (1965), focuses exclusively on the process of individual-level religious change. Although it extends the scope of focus beyond individual psychology to personal bonds or networks, these relationships are seen as being of an individual nature and the interactions with others are on an individual basis. However, when large numbers of Chinese are changing their religion now, but not in a previous era, we must look for explanations beyond individual personality and personal bonds in small networks.

Why *do* immigrants change their religion? Little research has been done on immigrant religious conversions in part because religious conversion among the immigrants is a new phenomenon. Earlier European immigrants by and large retained their traditional religion, be it Protestantism, Catholicism, or Judaism (Herberg 1960). Nevertheless, without existing theories to refer to, three assimilation explanations for immigrant conversions may be posited based on commonsense understandings.

One presumption would be that some people join the church without genuine conversion in order to gain material advantages as the well-known phrase "rice-bowl Christian" suggests. However, this cannot be the major motive for Chinese converts in the CCC for two reasons. First, like most Chinese American churches, the CCC has placed exclusive emphasis on evangelization. The church has had no consistent or systematic social service programs, such as job referrals or English-language classes for new immigrants. Second, most church members are well educated, have professional jobs, and live in middle-class suburbs. They do not need the church for material support.

Another speculation would be that because about 86 percent of Americans claim a Christian faith of one kind or another (Kosmin and Lachman 1993) immigrants join a Christian church in order to make themselves appear to be more American. However, this cannot be the major motive for the recent Christian conversion of new Chinese immigrants for several reasons. First, if assimilation were the goal, a good choice for these highly educated professionals would be to remain nonreligious. In contemporary American society it is no longer necessary to have a religion. Nonreligious persons are accepted, especially in professional working environments, and religious expression is discouraged in the highly secularized, private, high-tech companies or government offices in which many Chinese work in the Washington, D.C., area. Nonetheless, these professional Chinese immigrants have converted to conservative Christianity despite risking derision from colleagues. Second, if these new immigrants want to assimilate to American society through a church, a better choice would be to join a non-ethnic one. Many of these Chinese immigrants have reasonably high socioeconomic status, speak fluent English, and live in racially mixed middle-class suburbs. Many nonethnic churches in the neighborhoods in which they live welcome and invite nonwhite people to join them. However, these Chinese converts have joined ethnic Chinese churches and often drive twenty to forty minutes to attend them. Third, if these new immigrants intend to make themselves more like mainstream Americans by becoming Christian, a better way would be to join a mainline church. However, Chinese Christians have chosen evangelical or fundamentalist Christianity and subsequently have formed nondenominational ethnic churches.

Some studies of immigrant churches argue that a motivation for joining an ethnic church may come from social needs for ethnic-group belonging. This factor seems significant for many Korean immigrants (Hurh and Kim 1990; Min 1992; Kwon, Ebaugh, and Hagan 1997). However, the religious motive was found to be predominant over social or psychological motives in attending Korean churches (Hurh et al. 1978; Hurh and Kim 1990). In reality, Hurh and Kim (1990, 31) found that "among the majority of Korean immigrants, the religious need (meaning), the social need (belonging) and the psychological need (comfort) for attending the Korean church are inseparable from each other; they are functionally intertwined under the complex conditions of uprooting, existential marginality, and sociocultural adaptation for rerooting." Similarly, joining the ethnic church for ethnic purposes is not the primary reason for Christian conversion among Chinese immigrants. Moreover, unlike the Korean immigrant community in which the Korean church has been the most well-established social, cultural, and educational center, Chinese immigrants have had more numerous and diverse kinds of ethnic organizations and associations available to them, as discussed in Chapter 2. There are also traditional Chinese religious groups, such as Buddhist temples and semi-religious *qigong* (meditation) associations. To find some ethnic group to join is not hard for new Chinese immigrants. They do not have to go to a church simply for the purpose of meeting their ethnic needs.

Of course, the Christian church has some unique structures and functions that other ethnic Chinese organizations and associations do not have. The structure of congregations and an emphasis on fellowship groups help new immigrants find social belonging; weekly meetings provide opportunities for frequent and intimate interactions with compatriots; the proclaimed teachings help to create a loving and harmonious community where new immigrants can find spiritual peace and psychological ease; church activities and youth programs help to foster a moral environment for nurturing the growing second generation. No other ethnic Chinese organization or association serves these functions in the way that ethnic Christian churches do. These features of the church are attractive to many new immigrants. Nevertheless, at this evangelical church, people can hardly integrate themselves into it without religious conversion.

In the debates about reasons for the growth of conservative churches and declines of mainline churches since the 1960s (see Hoge and Roozen 1979; Roozen and Hadaway 1993), some scholars emphasize the importance of institutional factors (e.g., Kelley 1972; Iannaccone 1994; Finke and Stark 1992). Finke and Stark (1992) contend that in a religious free market, the growing churches are those that have efficient polity and clergy, attractive theologies and services, and good recruitment strategies. Institutional factors seem important in Chinese conversion to Christianity, especially to conservative Protestantism. First, some CCC members attribute their conversion to the influence of Western missionary schools in China and Southeast Asia. Second, the most active converting agents for the Chinese have been evangelical missionaries in Asia; campus evangelical organizations in North America, such as InterVarsity Christian Fellowship, International Students, Inc., Campus Crusade for Christ, and Navigators; and conservative Chinese churches and organizations in the United States. However, the importance of these institutional factors is probably only secondary. Historically, there were tremendous efforts put forth by thousands of Western missionaries in China and the United States, but "the missionaries' long-continued effort, if measured in numbers of converts, had failed" (Fairbank 1974, 1). Those missionaries who chose to continue to work among the Chinese in Hong Kong, Taiwan, and Southeast Asia after they left mainland China around 1950 found unprecedented openness toward Christian proselytization among people who had fled the wars and Chinese Communists. Had there been no such enthusiasm from these Chinese migrants, there would not have been so many Christian organizations working to proselytize among the Chinese. Similarly, in the United States, without the enthusiastic responsiveness of Chinese students, refugees, and new immigrants, there would not have been so many Christian organizations and churches working to evangelize them. In other words, the intensification of Christian institutional efforts is not only a *cause* for increasing Chinese conversion, but also a *reaction* to the increasing responsiveness to the Christian message among the Chinese.[11]

More important than the institutional factors are contextual changes that are internal to China. As discussed in Chapter 2, modern China has been in constant social and political turmoil. Most scholars of conversion acknowledge that some form of personal crisis usually precedes religious conversion (Lofland and Stark 1965; Bainbridge 1992; Rambo 1993). Any one life-threatening event can lead some individuals to religious change. Yet many contemporary Chinese have experienced more than one trauma in wars, social turmoil, political campaigns, and natural disasters, as we have seen above. Many Chinese were forced into unwilling migration, both physically and spiritually. For some of these unwilling migrants, the experience in the United States further intensified their spiritual needs. Because of the hardship of settling down anywhere in the world, some sojourners have a deep sense of homelessness and consequently seek permanence or eternity in the heavenly world promised by Christianity. Facing the difficulties of dramatic social change, some people cling to their traditional religions to find the meaning of life and the strength to live. However, during the turbulent process of modernization in China, Chinese cultural traditions have been mercilessly attacked, destroyed, and smashed to pieces, as discussed in the previous chapter. Without cultural traditions as barriers, the Chinese are now both free and bound to seek alternate meaning systems. As one of the available alternatives, Christianity sufficiently answers the spiritual quest for many Chinese who have experienced life-threatening traumas.

Why then, one may ask, did the Chinese not accept Christianity until recently? As we have already discussed, in the past the Chinese regarded Christian evangelism by Western missionaries as an integral part of Western imperialism. Christianity was seen as a *yangjiao* (foreign religion) and Chinese converts were treated as traitors to the nation. Today this political stigma has been largely removed for several reasons. First, Christian evangelists and preachers have made painstaking efforts to deconstruct modern Chinese history and uncouple Christian evangelism from Western imperialism.[12] These efforts have been effective to a great extent. Second, Western imperialism in China has been gone for many years. The Japanese invasion and Chinese alliance with the United States during World War II further superseded the historical memory of Western imperialism. Third, Christianity has increasingly taken on a "Chinese look" with the increase in the numbers of Chinese evangelists, Chinese pastors, and Chinese Christian believers. Fourth, for many Chinese, after decades of "modern education" or indoctrination in Marxist universalism, "foreignness" is no longer a problem in choosing a religious faith or moral authority. And finally, today the most advanced societies are "Christian countries" with Christian traditions. Chinese intellectuals, especially those under the influence of Chinese Communists, were once fascinated by the achievements of the Soviet Union and other Communist countries. However, the cruel reality of socialist experiments in mainland China and other countries has smashed their idealism. Many have subsequently begun to look to Western democracies as models of modernization. Some Chinese converts express the conviction that there is a causal connection between Christianity, on the one hand, and modern market economies and political democracy, on the other.

Besides contextual factors specific to the Chinese, there is also the American context or the universal challenges of modernity and modernization. On the one hand, modernity tends to relativize and trivialize conventional religious beliefs (Berger 1969). On the other hand, however, conservative religions combat modernity by asserting absolute beliefs and strict moral standards (Ammerman 1987). The challenge of modernity is universal to all people in the contemporary world, but it has particular weight for immigrants. Nancy Ammerman finds that American "Fundamentalism is most likely to be found at the points where tradition is meeting modernity" and that suburbs are often such meeting points where conservative churches are thriving (1987, 8; see also Ammerman 1991). Many contemporary immigrants moved first from the village to the city before immigration, then plunged into a highly developed modern or postmodern American metropolis. Living in this fast-changing, pluralistic, relativistic, and chaotic world, conservative Christians are assertive in proclaiming that the sole and absolute truth can only be found in the inerrant Bible. Evangelicals assure believers of absolute love and peace in this world and eternal life after death. For new Chinese immigrants, both premigration traumas and postmigration uncertainties in modern American society fortify their desire for absoluteness and certainty.

Moreover, as well-educated professionals living in middle-class suburbs, what concerns these new Chinese immigrants the most are not social justice issues, the main agenda of liberal Christians, but social group belonging and moral education for their children. For many Chinese immigrants no traditional Chinese religion, modern science, philosophy, or liberal Christian denominations can meet these needs as well as conservative Christianity does. Finally, the attraction of evangelical Christianity to Chinese immigrants also comes from its perceived compatibility with Confucian moral values. Absolute evangelical beliefs provide a foundation upon which Chinese church members can justify the strict moral and behavioral values that they impose on themselves and their children. I will return to this point in Chapter 5 when discussing Chinese traditional values.[13]

4

Becoming American

Does the Chinese immigrant church help its members assimilate into American society? The mechanism of the assimilation function of the church, as the literature reviewed in Chapter 1 shows, lies in the denominational hierarchy and in the American-born generations. The church hierarchy on the regional and national levels may impose measures for religious uniformity and Americanization onto immigrant congregations, whereas the American-born children often push the immigrant church to give up the original language and ethnic values in favor of English and American values (Buczek 1976). However, the Chinese Christian Church of Greater Washington, D.C., like many Chinese churches established since the 1960s, was founded by Chinese immigrants and has had no denominational affiliation. Does such a church still function as an agency of assimilation? If so, to what extent and in what ways does such a church help its members to integrate into American society and construct an American identity?

Like many post-1965 immigrants, CCC members have been well assimilated both in structural and cultural dimensions. They are middle-class professionals living in ethnically mixed suburbs and have adopted many American ways of behavior and values. However, their assimilation has two important caveats—Americanization begins before immigration, and structural and cultural assimilation in the United States is selective. In adopting the English language and American lifestyle the church reflects the growing Americanization of its members, but the church itself is not the major agency of acculturation in these particular aspects. The Chinese church affirms its members' structural assimilation in public spheres of school and employment but maintains the ethnic church; it teaches social and moral values that are in line with the American core culture but also rejects some other American values; and, more importantly, it proclaims the "Christian foundation of the U.S.A." The CCC is an independent church, but it is not socially isolated from American evangelical Protestant organizations.

Assimilation of Chinese New Immigrants

Following the general pattern of upper-strata new Chinese immigrants,[1] most CCC members are well assimilated in American society in various aspects. They are engineers, scientists, and professionals working in nonethnic companies, universities, and federal government agencies, such as the National Institutes of Health and NASA. Some are real estate agents, and only a very few are Chinese restaurant owners and workers. The professionals work among non-Chinese and participate in professional associations and social clubs. A majority of church members have attended American universities, and many hold master's or doctoral degrees. They send their children to public schools and push them to excel. The church has never considered establishing a parochial school, as many earlier European immigrant churches did. CCC members live in racially mixed neighborhoods in middle- and upper-middle-class suburbs in Maryland and Virginia. Moreover, virtually all immigrants who are qualified to become U.S. citizens have achieved citizenship. These membership characteristics are common in all new Chinese churches in the Greater Washington area, which are all located in middle-class suburbs in Maryland or Virginia. In fact, the vast majority of new Chinese churches nationwide are in metropolitan suburbs rather than in ghetto Chinatowns, and most church members are middle-class immigrants and their children (see AFC 1994; Chuck 1996; Pang 1995).

Contemporary Chinese immigrants usually achieve these aspects of structural assimilation upon or soon after arriving in the United States, rather than by gradually climbing the mobility ladder intergenerationally like earlier European immigrants did.[2] Actually, their high levels of structural, residential, and socioeconomic assimilation begin with selective immigration, the result of U.S. immigration laws that favor highly educated professional immigrants and their families.[3] Several of the founding members of the CCC came in the mid-1950s as political refugees from mainland China via Hong Kong, but they had received a college education in China or Hong Kong and entered graduate schools upon arriving in the United States. Others were students from Taiwan and Hong Kong attending colleges and graduate schools. Upon finding employment after the enactment of the

New Immigration Act of 1965, they changed from their original student visas to permanent resident status. In other words, they could become immigrants precisely because of their high level of education and professional employment. These well-to-do immigrants bypassed the Chinatown ghetto and settled in middle-class suburbs immediately after their university graduation.

This pattern—students becoming immigrants—has continued until the present with few exceptions. One exception is that some immigrants, after becoming U.S. citizens, have sponsored their less-educated parents and siblings for immigration. Another exception is that in the mid-1970s this church sponsored some Vietnam refugees who were ethnic Chinese. Even these family-based immigrants and refugees were not really lacking good educational and socioeconomic backgrounds, however. Many of them had a high school and college education before coming to the United States. The fact is that the parents of these professional immigrants were people who could afford to send their children to schools in China, and later to colleges and graduate schools in the United States. The Vietnamese Chinese were political refugees who suffered from the Communist revolution in part because of their wealth in Vietnam. This middle-class social status has been reproduced in the church: virtually all second generation children are expected to enter college, almost all grownup children have done so, and many have gone on to graduate school.

Another important dimension of assimilation is acculturation or the adoption of American behavioral patterns, values, rules, and symbols (Gordon 1964; Gans 1997). Dress, diet preferences, hobbies, behavioral mannerisms, ways of talking, and so on, are often culturally distinctive. Differences between Chinese and American traditions are notable; therefore, Chinese immigrants from the Far East need to adapt in many ways to the life in America. Classic assimilation theory assumes that acculturation begins after immigration. However, in the increasingly shrinking "global village," it more typically begins *before* immigration (cf. Rumbaut 1997).

Unlike earlier European immigrants who came from rural villages, most new Chinese immigrants came from urban areas even if some were born in the countryside. Before coming to the United States, many had learned English in schools and had been exposed to some aspects of American culture, especially popular culture, through the mass media, Hollywood movies, school curricula, and direct contacts with Americans traveling or working in Asia. Even without immigration, some Chinese have adopted American behaviors, such as using a knife and a fork instead of chopsticks, drinking coffee and cola instead of tea, eating hamburgers, listening to rock music, watching football and basketball, and wearing jeans or suits and ties.

Schools in China may have integrated American history, politics, society, culture and sciences into their curricula. Actually, the whole modern educational system in China has been very much Westernized or Americanized in form *and* in content. American values, such as individual freedom, equal opportunity, and democracy, have generally inspired the Chinese pursuit for modernization. In fact, "Westernization" or "Americanization" has been a major stream in the modernization process in China, although there have always been debates concerning the best routes to Chinese modernization. Americanization thus begins before immigration for many contemporary immigrants. Overall, Chinese immigrants to the United States are probably more Americanized before coming to the United States than their counterparts who do not emigrate. In fact, many new immigrants chose to come to the United States because they had learned and liked something in the United States, including American lifestyle.

After arriving in the United States, American mass media encourage further cultural assimilation. For the educated professionals who have little problem understanding English, the media are very influential. Watching television is an especially popular thing to do. Even if new immigrants cannot fully understand the English language on television, they can still imitate the fashions and manners shown. Chinese radio broadcasts, televisions, and newspapers also serve the immigrant community by introducing American politics, society, culture, and lifestyle. More important, the integrated school and workplace are two very important institutions for cultural assimilation. Through working or studying among non-Chinese and through daily encounters and interactions with non-Chinese, immigrants become aware of American ways and social norms. To survive and succeed, they adjust and adapt to American ways of seeing and doing things. In the public school, Chinese children follow the same rules and standards, succeed and excel among non-Chinese children. In this way Americanization is naturally brought about.

On the other hand, integration and interactions in ethnically-mixed schools and workplaces may also sharpen ethnic consciousness among many immigrants and their children.[4] Many Chinese immigrants came to America with an ideal of great universalism of all human beings and equality of every person. However, American society is still a racially and ethnically conscious society. The Chinese are physically distinguishable from Caucasians, blacks, and Hispanics and are categorized as Asian and Pacific Islanders in all kinds of school-related or work-related forms. Blatant racism may have become rare, but racism has not completely gone away. One church member, who had retired from a federal government job, said,

> I have never really experienced racial discrimination in my work. All Chinese employees work hard, and it is difficult for others to find faults with us. We deserve what we get and do not need to be clamorous. . . . Of course, it is still hard for us to get promotions to really high ranks. The "glass ceiling" no doubt exists.

His daughter, an ABC who recently graduated from a state university, told me:

> Most of my close friends in high school and college are Asian, well, actually Chinese. I don't know why. I didn't intend it that way. I had some [white] American friends. But those friendships didn't last long. I don't know why, but I find many ABCs are like me.

American institutions often enforce racial grouping, even among religious groups that proclaim racial equality. Harry Show immigrated with his parents as a small child from Taiwan. Growing up in the CCC, Harry wanted to get out of the ethnic enclave and mix with people of other races in college. He became a regular participant in activities organized by the InterVarsity Christian Fellowship (IVCF). However, IVCF organizes separate fellowship groups for whites, blacks, Chinese, and Koreans on this campus of a large state university. After two or three years' efforts, he realized that the racial and ethnic grouping was a hard reality for him to face. As an American-born Chinese, he could not simply become an American, or one that would have no ethnic or racial label. Later, in his junior year, this engineering student began to seriously read the history and social studies of Asian Americans.

As their ethnic consciousness is awakened or sharpened in their workplace and school, both immigrants and their children find the ethnic church is needed for social belonging, psychological comfort, and religious meaning. In other words, the social integration in the public spheres of work and school provokes a desire to congregate with fellow Chinese on the weekend.

One might assume that the high levels of socioeconomic integration in American society and premigration acculturation of these Chinese immigrants would naturally make the Chinese church look American or easily become American. Milton Gordon (1964) argued that there was not cultural pluralism in the United States because structurally separated groups based on race, ethnicity, and class were actually substantially acculturated or culturally assimilated. However, Chinese immigrant members are determined to be selective in their assimilation. The ethnic church, as part of the private sphere away from the integrated public spheres, is a social mechanism that immigrants use to fend off unwelcome aspects of American ways and values while adopting other aspects. Even adopting the English language is not a simple matter in this immigrant church.

Adopting English in the Church

Language is a common problem of immigrant churches. If English is not the original language of the immigrant group, the issue of adopting English in the church will be brought up sooner or later. Some people (e.g., Mullins 1987) assume that an immigrant church will evolve from a monolingual (non-English) stage to a bilingual (English plus the original language) stage and end with a monolingual (English only) stage. However, this pattern of "straight-line evolution" does not apply to Chinese churches in the United States. In many of the Chinese churches established before World War II, English has been adopted, but the original Chinese language (Cantonese dialect) has been preserved, and one more Chinese dialect (Mandarin) has been added. The first Chinese church in San Francisco, which was founded in 1853, has become trilingual (Cantonese, Mandarin, and English) instead of becoming monolingual. Similarly, the Chinese Community Church in Washington, D.C., which was established in 1935, today provides Sunday services in Cantonese, English, and Mandarin. Similarly, many new Chinese churches started monolingual but have become bilingual or trilingual. The Chinese Christian Church of Greater Washington, D.C., which started as a monolingual Mandarin church, has become a trilingual church with Sunday services in Mandarin, Cantonese, and English. There were even experiments to adopt more languages, such as Taiwanese and Vietnamese, but these did not work out. Continuous Chinese immigration is an important factor for the continuous use of Chinese dialects. Because of the linguistic diversity of new Chinese immigrants, ethnic Chinese churches in America have been overwhelmed by the task of absorbing newcomers and accommodating to their needs.

Past studies show that the pressure for the immigrant church to adopt English may come from the denominational hierarchy and the American-born generations (Buczek 1976). As a nondenominational church, the CCC has had no outside direct pressure to adopt English. Nonetheless the use of English has gradually increased in its forty-year history. The driving force for using English comes mostly from the American-born or American-raised children. However, in the national Chinese American population, American-born Chinese (ABC) have been outnumbered by overseas-born Chinese (OBC) since 1970. Similarly, ABCs remain a minority in many Chinese American churches. Consequently, the use of English is still limited in these churches. Tensions and conflicts are often characteristic in the process of adopting English in the Chinese church.

Sunday Services

The CCC began with a monolingual Mandarin Sunday service in 1958. About ten years later the Sunday service became bilingual in Mandarin and Cantonese. In the early 1970s English was added to the Sunday service. The trilingual Sunday worship service is a fascinating event to observe, although some participants find it difficult to follow. The sermon and the announcements are all spoken and interpreted in three languages. Often the worship leader and the preacher speak Mandarin, which is translated into English, sentence by sentence, by a person standing side-by-side with the speaker behind a wide pulpit. Another person, often invisible to the congregation, simultaneously translates every sentence into Cantonese, which is transmitted wirelessly to earphones in the designated pews. I have seen such setups of trilingual Sunday services at a number of Chinese churches in the Washington and other areas.

However, the trilingual translations were unsatisfactory for many people. In 1972 a CCC member who was fully trilingual made the first request for holding a separate English service each Sunday. He argued that monolingual services without interpretation would save time and allow the sermon message to be communicated more effectively to the congregation. The Official Board, composed of deacons, elders, and the pastor, responded to the request by carrying out an opinion survey in early 1973. It reported that 55 members opposed holding separate services, 42 members supported them, and 5 members were neutral. Among those who supported a separate English service, 9 had become inactive in Sunday attendance, citing their dissatisfaction with the trilingual service as a reason. However, the Official Board decided to continue the trilingual Sunday service. Church records show that some lay leaders feared that a separate Sunday service might lead to division of the church; some parents wanted to sit beside their

English-speaking teenage children in the same service; and some members found the bilingual or trilingual translation helpful for them to learn another language.

Pastor Frank Chao joined the young people in pressing for holding separate Sunday services. The church was growing fast and receiving several dozen new members every year in the early 1970s. Soon regular church attendance reached over 300, exceeding the maximum seating capacity of the sanctuary so that folding chairs had to be added every Sunday. Pastor Chao suggested holding two Sunday services in order to accommodate the increasing attendance and to invite more people to join the church. However, several lay leaders spoke in strong opposition and wanted one service to preserve church unity. An elder said,

> We do not need two services. In our evangelism visits we can recommend people to join nearby churches in their neighborhoods. They do not have to come to our church. Our goal is to evangelize them and to let them know the Lord, not to make our church bigger.

Instead of breaking down into two services, the lay leaders suggested installing a closed-circuit TV in an overflow room.

The growing second generation became increasingly demanding. Mr. Peter Luo, a new seminary graduate who grew up in this church, joined the Official Board as the pastor's assistant. At an Official Board meeting in October of 1975, Mr. Luo complained on behalf of the young people:

> We haven't done enough for the ABCs [American-born Chinese]. We need to pay more attention to them in the ministry. A separate English service is necessary in order to effectively meet their spiritual needs.

Mr. Luo and Pastor Chao pressed hard against the lay leaders by calling for special Official Board meetings to discuss the possibility of holding separate services. They pushed to start the separate English service at the beginning of 1976. But resistance also grew. After lengthy discussions, the Official Board finally granted a probationary period of holding a separate English Sunday service. In order to improve the English ministry to the growing youth, Rev. Chao also wanted to hire Mr. Luo as the assistant pastor. However, some members strongly opposed ordaining and hiring Mr. Luo. They argued that Mr. Luo was not qualified to be a pastor of this Mandarin church because he did not speak Mandarin well. Pastor Chao's proposal was turned down by a ballot vote at the congregational meeting in January of 1976. Rev. Chao continued to press on and eventually succeeded in hiring Mr. Luo and starting the English service. However, these successes preceded a bitter split.

Beginning in early 1976 many controversies emerged involving Rev. Chao and Rev. Luo, including suspected mismanagement of church funds and relationships with church members. A series of special congregational meetings were called for clarifying the controversies, but the meetings were filled with emotional confrontations. Finally, Rev. Chao resigned in May. But the problems and conflicts persisted and eventually ended in a schism in August of 1976. Assistant Pastor Luo, two elders, most of the deacons, and about half of the church members suddenly withdrew from the CCC and started another church. The separate English Sunday service was not the major issue in the conflicts leading to the schism. Nonetheless, the experiment of an English service had to be discontinued because the total Sunday attendance suddenly dropped to about 160. It took another ten years before the English service was reintroduced at the CCC.

The 1976 schism resulted in instability in leadership. After several years of difficulty, the church finally hired Rev. Philip Hung as the pastor in 1982, then hired Murray Hwang, a young American-born Chinese, as the assistant pastor in 1985. One year later the church formally started the separate English Sunday service that continues today. The English service was held at 9:30 A.M. in the sanctuary, finishing by 10:45 A.M. to clear out for the Chinese service at 11:00 A.M. To preserve and signify unity as one church, a combined bilingual communion service has been held on the first Sunday of each month.

The English Congregation and the Caucasian Pastor

In the 1990s because English-speaking young people have increased in number, the church hired Rev. Allan Houston as the assistant pastor for the English ministry. The Houstons, in their mid-thirties, were white Americans. When he was a seminary student at Capitol Bible College in the Washington, D.C., area, Allan served as a youth intern at the CCC in 1982–83. He was then invited to speak to the youth at the church summer retreats in 1984 and 1985. After Timothy Han resigned in 1988 to continue his graduate study, the Pastor Search Committee recruited Houston, who had been ordained by then and was teaching at a Bible college in the South. English-speaking young people at the church welcomed Houston's coming. However, some church leaders and immigrant members found it difficult to communicate with Houston because of language difficulties and cultural differences. Tensions and conflicts accumulated. One year later, Senior Pastor Philip Hung resigned and left for a Chinese church in Oklahoma. One of the reasons leading to Hung's resignation, although never made explicit, was probably that he as the senior pastor had a hard time working with the Caucasian assistant pastor.[5]

After Rev. Hung left, Rev. Houston became the only pastor of the CCC. To maintain a normal operation of the church with an average total attendance of about 240 people, Rev. Houston naturally assumed greater responsibility. Feeling the overload of ministering to the whole church, he recommended hiring another Caucasian man to be the youth pastor. However, some older people, who were mostly parents of immigrant professionals and spoke little English, felt threatened by the increasing presence of non-Chinese speaking ministers. They wrote an opposition letter to the Official Board, calling for a review of the history of the church as a *Mandarin* church, and asked that attention be paid to those who did not speak English. They asked pointedly, "If two pastors both speak English only, how will the Chinese-speaking people be taken care of? Does this move suggest that no Chinese-speaking pastor will be hired?" This emotional campaign by senior people successfully confined Rev. Houston to ministering to the English-speaking young people. The second Caucasian man left the church after a few months of service without having a pastor's title. Moreover, the church quickly proceeded to hire a Chinese-speaking pastor.

In 1991 Rev. Daniel Tang became the senior pastor. He could speak several Chinese dialects as well as English. Backed by some members and also out of his own interests, Rev. Tang tried to take over both English and Chinese Sunday services. He insisted on preaching at both English and Chinese services on a given Sunday at least once a month, and wanted Assistant Pastor Houston to act as his assistant. However, Houston was hired by the congregation and was thus responsible to the congregation, not to the senior pastor. He resisted Rev. Tang's claims of power and authority. Rev. Houston was well received by the English-speaking members and had the support of some immigrant members as well.

In the meantime, the grownup ABCs began to express their desire to have greater participation in the decision making of the church. In 1993 a young man of around thirty years old wrote a six-page open letter complaining about the lack of leadership opportunities for young people. He requested establishment of a leadership board for the English congregation independent of the immigrant-dominated Official Board. Rev. Houston backed him up and mobilized support from both the English congregation and some immigrant members. They claimed that an independent leadership team would get more enthusiastic participation of the young people. Despite opposition from the senior pastor and some lay leaders, Rev. Houston successfully developed the leadership team for the English congregation. He also changed the time of the English service from 9:30 A.M. to 10:30 A.M., which he claimed would make it easier for the young people to invite their non-Christian friends. The time change made it impractical for the senior pastor to preach at both services on a given Sunday. This change not only pleased the English-speaking younger generation, but also attracted some immigrants. Those immigrant parents who wanted to be with their children could attend the same English service without missing the Sunday school class or having to come to the church early. They could understand the English preaching or at least found it tolerable to sit through the service. Some non-American born graduate students or young professionals found the English sermon by Pastor Houston more interesting than the Chinese sermon by Pastor Tang. Some also found English sermons helpful in improving their English language ability. Therefore, following the changes in September 1993, attendance at the English Sunday service immediately jumped. However, after Pastor Tang was ousted in the summer of 1995, many of these people returned to the Chinese service. The religious message seemed to take priority over language improvement for these immigrant Chinese.

English Usage at Other Church Meetings

Besides Sunday worship services, two church gatherings important to the whole church are the congregational meeting and the Official Board meeting. The regular congregational meeting is held three times a year, and the Official Board meeting is held monthly. The Official Board meeting is attended by the annually elected deacons and the pastors. Until the end of the 1970s, the minutes of congregational meetings and Official Board meetings were recorded in Chinese only, although the meeting often provided English and Cantonese interpretations. Church records show that some dissatisfied members made several requests to restore Mandarin as the only working language at all church meetings. They argued that this would save precious time and make the meetings more efficient. They also suggested that non-Mandarin-speakers ought to learn Mandarin, the national language of China, and that they could learn it in the church-sponsored Chinese School. However, instead of maintaining Mandarin as

the official language of the church, English became increasingly necessary. In the 1980s the church had to keep two versions of the minutes of
congregational meetings. Furthermore, English has become dominant at
Official Board meetings, and the minutes of the Official Board have been
in English only since 1990. The increasing use of English is partially because
of the presence of Assistant Pastor Allan Houston, who speaks no Chinese,
and partially because of one or two younger deacons who do not know
Chinese well. Whenever these non-Chinese-speaking people are present,
the meeting has to be conducted in English. Sitting in at some Official
Board meetings, I observed that some immigrant deacons were sometimes
left out in intense debates or discussions because of their lack of English
proficiency. The chairman of the Official Board told me that English was
not the required working language; therefore, it was possible for them
to speak Chinese and let others interpret into English for the English-
speaking leaders. However, speaking English is probably a mark of success
for the young professionals who are working hard to enter the American
mainstream society, which means that they might feel embarrassed by not
speaking English. Nonetheless, the change toward more use of English is not
straight-line evolutionary. The most recent Official Board has some recent
immigrants in their fifties. Unlike those young professionals in their thirties, these older immigrants appear to be more confident and insistent on
speaking Mandarin at the meetings. Bilingual interpretations thus become
necessary again. Also, Rev. Allan Houston resigned and left the church in
1997. These changes make the use of the Chinese language more prevalent
than it had been in preceding years.

The English Problem and Continuous Immigration

Immigrant and ethnic churches often provide community services, including teaching English to new immigrants. However, the CCC has not provided an English class for new immigrants for any significant period. There
are several reasons for this lack. First, most Chinese immigrants coming
to the church are highly educated people. Many learned English before
coming to the United States. Graduate students or college students learn
and/or improve their English at American universities. Immigrant professionals use English at work. Second, those immigrants who need to learn
or improve their English can either afford to go to language schools or
attend government-sponsored English programs for immigrants. Some non-
Chinese churches also provide English classes with or without government

funds. Third, as pointed out in Chapter 3, evangelism has been the mission of this evangelical church. Occasionally, some ABCs volunteer to teach an English Bible study class for those immigrants who want to learn English and Christianity; however, they are not enthusiastic about teaching English only. Major resources for Chinese immigrants to learn English come from organizations other than the Chinese church, including schools (both those in the original countries and in the United States), government programs, and other social organizations.

The American-born or American-raised Chinese learn English in public schools. Most immigrant parents are bilingual professionals who want their children to succeed in mainstream America. These bilingual professionals have shown flexibility and willingness to change toward greater use of English. However, older immigrants who speak little English still insist on Mandarin and on teaching Mandarin to ABCs. Some new immigrants from China, even though they may have learned English, still prefer to use Chinese. Therefore, as long as Chinese immigrants and Chinese students continue to come to the United States, as long as the church keeps its door open to Chinese newcomers, Chinese language will continue to be important in this Chinese church. Also, the rise of "Greater China" (including Hong Kong, Taiwan, Singapore, and mainland China) and the increasingly globalized economy provide incentives for young people to become fully bilingual or multilingual. When American-born young people see learning Chinese as rewarding in their future careers, attending Chinese services or bilingual services can become attractive for them, as we will see in the next chapter.

The Protestant Ethic

Although adopting American lifestyle and English language are carried out mostly outside the immigrant church, the CCC does promote social and moral values that are in line with what Milton Gordon called "the American core culture" (1964, 72). The dominant social and moral values at this Chinese Protestant church can be described as what Max Weber called the "Protestant ethic" or "this-worldly asceticism." The CCC promotes the values of success, thrift, delayed gratification, and spiritual rewards; and it concurrently opposes American consumerism, eroticism, and radical individualism. Concerning gender equality and democracy, however, there are conflicting opinions in this evangelical church.

Success

CCC members are successful people in terms of educational and career achievements. The great majority have received a college education, and many hold master's and doctoral degrees. Most are engineers, scientists, and federal technocrats. The few entrepreneurs are successful in their businesses, such as owning Chinese restaurants or construction companies. More important, church members are success-oriented people who highly value their educational and career achievements. During my interviews with church members, many of them proudly showed me the awards they have won or explained to me their career accomplishments. Young people in an early stage of career look up to well-established members as role models and often consult them for advice and suggestions. Those who have school-age children also emphasize the importance of success. Fellowship groups often hold special meetings to discuss how to better educate their children. At one such meeting the speaker said,

> Among Chinese parents we have a joke. Their responses to their children's grades commonly like this: C is "no-no," B is "so-so," A is "OK." If the kid got a D, the parent would ask, "What's that?!" We ought to have high expectations of our kids. That's for sure. However, you should not over-press the kids. For example, don't become angry when your kid gets a B. You may give some helpful punishment in order to make improvements. For example, if he got a B in composition class, you may ask him to *write* out why he got a B. This punishment would become an opportunity for him to improve his composition ability.

Immigrant parents' emphasis on educational achievement appears to have been successfully passed onto their children. A mother told me about her daughter in middle school. Coming home from work one day, the mother found the girl sobbing quietly. Upon asking, the mother learned that it was because she got a B in a final exam. When the mother comforted her by saying that a B was all right, the girl responded, "Don't say that. I know a B is *not* all right. I don't feel all right. I wanted an A. I wanted straight A's."

Why should one succeed? What is the purpose of success? This would be an important research question. However, I could not even ask this question directly during my interviews because it would sound silly or out of place. Success is a goal that is taken for granted. Nevertheless, I had many opportunities to hear this question being touched upon in public speeches or during informal conversations. For these Chinese Christians, success has a religious motivation. Although church members acknowledge that success leads to a decent life or brings material rewards and respect, they emphasize the religious justifications. It was common to hear words like this:

> As Christians, the glory of our successes in the world belongs to the Lord. Without God's blessing we cannot succeed. God has His purpose on us in our everyday life, including our career. We want to praise God by all means. We want to show the good fruits of our faith to non-Christians.

Indeed, the school and career successes of many church members have impressed many enquirers. Educated Chinese commonly believe that all religions are synonymous with superstitions. They think that Christians, just as other religious people, may be nice people, but they probably lack intelligence. This view is at least shared by many students and visiting scholars from the People's Republic of China. When these people come to the church for a fellowship occasion, many are surprised to meet university professors, scientists in physics or biochemistry, and engineers working on advanced research projects. Many times such a surprise has preceded serious inquiries about Christian beliefs and eventual conversion to Christianity. For these educated people the most welcomed evangelistic speakers are not pastors or professional evangelists, but lay people with career accomplishments.

However, worldly success is seen as secondary to religious service. Some church members retire early to work voluntarily on church ministries or do personal evangelism. One man retired at age fifty-eight. After showing me all the trophies and badges of awards he had collected, he said, "What is the use of all these? Nothing. It's better to do more service in the church. The church needs more people to work." He found the voluntary work at the church more meaningful. Several other people also retired before age sixty, took some seminary courses, and subsequently went abroad for short-term evangelism missions.

Many church members live in the middle- and upper-middle-class neighborhoods of Potomac, Rockville, Gaithersburg, and Silver Spring, Maryland. Some families have very large houses, a few with large yards, private pools, and tennis courts. Again, the justification they give for purchasing a larger house is often religious. They would say that they purchased the big house in order to host fellowship group meetings. Because of the existence of about a dozen fellowship groups and the regular fellowship meetings at members' homes, this justification is apparently commonly accepted. Many people move to large houses for the sake of their children's education. Good public schools are very often in upper-middle-class neighborhoods. Parents who want to put their children in the best public schools have to purchase expensive houses in those neighborhoods even though this may mean working longer hours to pay the mortgage.

Thrift

The CCC is affluent but frugal. The church has very good income from tithing and offerings. In the early 1970s they constructed a two-story sanctuary and a three-story education building within four years, relying completely on members' donations without bank loans or outside donations. In the 1990s the church sent out more than $100,000 every year to support missionaries and Christian organizations. The CCC also pays two pastors good salaries and provides generous subsidies for their continuous education in theology and their transportation.

In 1995 the average offering per person attending Sunday services was between $20 and $30 per week (including teenagers and visitors who probably donate little or nothing). However, church life is frugal. The well-maintained church buildings have little interior or exterior decoration.[6] Air-conditioners, heaters, and lights in the buildings are always turned off unless there are group activities. The church budget is subject to item-by-item scrutinizing by church members at congregational meetings. Church leaders have to justify every item of the budget in detail. At one time, when a fellowship group of college students purchased a portable overhead projector, the treasurer made strong remarks about it at a monthly Official Board meeting:

> American society is a consumerist society. This consumerism has influenced our American-born kids. They want to buy this and buy that without thinking of necessity. The kids are indulged too much. Parents often buy whatever things their children ask. It may be OK because the parents can afford it. But our church should not encourage this. Every penny is given by God and we should carefully manage God's property. We already have two overhead projectors. Why not just use those?

Some deacons explained that those overhead projectors were too heavy to carry to fellowship group meetings and that the church sometimes did need several for simultaneous activities. Eventually the treasurer agreed to reimburse the expense for the new projector, but he declared that this would be the last time he would do it.

The big houses of many members were easily observable and might suggest a life of luxury. However, as already indicated, many families bought those houses so their children could enter good public schools in affluent neighborhoods, and with the justification of hosting fellowship group meetings. Without these justifications, purchasing such a house could become unacceptable. In this regard, Rev. Daniel Tang received some criticism about his lack of frugality. The Tangs had two teenage children. After becoming the senior pastor in 1991, Rev. Tang purchased a house costing over $350,000 in Potomac, a very affluent neighborhood. Rev. Tang told me that some church members showed disapproval of this seemingly luxurious purchase. He defended himself by saying that his house was not the best and that some church members had better houses than his. This was true. But few people accepted his defense. To show the goodwill of the church toward the newly hired pastor, the Official Board decided to provide a noninterest loan for the pastor after he made the purchase. But some older members criticized the pastor. A lay leader commented in an interview:

> We should keep expenditures within the limits of income [*liang ru wei chu*]. This is a good Chinese tradition. A good Christian should follow this principle even better. When you take up a huge financial burden [like Pastor Tang did], how could you live in peace and focus on ministries for the Lord?

In the summer of 1995, Rev. Tang was voted out by the congregation.

Temperance

Temperance is the norm among these Chinese Christians. They are explicit about their interest in good food and enthusiastic about dinner occasions. Fellowship groups often hold potluck gatherings, to which every family brings a home-cooked dish. In those gatherings I always found excellent dishes of various Chinese cuisines. Around the table people are relaxed and comfortable in talking with each other. Exchanging recipes at the gatherings is a favorite topic among both men and women. However, all of the group gatherings that I attended were "dry"—no wine, beer, or other alcohol were ever served. Also, I never saw any person smoke at the church or group gatherings. At first I did not pay any attention to the absence of smoking because I myself was a nonsmoker. Later I found that this was in the implicit moral code of this and other conservative Chinese churches. The pastor of the Chinese Bible Church of Maryland said this in an interview:

> I once served a Chinese church in another city for several years. One time a man was elected as a deacon by the congregation. I knew he was not a good Christian. He had moral problems. He smoked. Sometimes he even could not hold out in a Sunday service and had to rush outside to light a cigarette. I knew he had this problem. Smoking was an indication of other problems. How could such an addicted person serve on the church council? He was not able to sit through the board meeting. He had to interrupt the discussion by going outside to smoke. However, some church members did not know what should be the criteria of deaconship. I made efforts to improve it.

In this remark smoking is taken as indicative of other deeper, moral and spiritual problems. A deacon explained to me in an interview that alcohol can be consumed for medical reasons and that Christians may have a drink on occasions to befriend non-Christians, but that habitual alcoholism is definitely un-Christian: "If one cannot resist alcohol or smoking, how can one resist other temptations?" His view apparently is shared by people in most Chinese evangelical churches. In their conversion testimonials some people said that they used to smoke or drink before conversion. Upon my enquiry about the necessity of quitting smoking or drinking, some respondents asked a question in reply: "When you know smoking is not good for your health, why should you do it anyway? Yes, the Bible did not say that Christians cannot drink. But what is the good of drinking?" Although smoking or drinking never became a topic at the CCC during my field work, the implicit moral code was clearly against it.

There seemed to be no clear rules against seeing movies or watching sports, although these were vaguely discouraged in favor of work or study. Chinese parents often invest time and money in their children's extracurricular activities, such as learning to play piano or violin, or participating in volleyball or swimming. They want their children to develop in an all-around way. However, church leaders and most parents discourage children from entering sports as a profession.

Sexuality and Marriage

Church leaders and parents definitely discourage dating among high school boys and girls. A mother of three teenage boys once told me:

> I was worried for my second son. He is a high school student. The teens fellowship group once was on the edge of becoming a social and dating club. Several parents were worried about this when they sensed the tendencies, but we didn't know what we could do. These are youth at a rebellious age in this free American society. But God is really wonderful. Right then the assistant pastor gave a sermon: "True Love Waits." It was an excellent sermon. My boy understood the preaching very well and liked it very much. The pastor asked these young people to make a commitment to God, write it down, and keep it for themselves, that they would wait for the true love. After that the teens fellowship returned to normal.

To guard against bad influences the parents rely on the church for meaningful and attractive youth activities. They also try to fill their children's schedules by sending them to camp meetings, pressing them to study the Chinese language, and bringing them to private music and sport classes. These efforts are quite successful. Some common problems in American society, such as drugs, teenage pregnancy, and homosexuality, have been very rare among the young people in Chinese Christian churches. I heard of no case of such problems during my field work period at the CCC and found no such things in church records of the CCC.

Chinese parents are in constant fear of bad influences in American society. One of the most frequent topics at fellowship group meetings is how to bring up children in the free American society. Freedom and opportunities are appreciated, whereas the common problems are feared and various strategies are suggested. The most recommended strategy is, as I heard many times, to "bring the kids to the Lord." Once the children become true Christians who love God, the reasoning goes, parents will not need to worry about them any more.

Intact and traditional marriage and family life are highly valued in the Chinese church. The vast majority of adult church members are married. The few singles in their thirties or early forties are usually seen as yet-to-be married. Marriage problems do exist among some church members. However, family problems are generally not made known to the public, and divorce cases have been rare. After reading through several boxes of church records, I finally found records on one divorce case in Official Board meeting minutes. I tried to follow it up, but found that the involved couple had left the church. One informant told me that the man later remarried a white American and was attending a non-Chinese church with his new wife. The divorced woman had lost contact with this church. When I asked why they had left the church, the informant said that although the church did not have a policy against the divorced, almost all church members had good marriages, and divorced people might feel uncomfortable with other church members. Apparently, the Chinese church promotes good married life and continues to be a community of intact marriages.

"Be Proud of Yourself" and "Dare to Be Different"

Living in the pluralist society of contemporary America, group identification is a necessary choice one has to make. Differences, be they racial, ethnic, religious, moral, or political, are normatively and frequently highlighted in the American context. The adaptation of the Chinese Christians is expressed typically in two statements: "Be proud of yourself" and "Dare to be different."

To be proud of oneself, beyond personal success, one needs to appreciate one's group social status and cultural heritage. Generally speaking, Chinese culture is known for its cultivation of a cultural pride that is a result of five thousand years of uninterrupted and expanding civilization. In modern times, however, the Chinese nation has been repeatedly humiliated by Western and Japanese powers. In the United States the Chinese were the first people excluded from immigration and naturalization. The phrase "a Chinaman's chance," the generic name of Charlie for Chinese laundrymen, and the "coolies" are humiliating images of the Chinese in America (see Barth 1964; Miller 1969). During those anti-Chinese decades, it would have been hard for Chinese immigrants and their children to achieve a sense of "being proud of oneself" in American society.[7]

Only after World War II did the Chinese nation and Chinese Americans start to rise in social status. New Chinese immigrants arrived in the United States after this upturn, and thus are able to claim self-pride. To justify one's pride, an appreciation of one's own cultural traditions is necessary but not always adequate. Multiculturalism in American society presses for critical reflection on all cultural traditions. In this regard, conservative Christianity may provide an absolute moral foundation on which believers can claim their pride in the name of following the absolute biblical teachings.

Therefore, personal achievements in education and career, the rising status of the ethnic group in America backed by a long and rich civilization and a rising nation, and the absoluteness of the Christian faith, together, enable these Chinese Christians to assert their pride.

"Dare to be different" is a complementary statement of "Be proud of yourself." American society is at once a society of conformity and a society of contention (Bellah et al. 1985). Peer pressure for conformity is pervasive in school and in work. At the same time, individuals and groups have to assert their distinctiveness or uniqueness to get recognition or respect. Talking about educating children, a popular woman speaker of the CCC spoke at a fellowship meeting:

> Having American friends is necessary for your kids, but only to a certain degree. There are too many problem teenagers in American society. Some Chinese children become problem teenagers because they are too Americanized. They conform too much to the peer pressure. Don't say we must immerse ourselves into American society. What is American society? Students who are participating in math contests are seen as nerds by [white] American girls. We need to teach our kids "dare to be different." Teach them to have self-confidence about what they do and be proud of what they are. We must have rules. For example, don't allow your kids to stay overnight with other kids. Peer pressure may be strong on your kids. But after two or three times, others will accept the differences, and even respect your kids, and would let your kids go home before midnight without problems.

She went on to say that white American parents, including those who attend churches, often have low expectations of their children. They ask their children to "do your best," which is often only an excuse for failure. Mixing with such children could bring bad influences on Chinese children. She suggested that it would be more desirable to mix with children of immigrants, such as Asian Indians or Koreans, because they were more conservative in moral values. Better yet, she suggested, bring your children to the Chinese church:

> It is necessary to have friends after school. It's better to include several families. The Chinese church provides this. In the fellowship group it is easier to provide such an environment. We Chinese have a proverb: "He who stays near vermilion gets stained red, and he who stays near ink gets stained black" [*jin zhu zhe chi, jin mo zhe hei*].

> Mencius' mother moved three times [*meng mu san qian*] [in order to have good neighbors for her child]. It is very important to have proper friends.

The pastor told a story in a sermon that echoed that of the woman speaker: A Chinese family used to attend an American church. The parents became unhappy about their daughter's getting some B grades in school. When they asked about it, the girl replied, "I have done my best." When they asked again, she ruffled, "I am doing better than many of my friends in school and church. They got C's and B's but their parents still love them without a fuss. Why are you so harsh on me?" The daughter felt disappointed to be Chinese, and the parents felt helpless to respond. Later, they found a Chinese church and switched there. After a while, the girl came to tell her parents, "Compared with other parents in the church, you are not really harsh." Her gradual change pleased the parents. A changed reference group and her growing Chinese identity, nurtured in the Chinese church, helped this girl to excel in school.

What is interesting here is not that these Chinese proclaim "Dare to be different," because many other Americans do the same. The interesting change for these Chinese Christians is that they claim their "differences" are based on the supposedly universal principle of Christianity more than on the particularity of Chinese traditions. The absolute and universal claims of evangelical Christianity make it easier for them to justify and defend their differences from the surrounding society. The Chinese church is a plausible structure that helps these immigrants and their children maintain their distinctive value system (Berger and Luckmann 1966).

Democracy

The Chinese immigrant church is an institutional setting in which immigrants learn to exercise democracy, an important American principle.[8] Democracy, the CCC proclaims, is based on the Christian belief that no person is perfect, thus no person should hold power without checks and balances.

From its outset, the CCC has exhibited a spirit of equal and democratic participation of individual members. In the first congregational meeting in 1959, the participants chose three "co-workers" to be church leaders with one-year terms. For each position, they first nominated three candidates before holding an anonymous vote. When two candidates tied, a second round of votes was cast. Eventually, none of the co-workers received more than eight votes out of the total number of fifteen participants. The meeting was utterly democratic. The same pattern continued in the following congregational meetings.

Every year deacons are democratically elected from and by church members; no one may hold the position for more than two consecutive years. All important decisions must be made by congregational meetings, which are held two or three times a year. In the 1960s there were several attempts to select lay "elders" for the purpose of long-term planning and church stability, but some members were strongly opposed. They argued that there was no such need, and even if there were, no one was qualified to be an elder since the title conveys a meaning of authority with senior status, whereas church members were all in their twenties and thirties.

After Rev. Frank Chao became the pastor in 1969, the CCC underwent important organizational restructuring. The immigrant pastor pushed to ordain three permanent lay elders. The Elders Board, chaired by the senior pastor, claimed the highest authority, whereas the Official Board, composed of elected deacons, was relegated to take care of administrative matters. Rev. Chao further suggested that the Elders Board be the *de facto* Deacons Nomination Committee. Thus the congregational meeting became no more than a place to get decisions announced and confirmed. These changes caused grave concern, quiet resistance, and open opposition in the congregation. One highly respected lay leader refused to be nominated for elder, citing his Baptist conviction. In 1973 the Elders Board made the nomination of candidates for deacons. These candidates were elected, but none of them received majority votes at the congregational meeting. Church members expressed distrust in the Elders Board and subsequently returned nomination responsibility to the congregational meeting.

After failure to change the church according to his wishes, Rev. Chao sometimes went ahead with his own decisions in financial and personnel issues without going through due processes. This caused resentment from some lay leaders and members. Many members wanted to restore the congregational meeting as the highest authority of the church, whereas the Official Board subsequently declared that it had sole responsibility for budget planning and other decision-making. A retiring chairman of the Official Board made a speech at a handing-over meeting attended by all deacons of both years, all elders, and the pastoral staff. He asked the elders not to play the role of super-sovereign emperors (*tai shang huang*) over the deacons, and asked the pastor not to act like the pope. Responding to this and similar criticism, Rev. Chao wrote an open letter to the congregation and declared: "We pastors are sent here by God to lead, rather than to be led by people." Amid heightened conflicts, some lay leaders sided with the pastor and argued that mass democracy was not biblical. However, the congregation eventually forced Rev. Chao to resign, which precipitated the split in the summer of 1976.

After the schism the CCC passed a new church constitution after repeated open debates and several drafts. The adopted constitution made it clear that all important decisions should be made at the congregational meeting. Until today, the Official Board has no right to spend more than $500 without prior approval from the congregational meeting. The constitution has kept clauses about eldership and the Elders Board. However, in 1978 a pastor from a Baptist background clashed with the remaining elder. A year later the pastor was voted out by the congregation and the weary elder became inactive in church attendance. Since then the CCC has had no elder. The church constitution also explicitly limits the power and the term of the pastor: every two years the pastor is subject to review by the whole congregation; without at least two-thirds majority approval, the pastor must go. In the 1990s Rev. Tang tried to select some elders, but his attempt ended with bitter failure, and he himself was voted out in 1995. The specifics of the church polity vary in different Chinese churches, but the principles of checks and balances and democratic procedures are favored by immigrant members in most churches that I have visited.

Before the vote on Rev. Tang in the summer of 1995, some people voiced their opposition to voting on any pastor. They argued that the authority of the pastor comes from God so it should be respected rather than decided by church members; democracy in the church was not right, not biblical. An observer might expect that Chinese immigrants from nondemocratic societies would oppose church democracy. However, most of the dissenters were actually American-born or American-raised young people. In contrast, most immigrants insisted on the principle of democracy in the church. "This is America," they argued, "where democracy is the norm."

Gender Equality

Gender equality is an issue about which there is disagreement among church members at the CCC. In education and occupation women members are generally not much different from the men. For some couples, both the husband and the wife are Ph.D. holders and both have good careers. While a few women are homemakers, especially when they have small children, most women have their own jobs. At home and in the society these women and men are not much different in status. General participation in the church is quite equal as well. Every Sunday volunteers prepare the Sunday lunch for the whole congregation. Most of the time husbands and wives do the cooking together. The participation of women in the church has been active and enthusiastic. Women sing in choirs, teach children's Sunday School, and coordinate group and church activities. Women have served in various leadership positions. The family is the basic unit in most church activities, and women attend church or group activities with their husbands. There has been a women's fellowship, but it did not hold regular activities in the period of my field work. Only two church members were listed as members of the women's fellowship in the 1996 church directory, whereas other fellowship groups had at least a dozen people.

Taking a historical perspective, these manifestations of gender equality are in accordance with the roles Christian churches played in the past among Chinese immigrants. In the first half of the twentieth century, Chinese Christian churches made a significant contribution to the emancipation of Chinese immigrant women and American-born girls from footbinding, ignorance, and confinement within the domestic sphere (Yung 1995). The churches provided Chinese women a social space and supported their social activities and public education.[9] Today, Chinese American women at the church seldom need to fight battles for social participation, education, and democratic procedures of the church.

However, the testing ground now concerns leadership roles. At this Chinese evangelical church men hold most of the leadership positions. Since its early days the church has had some deaconesses. But the chairperson of the Official Board has always been a lay man and the majority on the board have been men.[10] All of the past and present pastors have been men.[11] Furthermore, upon taking up the pastor's position in 1982, Rev. Philip Hung requested at an Official Board meeting that no woman should be the Sunday service leader. There was no record of this having been made an explicit rule, but I did not see any woman presiding at a Sunday service at the CCC.

When Rev. Allan Houston became the assistant pastor in 1989, he further suggested that no woman should serve on the Official Board. When Rev. Houston was the only pastor in 1990, he and some conservative lay leaders succeeded in nominating only men as deacon candidates. Some women who had served as deaconesses protested, but it was too late for that year. In the following year, however, some women were elected to the Official Board.

During that period, Rev. Houston also brought in another Caucasian man as the youth pastor. Some church members opposed the increase of non-Chinese-speaking pastors. When that man left the church after serving for several months as a staff worker without a pastor's title, Rev. Houston told me that he left because he disagreed about having women as deaconesses and felt this church was too liberal for him. Rev. Houston adjusted his own position from opposition to reservation, justifying his position by saying that deacons and deaconesses were not really spiritual leaders.

After Rev. Daniel Tang became the senior pastor in 1991, he expressed his support for women leaders. However, some lay leaders bluntly confronted Rev. Tang. Those outspoken men and women were taking courses at a fundamentalist Bible college. A professor of biblical theology, a white man, taught them that according to the Bible, no woman should be a spiritual leader—pastor or elder. American fundamentalists seem to have exerted significant influence in this regard.

The fundamentalist influence was further manifested in the discussions about a candidate for senior pastor. One year after Rev. Tang left the church, the Pastor Search Committee finally recommended a candidate to the congregation. This candidate seemed to be very qualified in terms of his theological training, ministry experiences, and linguistic capability. The only problem was that his wife was also an ordained pastor. Many members spoke against the candidate because of his wife's pastoral status. Again, one might assume that Chinese immigrants would be conservative while American-born young people would be more open on this issue. However, several American-born young people voiced firm opposition to this candidate simply because of his wife. They argued that if the biblical principle of no female spiritual leadership could be broken, no biblical principles would be unchangeable. To protect the integrity of the faith, faithful Christians should not accommodate worldly trends in anything. This is a powerful argument at this evangelical church whose members are in need of certainty. The Pastor Search Committee was composed of five people. Except for Rev. Houston, all the other four committee members were first-generation Chinese immigrants in their fifties or sixties. Rev. Houston clearly stated his disapproval of having a woman pastor, but he had decided to resign from this church by that time. Although they did so with hesitation, the committee members recommended this candidate to the congregation. When I heard the English-speaking young people opposing this candidate, it became clear to me that Rev. Houston, a very conservative American, had made a significant impact on those he had nurtured in the past eight years.

These incidents clearly show the influence of American Christian fundamentalism upon this immigrant Chinese church. It is true that the equal status of women was not recognized in traditional Chinese culture. But most church members have been educated in China and the United States and have experienced equality between men and women. The opposition to gender equality at this Chinese church is puzzling. The only noticeable factor is the influence of Christian fundamentalism in the United States, which has been on the rise in the last few decades. However, why does this Chinese church voluntarily accept the influence of American Christian fundamentalism? Further explorations of this question will follow in the next chapter.

The Christian Foundation of the United States of America

In the United States a majority of people claim a Christian faith. The historical and social affinity of Christian and American identities may suggest easy identification for Chinese Christians with the United States. However, Chinese immigrants and their children at the CCC share many of the feelings and concerns of conservative Christians, including evangelicals and fundamentalists, who often claim their minority status in a sea of secularism and atheism. Chinese Christians also see themselves as a minority, not so much in the ethnic as in the religious sense. They say that although many Americans claim to be Christian, only a few are true Christians—those who are born again.

A young Chinese preacher at the Chinese Bible Church of Maryland clearly enunciated this sense of religious minority in a sermon in the fall of 1995. That sermon, entitled "Suffering and Peace," began with the reading of the biblical verse from John 16:33 (NIV): "I have told you these things, so that in me you may have peace. In this world you will have trouble. But take heart! I have overcome the world." The young man preached in Mandarin:

> Christians will suffer the sufferings that Jesus once suffered. We suffer just because we are Christians. The disciples of Jesus were persecuted and hated by their contemporaries. . . . Christians have been suffering since the foundation of the church. It is not exceptional in the United States. Christians are often ridiculed by the media, by our

colleagues, and even by our own family members. Not long ago a
TV program showed an interview with a pastor. The pastor has been
active in the anti-abortion movement. A woman who once fought on
the frontline for the right of abortion suddenly converted and was
subsequently baptized by this pastor. During the interview, the jour-
nalist asked the pastor, "Are you going to use her for your purpose?"
As the pastor barely said "No," without being able to complete his
sentence, the newsman immediately said, "*suan le ba* [come on]!"

The phrase "*suan le ba*" plainly conveyed the unspoken words, "No doubt
you will use her. How ridiculous you are for even trying to deny this." The
preacher continued:

> If a person never suffers for his belief in the Lord, this person does
> not truly belong to Christ. . . . I would like to challenge everyone:
> Have you ever experienced torment, derision or bigotry because of
> your faith in the Lord? Are you willing to suffer for the Lord? Do
> you dare to face derision for your Christian beliefs? . . . Those who
> suffer for the Lord will be blessed by the Lord. We must be prepared
> to endure sufferings as Christians, even in the United States.

He pointed out that to be a faithful Christian incurs a cost in the world,
including in American society. CCC members and many other Chinese
American Christians share the concerns of American evangelicals, including
views concerning school prayer, abortion, and the perceived moral decay.

On the other hand, many Chinese Christians do see their Christian identity and American identity overlapping to a certain degree. Some immigrants
who had been Christians before coming to America looked up to the United
States as a Christian nation. Only after they found the secularized reality of
American society did they become somewhat disappointed. Nonetheless,
most people believe that the United States is the best country on earth.
Although true Christians are only a minority in the United States, the
proportion is nevertheless larger than in European and Asian countries.
There are occasions where conservative Christians are derided, but there
is no political persecution against Christians in America. Moreover, many
converts came to know the Christian God only in the United States.

More importantly, this Chinese immigrant church proclaims the "Christian foundation of the U.S.A." Like many conservative Christians, most
Chinese Christians dispute the notion that the United States is a Christian
nation. However, many of them believe that it has a Christian core or a

Christian foundation. These evangelical Christian Chinese are willing to identify with this Christian America; hence, this theme frequently appears in sermons, group discussions, and written articles. One of the most welcomed speakers at the CCC was Mr. Yuan Zhiming, a dissident activist in the Tiananmen Square Democracy Movement in 1989. He fled to the United States in 1990 and converted to Christianity in 1991. After attending an annual Prayer Breakfast at the White House, he was so impressed by the Christian beliefs of American political leaders that he subsequently began to proclaim the Christian foundation of the United States by publishing articles and giving speeches. A young man from Taiwan also described his excitement upon discovering the Christian core of the United States. In an article in the church magazine he wrote:

> Three years ago I came to the U.S. to study computer science. Besides learning this newest and most advanced science and technology, I had a strong desire to find out what made the USA the strongest country in the world. Before coming here my knowledge about the U.S. came from Hollywood movies, which portrayed a dazzling world with myriad temptations, material prosperity, and severe corruption of young people. After I came to the U.S. and have observed with my own eyes, however, I find the profound influence of Christianity among the backbone elements of Americans. Many middle-aged and older people, who have good social status and great influence, are Christians. Their words and deeds have been deeply influenced by Christian beliefs. The founding spirit of the USA is originated from Christian doctrines. American laws and the humanitarian spirit all have roots in Christianity. Internally, this made the American social political system healthy, the nation strong, and the people prosperous. Internationally, then, the USA can advance her military, political, and economic developments, and has become the leader of the free world.

These words are written by a man from Taiwan, a close ally of the United States during the Cold War. Other immigrants may disagree with some of his points. Nonetheless, the article reflects the thinking of some church members, and this "discovery" preceded this young man's conversion to Christianity and his decision to stay in the United States.

Although the CCC does not celebrate Independence Day, Thanksgiving and Christmas are always major events for the whole church. A former CCC pastor from Hong Kong wrote in the church magazine:

> When I was young, I went to a missionary school [in China]. We were taught to sing the song "God Bless America." I was unconvinced and demurred. Why should God just bless America? By now I have lived in the U.S. for more than 20 years and visited 47 states. I realize that there are many reasons for God to bless America. One of them is the grateful hearts of Americans. Traditionally, the USA is a Christian country. Since its early days, every family would get together in November to thank God. Following this is Christmas in December when people often make donations to help needy people all over the world.

However, the Christian foundation of the United States is eroding, this evangelical church fearfully claims. This was a message I repeatedly heard at the CCC and at various Chinese Christian meetings. Many Chinese Christian leaders state that the United States is becoming less and less Christian. They point to the 1960s and the ban of prayer in public schools as the turning point, following which all kinds of problems emerged—violent crime, drugs, premarital and extramarital sex, teenage pregnancy, homosexuality, AIDS, and so on. These social evils have even penetrated into mainline churches, a frequent guest preacher said, and many American churches have become empty:

> There was a big church with more than a thousand seats located near a university campus. A group of Chinese Christian students and a group of Asian Indian Christian students rented the church for Bible studies and other religious activities. One day the pastor of the church asked the two student groups for a joint activity with his church in order to enhance communication. He asked Chinese and Indian students to prepare food while the host Americans would prepare the program. The food was of course very delicious, but the program was just unbelievable. The host church provided bingo games, a kind of gambling, and belly dancing. During the dance by a half-nude woman, the Christian students were so embarrassed that they all tried to hide their heads. It was just so awkward.
>
> This is the problem of American churches. They have become empty physically and spiritually. The social problems of teenage pregnancy, violence, crime, homosexuality, and so on are also found in many American churches and in some American seminaries as well. In these seminaries the Bible is taught as not credible or believable. There is no prayer. Professors of theology smoke in the class and

grow ponytail hair. How could these people speak God's words? . . . All failures of America today are because of their rejection of God.

Interpreting these problems as signs and consequences of the erosion of the Christian foundation of the United States, this Chinese pastor made a call to Chinese Christians:

> We have to work hard to uphold God's words in America. . . . We have seen the decline of the strength of the U.S. and the emptiness of American churches. We should have a sense of responsibility for this nation and for all people in the world. We must take up the burden to evangelize all peoples in America and the world, not just the Chinese.

This is a call for Christian evangelism, not a call for political action. As a conservative church, the CCC usually does not promote political actions other than encouraging members to be good citizens and to vote in national or local elections. However, before the 1992 presidential election, I found some flyers and campaign letters at the church. One flyer, taken from the "California Voter's Guide" and translated into Chinese, compared the positions of the Republican incumbent George Bush and the Democratic candidate William Clinton on homosexual marriage, pornography, sexual education in public schools, prayer in public schools, abortion, and so on. All these concern moral issues. The tone was clearly in favor of incumbent George Bush. A letter distributed in the church entitled "The Voice of a Chinese American Voter" made a clear call to vote for George Bush. The letter accused Clinton of moral problems, warned of the slow brainwashing by the liberal media, and praised Bush for his moral concerns. "Although Bush is not the most ideal candidate, he nevertheless has moral values most compatible to those of us Chinese people. At least he is a gentleman who highly values the family." The authors who signed these letters were not church members; however, the presence of these flyers and letters at the church and the absence of anything positive for Democrat Clinton showed the general political tendency of these Chinese Christians.

Many Chinese Protestant churches of new immigrants are more Republican than Democratic. An interesting contrast is the Chinese Community Church in Chinatown, which is an interdenominational church founded by mainline churches and attended mostly by earlier Chinese immigrants and their descendants. Through interviews with its pastor and some members I learned that the Chinese Community Church was apparently more

Democratic. This might reflect a general political difference between older Chinese churches and new Chinese churches, which in turn may reflect some general differences between the earlier Chinese immigrants and the new Chinese immigrants. These two groups have had very different social experiences in the United States.

Some CCC members have become interested and involved in local politics. A young mother, an immigrant from Taiwan and an active member of the church, said to me that she had dreamed about the United States as the "beautiful country" (*meiguo*) before her immigration, but only was disappointed by the social reality:

> I am not a political person. However, I now find that you have to get involved at least in the local politics. All things are changing, and often changing toward bad and worse. For example, the public schools in this county may make some liberal changes. We cannot keep silent about this. We have to make our concerns known. I don't like the way of American politics—the noisiest gets most attention. But we have to make our voice heard in order to protect our own interests, to secure a clean social environment for our children, and for the good of our children's education. We have to get involved in the neighborhood organizations, in the county school board, and in the city government. Morality in America is declining. As Christians we have the commission of evangelism. As American citizens we have the responsibility for preserving the good society.

For her, and for many Chinese Christians as well, the Christian church provides a ground to stand on to assert their moral concerns in American society. The proclamation of "the Christian foundation of the USA" empowers them to assert their American identity and to join the forces pulling American society in certain directions.

Independence and Integration

The CCC, like many Chinese churches in contemporary American society, is an independent church without denominational affiliation. Does non-denominational status mean a self-chosen separation or isolation? Does it reflect the lack of social integration or structural assimilation? These are important questions, but there are no simple answers. Past studies of Chinese American communities tend either to stress the assimilation intention of Chinese converts or to highlight the assimilation efforts by white American missionaries. However, the intentions and consequences of both white Christians and Chinese converts need to be examined carefully.

Earlier Missions Revisited

As has already been noted, Chinese mission stations were established by American mainline denominations soon after Chinese laborers arrived in California in the mid-nineteenth century. Those white missionaries tried to Christianize the heathen Chinese and also Americanize them culturally. Two motivations were most obvious for doing that. One was to Christianize the Chinese and send them back to China to help American missionaries there; the other was colonialist concerns. By and large, however, their intentions were usually not to include those Chinese laborers as equal members of American society.

First of all, the nineteenth-century missions among the Chinese in America were extensions of China missions. When the Presbyterian denomination established the first Chinese church in San Francisco, that mission was under the sponsorship of the Presbyterian Board of Foreign Missions. Other denominations similarly treated their missions among Chinese in America as extensions of foreign missions. The primary goal of these missions was to produce missionary helpers to China. They wanted these Americanized converts to go back to China, rather than settle down in the United States. In his study of these missions, Timothy Tseng concludes, "Winning the Chinese in America for the sake of the Chinese in China would be echoed repeatedly into the twentieth century and became the *raison d'etre* for missions to the Chinese in America" (Tseng 1994, 59). Reluctantly, Tseng points out that most white American churches refused to receive Chinese converts as church members. He painstakingly tries to show the sincerity of the missions and missionaries' protection of Chinese laborers against exclusion and repeatedly states that only "a minority of white church members" resisted the Chinese. However, this "minority" claim might be true in the number of those Christians participating in violence against Chinese or open opposition to accepting Chinese converts into their church, but in a footnote Tseng acknowledges that probably "as many as 90% of the Protestants in California opposed Chinese immigration" (1994, 166). Apparently, social integration was not a goal of earlier Christian missions among Chinese in the United States.

Secondly, those earlier Christian missions among Chinese in America were also motivated by American colonialist concerns. For example, after the abolition of slavery, plantation owners in Mississippi made efforts to import Chinese coolies as indentured laborers. To weigh the cost and benefit, a newspaper editor representing the plantation owners stated,

> Emancipation has spoiled the Negro, and carried him away from fields of agriculture. Our prosperity depends entirely upon the recovery of lost ground, and we therefore say let the [Chinese] Coolies come, and *we will take the chance of Christianizing them* [stress added]. (Quoted by Loewen 1971, 22)

For these plantation owners, Christianizing the Chinese was closely associated with their need for docile laborers.

Some historical studies (Woo 1983; Fung 1989) of the early missions among the Chinese in California also argue that missionary motivations and work at that time were racist, nativist, and paternalist. Missionaries regarded Chinese culture as inferior and tried to change the Chinese to be like themselves. They feared that the heathen Chinese might demoralize America. Timothy Tseng provides ample evidence to show that "from the start, missionary zeal to convert the Chinaman was augmented by a concern for national homogeneity" (1994, 59). Evidently the colonialist or imperialist drives to "make others like us" were not accompanied by a willingness to integrate Chinese into their own institutions. In Mississippi, as well as in other areas, the dominant whites strove hard to maintain racial segregation (Loewen 1971).

Earlier Chinese Churches Revisited

What were the motivations of Chinese converts to Christianity? Looking at earlier missions among the Chinese, one can doubtless point to the impact of social pressure on Chinese laborers for becoming Christian. An old Chinese man quoted by Quan in his study of the Mississippi Chinese (1982, 37) stated, "It's hard to be a Buddhist in a Christian sea." The ethnic ghetto Chinatown could resist social pressures to a certain extent, but the dispersed Chinese in Mississippi were apparently subject to greater pressures from white Christians. Responding to Christian proselytization efforts as well as to the "Christian sea" surrounding them, many Chinese declared Christian faith, but they had to form their own church rather than joining the existing white churches.

On the West Coast, there were some "integrated" churches, or more appropriately, some efforts to integrate Chinese converts into white churches. However, these efforts largely failed. Tseng (1994) shows that the denominational hierarchy of the Congregational church held an "integration" policy in the late nineteenth century: "Congregational churches along the Pacific Coast were encouraged to open their doors to provide English education to the Chinese. Chinese converts were encouraged to unite with the church that sponsored the school mission" (53). However, "many white congregations resisted accepting converted Chinese into membership" (54). Integration ultimately failed among Chinese Congregationalists, and eventually, a separate Chinese Congregational church emerged in the early 1900s. In Mississippi too, the dispersed Chinese established their own Baptist church (Loewen 1971).

It is interesting that these Chinese Christians seemed to be able to claim their American identity more effectively through the separate Chinese church than through the integrated church. This seems paradoxical. However, internal racism and external imperialism were important factors. Those Chinese in America wanted to become equal members of this society, whereas many white Christians refused to accept them, with or without noble justifications. Consequently, Chinese Christians had to set up their own churches. Through the ethnic church they hoped to claim their equality as Christians *and* as good Americans. It is not clear how much these Chinese Christians in the separate Chinese churches were accepted by white people, but undoubtedly the Chinese church provided an institutional base for Chinese converts to claim their equal American identity.

Before World War II, most Chinese churches in the United States were mission churches supported by white Christians. However, these churches moved to claim independence or autonomy as soon as they could. Many remained in the denominations but secured independence in leadership and administration (Lau 1933). After World War II, along with the decline of mainline denominations and the continuous growth of conservative churches, many nondenominational Chinese churches emerged. Among the denominational Chinese churches, the largest groups are the Southern Baptist Convention (SBC) and the Christian and Missionary Alliance (C&MA).

It might seem strange to see the rapid increase of Chinese SBC churches since the SBC was notorious for its racist positions. However, there may be a historical reason for the large number of Chinese SBC churches: the success of the SBC in China missions. Chinese immigrants who had become Christians under the influence of Southern Baptist missionaries may tend to continue to stay in the SBC in the United States. However, a more important reason is probably the congregational autonomy within the SBC as well as its conservative theology. The local congregation has a great degree of independence from the denominational hierarchy. Meanwhile, the SBC has also encouraged the formation of "homogeneous worshiping units" or ethnic churches.

In contrast, many mainline denominations have insisted on the principle of racial integration since the Civil Rights movement in the 1960s. Some historically Chinese churches on the West Coast were pressed by the denominational hierarchy to drop the Chinese label from their church names. However, this insistence on the integration principle may have alienated Chinese Christians who wanted to preserve their Chinese ethnicity (cf. Fung 1989). This is another paradox—that an insistence on integration produced fewer affiliated churches, whereas a policy of encouraging independence attracted more ethnic churches for affiliation.

Independent, but Not Isolated

The Chinese Christian Church of Greater Washington, D.C., has been a nondenominational church, but it is not isolated from the larger society. First of all, church members are well integrated into American society in public spheres—schools, work places, and professional associations. Their church, like their family, is only part of their private life. It provides a sense of social belonging for Chinese immigrants and forges a close-knit community for their children's moral education. These needs are not easily met in nonethnic churches.

Second, although the CCC is by definition a Chinese church, it is not completely exclusive. White Americans have served the church as youth interns and pastors. Allan Houston served the church for eight years although he and his wife spoke no Chinese and showed little interest in Chinese culture. The church has sometimes had non-Chinese preachers for Sunday services, missions' conferences, and other functions. Many church members have taken courses at non-Chinese seminaries and Bible colleges. In fact, as I described earlier in this chapter, these non-Chinese seminary professors have had a significant influence on some church members. CCC members have attended Promise Keepers gatherings and leadership training seminars by American Christian organizations. College students commonly participate in activities organized by InterVarsity Christian Fellowship and Campus Crusade for Christ. ABC and ARC members have frequently brought their non-Chinese friends into the church, although few of them could stay long. Meanwhile, the church financially supports non-Chinese missionary and Christian organizations. The church and some church members subscribe to magazines from non-Chinese Christian organizations such as Navigators and Moody Bible Institute. Church records show that these non-Chinese magazines have made a significant impact on this church.

In brief, although there is no formal organizational affiliation with any American denomination, informal networking and personal contacts are many. An important difference between organizational affiliation and informal networking is the voluntary nature in the latter relationship. Only through mutual benefits can the relationship be built and maintained. No hierarchical coercion is acceptable. Of course, as the number of Chinese religious organizations is increasing, as more Chinese Christian leaders are emerging, there may be a tendency toward fewer contacts with non-Chinese Christians and Christian organizations. However, the growth of an English-speaking second generation will make complete isolation impossible.

In sum, members of this Chinese immigrant church are well assimilated in public spheres of school and work and in adopting American lifestyles and values. However, their assimilation is determinedly selective, maintaining the ethnic church and rejecting some American values. Most important, this independent Chinese church proclaims the Christian foundation of the United States of America, a conservative version of the American identity. The construction of American identity is an ongoing process that is simultaneously a process of selective preservation of Chinese cultural traditions.

5

Preserving Chinese Culture

According to Will Herberg, immigrants in the United States would give up everything but their traditional religion:

> Sooner or later the immigrant will give up virtually everything he had brought with him from the "old country"—his language, his nationality, his manner of life—and will adopt the ways of his new home. Within broad limits, however, his becoming an American did not involve his abandoning the old religion in favor of some native American substitute. Quite the contrary, not only was he expected to retain his old religion, as he was not expected to retain his old language or nationality, but such was the shape of America that it was largely in and through his religion that he, or rather his children and grandchildren, found an identifiable place in American life. (1960, 27–28)

However, for Chinese immigrants who have even forsaken their traditional religion and converted to Christianity, what is left for them to preserve? This question is especially important for Chinese immigrants because of the historical conflicts between Christianity and Chinese culture and between Christian and Chinese identities (see Chapter 2). For immigrant converts, the Chinese church is not a transplant from the old country but a new invention in American soil. These immigrants are uprooted socially, culturally, and religiously as well. Chinese Christian churches in the United States are self-defined as *Chinese* churches. In what sense do Chinese Christians in America claim their Chinese identity? What Chinese traditions does the church preserve?

Many scholars believe, as reviewed in Chapter 2, that the nature of the Chinese culture was fundamentally defined by Confucian values and notions, or by the Confucian orthodoxy (correct belief); whereas some anthropologists argue that orthopraxy (correct practice) reigned over orthodoxy as the principal means of attaining Chinese identity and maintaining cultural unity among the Chinese. In this chapter I will examine the CCC's preservation of traditional praxes (what people do), including the Chinese language and traditional rituals and symbols, and then analyze the church's different attitudes toward traditional value systems of Confucianism, Daoism, and Buddhism. Generally speaking, when they are able to de-religionize a specific Chinese tradition, these Chinese Christians claim it as compatible with the Christian faith; when it seems impossible to de-religionize a tradition, they reject it; when it looks possible but difficult to separate the religious dimension from the cultural dimension in a tradition, they manifest ambivalent anxiety and tend to avoid it. Overall, the Chinese church helps its members to selectively preserve certain aspects of Chinese culture with transformative reinterpretation.

The Chinese Language

Classic theories of immigrant assimilation regard losing the original language as inevitable. Many European ethnic groups strove to preserve their original language, but most fought a losing battle (Buczek 1976). Preserving the original language would be more difficult for Chinese immigrants because the Chinese comprise only a tiny minority in American society and China is far away on the other side of the globe. Furthermore, English and Chinese are radically different languages, and Chinese immigrants have brought many dialects that are mutually unintelligible. On the other hand, many people agree that the unique Chinese language provides a constant reinforcement of Chineseness across time and space (see Chapter 2). Preserving the Chinese language is thus important in maintaining a Chinese identity.

At the CCC, the use of English has increased along with the growth in the number of American-born children, but the church remains a trilingual church using Mandarin, Cantonese, and English. Indeed, forty-years after its founding the Chinese language continues to be dominant. The Chinese-speaking Sunday service continues to have a larger attendance than the

English service because of the continuous coming of new immigrants, and the immigrants continue to dominate in church leadership as well. Meanwhile, the church has made many efforts to preserve the Chinese language and pass it on to American-born children.

Mandarin as the Official Language?

From the 1970s to the 1990s, some church members made several formal requests to the Official Board to restore Mandarin as the official language for conducting church business meetings. In 1972 a man who could speak fluent English, Cantonese, and Mandarin made the first request to hold separate English services for the purpose of effective and efficient preaching. In the same letter to the Official Board he also proposed adopting Mandarin as the only working language at congregational meetings for purposes of saving time and preserving Chinese culture. He suggested that non-Mandarin-speaking people ought to learn Mandarin, the national language of China (*guoyu*) that every Chinese should learn to speak. In the 1990s some non-English-speaking people won a battle to preserve the prime status of the Chinese language. As we have seen in Chapter 4, the presence of a Caucasian assistant pastor brought an increase of the use of English at the Official Board and other meetings. He also helped the English congregation to achieve greater independence from the immigrant-dominated Official Board. When he tried to push the church to hire another Caucasian pastor, however, some Chinese-speaking seniors voiced strong opposition and successfully curtailed the development. After that incident, several senior members also publicly expressed disapproval of having a non-Chinese assistant pastor in this Chinese church. They called for the church to consciously take up the responsibility of passing on Chinese culture and the Chinese language to the young people.

   Although the church has never made Mandarin the official language, it does have written rules of the language requirement for the pastors. The church constitution and bylaws specify that the church can only hire Chinese-speaking men as the senior pastor and associate pastors. Because of this clause, Rev. Allan Houston was never conferred the title of associate pastor. Even though he served this church for eight years and acted very much like an associate pastor with independent responsibilities to the English congregation, he remained an "assistant pastor." This church is unlikely to drop this language requirement in the near future.

Speaking Chinese, Which Dialect?

Linguistic challenges come not only externally from English, but also internally from diverse Chinese dialects. First, there are many mutually unintelligible Chinese dialects, although Chinese written characters and grammars are much the same.[1] Among CCC members, there have been sizable groups of people speaking one of the dialects of Mandarin, Cantonese, Taiwanese (Minnan or Southern Fujian dialect), and so on. Some ethnic Chinese from Southeast Asia speak little of a Chinese dialect but instead speak Vietnamese or Malay. The "place of origin" of CCC members suggests the diversity of dialect subgroups and different social and cultural backgrounds (see Table 7). Linguistic and cultural differences are obstacles of communication and integration.

Second, various dialect groups sometimes compete for defining the authenticity of Chineseness. Dialects are associated with cultural and social status or political intentions. Before World War II, Taishanese, a dialect commonly spoken by immigrants from certain rural districts of Guangdong, was regarded as the *true* Chinese language in American Chinatowns. Later, Standard Cantonese, as spoken in the cities of Hong Kong, Macau, and Guangzhou, replaced the Taishan dialect as the common language because it signifies more genteel urban backgrounds (B. P. Wong 1994, 238–41). With the increase of new Chinese immigrants from all over China after World War II, Mandarin has become increasingly prevalent. Mandarin is the official language of China (both mainland and Taiwan) that every educated Chinese is expected to be able to speak. Since the 1970s the rising Taiwan independence movement has become associated with an insistence on speaking Taiwanese.

At the CCC, various dialect groups sometimes become contentious about the adoption of a particular dialect. The CCC was founded as a Mandarin church in 1958. Before long it opened Sunday school classes in Cantonese and English as well. In 1967 Cantonese was added to the Sunday worship service. In 1973 some members asked for a separate Sunday school class in Taiwanese, claiming that the existing classes in Mandarin, Cantonese, and English could not satisfactorily meet their spiritual needs. In 1975 and 1976 the church also hosted a Sunday service in Vietnamese primarily for the Vietnamese refugees. Both the Taiwanese Sunday school class and the Vietnamese Sunday service were short-lived. Throughout the church's history there have been many attempts to restore Mandarin as the sole official language; however, Cantonese-speaking people have fervently defended the

Table 7.   Members of the Chinese Christian Church of Greater Washington, D.C.: Place of Origin, 1976 and 1995

Place of Origin	Main Dialect	1976		1995	
		N	Percent	N	Percent
China (not specified)	Mandarin?	17	4	15	5
Guangdong[a]	Cantonese	95	21	32	11
Hong Kong	Cantonese	31	7	25	9
Taiwan[b]	Mandarin/Minnan	48	11	40	14
Fujian	Minnan/other	26	6	11	4
Zhejiang	Local[c]	34	8	24	8
Jiangsu	Local	27	6	8	3
Shanghai	Local	24	5	13	5
Shandong	Local(Mandarin)	18	4	1	0
Sichuan	Local(Mandarin)	12	3	3	1
Other provinces[d]	Various	69	16	34	12
Diaspora Chinese[e]	Various	16	4	12	4
USA and Canada	English	23	5	69	24
Unknown		5	1	4	1
Total		445	101	291	101

NOTE: "Place of Origin" is either birthplace, ancestral place, or place from where one comes (see Chapter 3).

[a] Some people are from Hainan and Chaozhou (Swato), whose dialects are unintelligible to Cantonese-speaking people.

[b] Major Taiwan dialects are Taiwanese (*Minnan* or Southern Fujian dialect) and Hakka. Many people from Taiwan were mainland-born Chinese who went to Taiwan in the 1940s and the 1950s. They may speak no Taiwan dialect but Mandarin and their original dialects.

[c] Zhejiang, Jiangsu, Shanghai, and many provinces south of the Yellow River have unique and mutually unintelligible local dialects. Dialects in Shandong, Sichuan, and most provinces north of the Yellow River are distinctive variants of Mandarin.

[d] Including southern provinces (mutually unintelligible dialects): Anhui, Guangxi, Guizhou, Hubei, Hunan, Jiangxi, Macao, and Yunnan; and Northern Provinces (local dialects of Mandarin variants): Beijing, Gansu, Hebei, Heilongjiang, Henan, Jilin, Liaoning, Shaanxi, Shanxi, Tianjin, and also Xinjiang. Fewer than 10 people were from each of these provinces in 1976 and 1995.

[e] Including Indonesia, Japan, Malaysia, Peru, the Philippines, Singapore, Thailand, and Vietnam.

use of Cantonese. As a consequence, the church remains a trilingual church of Mandarin, Cantonese, and English. Notwithstanding, in the combined Sunday worship service on the first Sunday of each month, which is bilingual in Mandarin and English, Cantonese is sacrificed.

Many Chinese churches in the United States today are trilingual churches with varied combinations of Cantonese, Mandarin, Taiwanese, and some other dialects or languages besides English. These churches usually started monolingually, but in five to ten years English and another Chinese dialect had to be added. The Chinese Community Church in Chinatown, Washington, D.C., was founded in 1935 as a Cantonese-speaking church. Now it holds Sunday services in English, Cantonese, and Mandarin. In the mid-1970s a Taiwanese-speaking Presbyterian church was founded in the Washington area. When I visited it in 1994, the Sunday service was also trilingual in Taiwanese, Mandarin, and English.

The Chinese Language School

The Chinese Language School (*zhongwen xuexiao*) has been an important means of preserving the Chinese language as well as passing on Chinese values. Unlike earlier European immigrants, Chinese immigrant churches do not have parochial day schools or other kinds of private schools. They want their children to mix with others and succeed in public schools. Meanwhile, they invented a new form of school—the weekend language school—for the purpose of preserving their traditional language and culture.[2] The CCC launched the Chinese Language School in 1971 after moving to the current location in a suburb. It opened classes on Saturdays, teaching conversational Chinese, Chinese writing and composition, and Chinese customs and history. Most students were children, but occasionally there were some adults. It should be particularly noted that the CCC Chinese language school was the first one established to teach Mandarin in this metropolitan area. Before that the Chinese Community Church had intermittently offered some Cantonese classes, although there had been many other ethnic Chinese associations and organizations. This fact shows that the Chinese identity of Christian Chinese was stronger, or at least no less, than non-Christian Chinese immigrants. It is not rare for Chinese churches to have an affiliated Chinese weekend school.

The church's Chinese Language School has explicit Christian imprints. The "founding principles" (*jianxiao yuanze*) were "(1) carrying on Chinese culture, (2) assisting evangelist work, and (3) leading unbelieving parents and children to the Lord." The school constitution specifies that all teachers must be born-again Christians. Since the 1980s many Chinese language schools have been established in this metropolitan area, most of them not church affiliated. In the 1990s, facing increasing competition from other Chinese language schools, the CCC's Chinese school purposely highlights its uniqueness as one sponsored by a Christian church in its advertisements in the local Chinese newspapers. The Christian label of this Chinese school is meant to convey several messages: it would provide a loving atmosphere and loving care to children by Christian teachers; it would teach moral values besides language skills and cultural knowledge; and it would stand aloof from political inclinations.

The nonpolitical stand is important because Chinese in America are often divided into conflicting groups: some are pro-ROC, some pro-PRC, a few pro-Taiwan independence, and so on. A pro-ROC Chinese school adopts textbooks from Taiwan and teaches the spelling system of *bopomofo* (*zhuyin fuhao*), whereas a pro-PRC school adopts textbooks from the PRC and teaches the spelling system of *hanyu pinyin*. The advertisement of the CCC Chinese Language School particularly specifies that it adopts the Yale University Press textbooks and teaches the Yale spelling system, an American spelling system for the Chinese language, rather than those from either the ROC or the PRC. This emphasis on nonpolitical textbooks shows an important strategy of the church in reconstructing Chinese identity—to avoid conflicts involving China's politics, the church resorts to an "American standard."

Defining Chineseness: Is the Language Indispensable?

Chinese is not an easy language for many American-born children. ABCs often complain about the vast differences between English, their first language, and Chinese. Many see learning Chinese as a burden because it is extracurricular and demands consistent efforts and time. Many middle-school and high-school students resist and even refuse to learn it. Some would stop learning it if their parents did not insist. Nonetheless, most ABC children at the church have learned to speak at least some Chinese. This is because the church is an immigrant and ethnic community where American-born children frequently interact with the immigrants beyond their own immediate family. Away from their peers in the public school and mixing with Chinese immigrants and youths, the Chinese church creates a favorable atmosphere for the children to learn the Chinese language and culture.

After entering college, these young people who grew up in the Chinese church take divergent paths. Far away from their parents while attending prestigious universities, some ABCs and ARCs completely abandon the Chinese language and disconnect themselves from any Chinese groups, whereas others take Chinese language courses and become fully bilingual and bicultural. The incentive for mastering the Chinese language may come from the booming Asian economies and the changing Chinese societies, which promise good career opportunities. In 1994, when I visited a Taiwanese

Presbyterian church in the Washington area, I talked with the pastor's son, who was a law school student at that time. After visiting Taiwan several times and spending a summer in mainland China, he realized that there would be many opportunities for a fully bilingual lawyer. During our conversation, he insisted on speaking Mandarin with me and said he would not miss opportunities to practice his Mandarin. Many college students who grew up at the CCC have made trips to Taiwan, Hong Kong, and mainland China. Some spent months there to learn Chinese language, to teach English, and to do evangelistic mission work. In retrospect, some grownup young people expressed appreciation to the church and the Chinese Language School for teaching them the Chinese language and culture.

Meanwhile, quite a number of American-born and American-raised Chinese at the church speak little Chinese. These non–Chinese-speaking persons have presented difficult challenges to the construction of Chinese identity. Their presence has pressed people to rethink and redefine the meaning of Chineseness. Originally, this Chinese church had a stringent definition of Chineseness that considered speaking Chinese as essential. This definition was formalized when the church sponsored refugees from Vietnam. Concerned about the refugees, especially those who were ethnic Chinese, the CCC organized a special committee and mobilized church members to donate money, provide jobs, and receive refugees to live in their homes. To select people from refugee camps, the special committee set a priority order: Chinese Christians would have the first priority, Chinese non-Christians the second, and all others the third. To make this priority scheme operative, during interviews with refugees they considered only those who could speak a Chinese dialect as Chinese.

Gradually, however, people realized the problems of this stringent definition of Chineseness. First, some children of church members refused to learn the Chinese language. Their parents could not reject these children as non-Chinese. Second, some Chinese descendants who spoke no Chinese, such as third- or fourth-generation Chinese Americans, came to join this church. This evangelical Chinese church could not reject these people as long as they identified themselves as Chinese. Consequently, the definition of Chineseness had to be changed by dropping off the language requirement. The Chinese language became nonessential in Chinese identity.

Moreover, some Chinese immigrants even abandoned their Chinese names. Most Chinese in America maintain the family name (surname, last name, or *xing* in Chinese), but have romanized it in this English society. Many people have taken an American first name (given name, or *ming* in Chinese), such as John or Jenny, besides the original Chinese name. A few

CCC members have even abandoned their Chinese *xing* (family name) and *ming* (given name). For example, one young man anglicized his family name *Shi* to Stone,[3] so his official name became John Stone. A Chinese family from Thailand had the family name Voraritskul. The appearance of these names leaves no trace of their ethnic Chinese origin. However, such cases have been few up to now, and the Stones and Voraritskuls have left the CCC.

Chinese Rituals and Symbols

Traditional rituals and cultural symbols are important in defining Chineseness because of the historical orthopraxy that united Chinese people in diverse local cultures and plural religions. Chinese Christians have tried to differentiate traditional symbols and rituals of religious nature from those of secular nature, and have rejected religious ones while accepting secular ones.

Funerals and Weddings

Anthropologists have written intensively about Chinese funerals and weddings (see Watson and Rawski 1988). The argument about Chinese orthopraxy as the core of Chinese identity was largely based on studies of Chinese funerals, which they found quite uniform in structure across the vast land of China. I did not have a chance to observe funerals at the CCC during my field work period, but from interviews and informal conversations I learned that their funerals generally followed Western Christian styles. For example, there would be memorial services both at the church or the funeral parlor and in the cemetery. A pastor would officiate at the funeral. His speeches would honor the dead and comfort the relatives and friends. Following the funeral people would be invited to have a dinner at a Chinese restaurant. Many of the Chinese traditional funeral rites were lacking—no performative wailing, no donning of white mourning attire, no burning of "paper moneys" or other offerings, no setting up ancestral tablets, and so forth. The lack of traditionally Chinese rites is common in Chinese Christian funerals in other churches, as my interviews with Chinese Christians in other metropolitan areas revealed. A study of a Chinese Christian community in Hong Kong finds the same phenomenon (Constable 1994). A Chinese pastor in Houston was willing to conduct a funeral for a non-Christian as long as the family invited him. However, he would use this opportunity to comfort the family *and* to evangelize by explaining the Christian beliefs about the meaning of life. He saw the funeral as an unusual opportunity to challenge non-Christian Chinese who otherwise might never step into a church or talk to a pastor.

The weddings I observed at the CCC and other Chinese churches were all in Western Christian style. At a special wedding service, commonly held on a Saturday at the sanctuary, the bride and the groom would take vows and exchange rings in front of the pastor. Then a reception would follow at the fellowship hall and/or a dinner banquet in a Chinese restaurant. There were no traditionally Chinese wedding rites of kowtowing to the Heaven and the Earth (*bai tiandi*), to the husband's parents, and between the groom and the bride. An interesting comparison was a "Buddhist wedding" that I observed in 1994 at a Chinese Buddhist temple in Chicago. The groom wore a Western style suit and tie, and the bride was in a long white wedding gown. Seeing the Western-style wedding dress, it was surprising for me to watch their kowtowing to the Buddha statue and making three prostrations in front of the monk. The bride seemed to have a hard time because of her high-heeled shoes.

Chinese Christians in America do not follow Chinese traditional ways in weddings and funerals because they do not believe that the traditional orthopraxy in weddings and funerals defines Chineseness. Actually, many non-Christian Chinese have stopped practicing the traditional rites as well. In mainland China those traditional rites have been viewed as feudal super-stitions, and the Communist government has made great efforts to abolish them (*yifeng yisu*). In Taiwan and Hong Kong many people have followed similar modernist reasoning against "feudal superstitions" and abandoned them as well. In the construction of Chinese identity, besides the Chinese versus non-Chinese dimension, there is also the premodern versus modern dimension. Many Chinese, both Christian and non-Christian, regard giving up traditional funeral and wedding rites as giving up something backward, rather than as giving up the Chinese identity.

The Chinese New Year and the Mid-Autumn Festival

The Chinese New Year and the Mid-Autumn Festival are the two most important traditional festivals.[4] Both are based on the traditional Chinese calendar system, which is a system of lunar months adjusted to the solar year.[5] This system has been used for many centuries in China and thus has many cultural and religious meanings attached to special holidays, just as the cycles of weeks and seasons in the Western calendar system bear Judeo-Christian meanings. China officially adopted the Western solar calendar after the founding of the Republic in 1911. Some political holidays were set according to the solar calendar, such as the National Day on October 10 (or October 1 for the PRC since 1949). However, Chinese people continue to observe festival days according to the traditional calendar. Consequently, the Chinese today have a bi-calendar system, following the solar calendar (*gongli* or public calendar) in public life—government, school, and work schedules—and the traditional calendar (*nongli* or farm calendar, or *yinli* or lunar calendar) in private life—family, cultural, and religious activities. Chinese calendars are commonly printed with both systems.

Christian Chinese, like other Chinese, maintain the bi-calendar system. The week-cycle and Christian seasons bear significant meanings for their religious faith and practice. At the same time, observing Chinese festivals is habitual and also important for them to assure their Chinese identity. However, Chinese Christians celebrate only certain traditional Chinese festivals that do not have the overtones of traditional religious meanings. With a history of several thousand years, China has many traditional festivals, most having some religious meanings or implications. For example, *Qingming Jie*, which is around the Easter time, is a day to remember dead ancestors by visiting and cleaning their tombs. The Ghost Festival on the fifteenth day of the seventh month, like the Buddhist *Yulan Jie*, is a day to "feed" the vagrant ghosts. Traditional practices on these days include burning "paper moneys" and making other offerings to the dead.[6] Chinese evangelical Christians do not observe these holidays. On the other hand, Chinese Christians in America have no problem in celebrating Chinese New Year and the Mid-Autumn Festival. These days are not religious holidays, although different people may attach various religious meanings to them. The Chinese New Year's Day (*xin nian*), also called Spring Festival (*Chun jie*), marks the beginning of a year and the coming of spring. It usually falls in the early part of February in the Western solar calendar. In Chinese societies Spring Festival is a holiday season that, like Thanksgiving and Christmas in America, extends to many days before the New Year's Day and ends around the *Yuanxiao Jie* on the fifteenth day of the first month (*zhengyue shiwu*). Traditionally, Chinese families have all family members get together on this day, and many community activities are held during this season.

At the CCC the climax of the Chinese New Year celebration is a grand *jiaozi* (boiled dumplings) banquet. *Jiaozi* is *the* traditional New Year's food, as are turkeys for the American Thanksgiving day. The Chinese in America have to adjust their communal celebration day because they do not have paid holidays for celebrating the Chinese New Year. The *jiaozi* party at the CCC is always on a Saturday nearest to the Chinese New Year's Day or the *Yuanxiao Jie*. On that day in the years when I did my research, church members and invited friends would gather at the Fellowship Hall of the church and make lots of *jiaozi* together. Preparing dough and stuffing, making wrappers, wrapping, and boiling, everybody participates in this collective cooking. It provides an opportunity for people to chat and enjoy themselves, and it also creates a jolly family-like atmosphere. The "*jiaozi* banquet" is followed with entertainment programs, including performing Chinese dances, playing musical instruments, and singing gospel songs.

New Year's celebration is a nostalgic time for immigrants to remember the past, a joyfully educational time for the American-born children to learn about Chinese customs and cultural traditions, and a wonderful time to get non-Christian Chinese into the church. Chinese New Year is celebrated as a cultural festival, not a religious holy day. Unlike Christmas, which is celebrated in the sanctuary with special musicals, worship services, and thematic sermons, the entire celebration of Chinese New Year takes place outside the sanctuary. These Protestant Chinese celebrate Chinese New Year in a significantly different way than do other Chinese. I did not see "red-pockets" with lucky money for children. The church did not put up red paper couplets outside the doorways or burn incense or make ritual offerings to dead ancestors, nor did they make dragon and lion dances. Anything with any possible religious implications is omitted on this occasion in this evangelical Protestant church. They exercise great caution to avoid anything non-Christian and deliberately try to distance themselves from the possibility of pagan practices. This practice is common in other Chinese evangelical Protestant churches in the United States and also in a conservative Chinese church in Hong Kong (Constable 1994).

In comparison, I observed a very different celebration of Chinese New Year at a Chinese Catholic church in the Washington area, which adopted more traditional Chinese symbols and practices. At a special ceremony of the New Year's Day, these Chinese Catholics offered sacrificial pig heads and fruits to venerate ancestors, burned incense sticks in front of a memorial tablet labeled for "all Chinese ancestors" (*zhonghua liezu liezong*), and gave out red pockets to small children. These practices would not be acceptable to Chinese evangelical Protestants. In the past, the Roman Catholic Church forbade practicing ancestral veneration, causing the "rites controversy" in the early eighteenth century. However, it reversed this policy two hundred years later in 1939 (Ching 1993, 192–95), so that Chinese Catholics today integrate many Chinese traditional rites into their Catholic practices. On the

Protestant side, the attitudes of mainline Chinese Christians toward Chinese traditional practices may be changing too. In a recent book (Ng 1996), a group of Asian-American ministers and seminary professors of mainline Protestant denominations explore ways to integrate elements of East Asian traditions with their Christian faith. The book shows greater acceptance toward many Chinese (and Korean and Japanese) traditional practices. In sharp contrast to Catholics and mainline Protestants, Chinese evangelical Protestants today deliberately distance themselves as much as possible from any possible "pagan" practices in Chinese traditions. How these evangelical Chinese Christians change (or not change) will be interesting to watch. Nevertheless, the various attitudes among Chinese Christians suggest that the religious (or nonreligious) meanings of many Chinese traditional practices are elastic and are subject to various interpretations from different people in different times.

The Mid-Autumn Festival (*Zhongqiu Jie*) on the fifteenth day of the eighth month (usually in September of the solar calendar) is another important traditional Chinese festival. The moon on this day is said to be at its roundest and brightest. "Roundness" symbolizes the whole family being united together. It is a time for family reunion. The round moon-cake is the special food for this day.

In its early years, the CCC often held a special gathering in the night of the Mid-Autumn Day. The gathering was not purely for preserving the cultural tradition, however. It was transformed and attached with Christian meanings. For instance, the announcement about the celebration of the Mid-Autumn Festival in 1966 reads,

> Come to our Moonlight Prayer Meeting: During this good festival time when we are missing our family members and relatives, let us come together to pray for our dear family members and relatives, and to pray for our mainland compatriots in the sufferings [under the Communist rule]. After the prayer we will have moon-cakes and fruits, and a time for moon-appreciation.

In the 1990s, however, the celebration of the Mid-Autumn Festival has become less formal and less regular. It has become more a time for family reunion than for gathering the church community. Sometimes the church combines the celebration of the Mid-Autumn Festival with a welcome party for new students. These evangelical Christians regard it, like the Chinese New Year, as an opportunity to bring non-Christian Chinese into the church, especially lonely students who have just left their families in Asia.

Family Altars, Artworks, and Dragons

Traditionally, many Chinese families had family shrines, either to venerate ancestors or to worship certain gods, or both. However, I did not see any family shrines at CCC members' homes, neither ancestral tablets nor religious altars. In fact, the conversion to Christianity was sometimes marked by an act of removing a family altar. One example is the Zhao family, a couple with three teenage sons, who immigrated from Fujian, China, in the mid-1980s. The Zhao family owned a Chinese restaurant in Washington, D.C., and worked seven days a week, fourteen to fifteen hours a day. They lived in constant fear of black robbers in the neighborhood. The Zhao family used to have a home altar dedicated to *Guanyin*, a popular female Bodhisattva in China, and other gods. In 1994 the family was invited to the church to attend a dinner party for mainland Chinese. After that they attended some Sunday services and other activities. One year later the couple and their three sons were baptized. Mrs. Zhao wrote this testimonial on behalf of her family:

> We used to be very superstitious, like to worship idols and burn incense in front of *Guanyin*. After we began to come to the church, I stopped worshiping the idols. However, then I sometimes had visions of suddenly stumbling down or my hair burning. One night I had a horrible dream in which I was chased by lots of demons. I was extremely horrified and became almost breathless. Suddenly I remembered the Lord Jesus, so I cried out: "Jesus come to save me!" Immediately, I saw an angel wearing a white robe appearing in the sky, holding a shining cross. The demons were all scared away. In such a wonderful moment I woke up. I prayed to the Lord Jesus and all worked, so I came to know that Jesus Christ is good. He protects me and my family. He is more powerful than ghosts and demons.

Immediately, they got the pastor to their home and demolished the family altar, and soon the whole family was baptized.

Traditional Chinese paintings and sculptures sometimes have religious implications. However, in many cases it is not easy to differentiate the artistic values from religious elements. Many CCC members decorate their houses with Chinese traditional paintings and calligraphic scrolls, often with Christian themes and biblical verses. Most sculptures I saw at members' homes were of a modern artistic nature, and I saw very few Chinese traditional figures. I did see the "triple stars" of good luck (*fu*), officialdom (*lu*) and longevity (*shou*) at the home of a church member who was a restaurant owner. However, whether these statues have religious implications or not depends upon the personal beliefs of the owners. Chinese restaurants often have an altar of certain gods, sometimes including the triple stars; however, these figures can be appreciated solely as artistic works. One young couple had a small china statue of the "Happy Buddha" as an ornament on a table in the living room. The Happy Buddha, a popular legendary figure in China, has a grinning face and a round belly, which signifies lack of worry and broad-mindedness. The wife's parents came to visit them and lived with them. The wife's mother, in her late fifties, had no religion; however, she began to express some revering attitudes toward this statue. Once the young couple noticed this, they removed the statue.

The dragon has been an important Chinese symbol. Chinese people often call themselves "Dragon Descents" (*long de zisun,* or *long de chuanren*). A song written by a young man in Taiwan in the 1970s, "*Long de Chuanren,*" became a popular song among many Chinese in Taiwan, Hong Kong, mainland China, and the diaspora. In 1988 a TV commentary series, *The River Elegy,* criticized Chinese traditions and vilified the symbols of the dragon and the Great Wall. This caused emotional rejections by many Chinese people, including overseas Chinese, because they still regard the dragon as a totemic symbol for the Chinese people. The dragon is also a popular decorative image.

However, this sacred Chinese symbol presents some problems for Chinese Christians. In ancient Western cultures, the imaginary dragon is a vicious monster, as depicted in the New Testament book of Revelation and in stories of St. George the dragon slayer. I did not hear CCC people talking about the dragon; I saw no paintings or decorative images of the dragon at members' homes; and no dragon dances were held by these Chinese Protestants to celebrate the Chinese New Year. One lay leader, upon my enquiry, said this:

> The Chinese dragon and the dragon in the Revelation are totally different things. Their features and their characters are completely different. The Chinese dragon is a cultural symbol, which can be just like the eagle to Americans. Only when someone worships the dragon as an idol it becomes a problem. I once jokingly said to [church] people: if you have a rug with a dragon image, don't throw it away. Give it to me. When someone wears a dragon-shape tie pin, some Christians would say no-no. What is the problem? It should not be a problem.

However, he acknowledged that some Chinese Christians did not agree with him.

In 1996 a Taiwanese Presbyterian pastor published an article in the newsletter of the Taiwan Christian Church Council of North America in which he distinguished the evil dragon in the Bible from the auspicious dragon of the Orient. He attributed the problem to mistranslation of the Bible and said that the dragon in the Bible should be translated as beast (*guai shou*) instead of dragon (*long*). However, "a group of concerned readers" wrote a letter to the newsletter, which was published in the following issue, in which they insisted that the Oriental dragon was the dragon in the Bible, the image of Satan. No further discussions were published. Apparently the dragon symbol is still problematic for many Chinese Christians. While some people believe that the two dragons are completely different symbols, others insist that they are the same. Most Chinese Christians, however, hold no clear position either for or against the dragon. They simply avoid the image of dragon as much as possible.

Confucianism: Its Compatibility with Christianity

Many scholars hold that Confucianism was the Chinese traditional orthodoxy and that Confucian values still broadly define the nature of Chinese culture and Chinese identity. Understandably, Chinese Christians do not hesitate to claim Confucianism as their cultural heritage. They see most Confucian values as compatible with Christianity and regard them as valuable complements for life in contemporary American society. This positive attitude toward Confucianism is pervasive at the CCC and other Chinese churches.

The Living Water

In 1982 the CCC started a quarterly magazine for publishing testimonials and sharing ideas among church members. They named the magazine *Living Water* (or *Living Spring*) in reference to the biblical verses where Jesus says,

> Whoever drinks the water I give him will never thirst. Indeed, the water I give him will become in him a spring of water welling up to eternal life. (John 4:14)

If anyone is thirsty, let him come to me and drink. Whoever believes in me, as the Scripture has said, streams of living water will flow from within him. (John 7:37–38)

Interestingly, the editorial foreword of the very first issue also introduced the magazine with a poem by Zhu Xi (A.D. 1130–1200), the great Neo-Confucian master in the Song Dynasty:

> *A square pond opens up like a mirror*
> *In it glowing light and white clouds are waving together*
> *No wonder this lagoon is so clear*
> *Because from the springhead comes the living water*

The editorial foreword continued,

> The Word of God is the living water for our hearts. His love is encompassing. Would you open up your heart like the pond to receive the light and reflections of the love of God?

Quoting a poem by a Neo-Confucian master in the opening remarks of the church magazine is a clear indication of the profound influence of Confucian heritage in the hearts and minds of these Christian Chinese. What is more interesting is that there seems to be a perfect fit between this Confucian poem and the biblical verses. Zhu Xi likens the heart to the water in his philosophical writings, analogically stating that the clearness and cleanness of the heart/mind depend on the living water. What is the living water? It seems unclear in Zhu Xi's poem and other writings. However, when Chinese Christians read the biblical verses quoted above, they find a definite answer—the living water is Jesus Christ. They find not contradiction, but compatibility.

Love and Filial Piety

A core concept of Confucianism is *ren*, which may be translated as humanity, benevolence, or love. Confucianism regards *ren* as the foundation of good-ness and all virtues. Following the Confucian phrase *ren zhe ai ren* ('*ren* is to love people'), Chinese Christians equate *ren* to *ren-ai* (love) and regard this *ren-ai* as the quintessence of Confucianism. They see this Confucian core principle as very close to Jesus' new command of love. Jesus said to his disciples, "A new command I give you: Love one another" (John 13:34). Other New Testament passages say, "God is love. Whoever lives in love lives in God, and God in him" (1 John 4:16); and compassion, kindness, humility, gentleness, patience, and forgiveness, "over all these virtues put on love, which binds them all together in perfect unity" (Colossians 3:14). Apparently, both Confucianism and Christianity regard love as the foundation of all virtues. Citing these biblical verses and Confucian texts, these Chinese Christians firmly believe in the compatibility of Confucian *ren* with Christian love.

The foremost virtue in Confucianism is filial piety (*xiao*), which requires children to respect their parents and elders, to take care of them when in need, to honor them in deed by achieving successes, and to venerate them after death. In sermons, lectures, and interviews these Chinese Christians stress the importance of filial piety. They often cite the fifth of the Ten Commandments: "Honor your father and your mother, so that you may live long in the land the Lord your God is giving you" (Exodus 20:12). They like to point out that this is the only commandment that has a promise of worldly blessing, since Paul said, "Children, obey your parents in the Lord, for this is right. Honor your father and mother—which is the first commandment with a promise—that it may go well with you and that you may enjoy long life on the earth" (Ephesians 6:1–3). Several articles on filial piety have appeared in *Living Water*. One article in 1995 clearly manifests the fusion of Christian beliefs and Confucian teachings to justify the necessity of filial piety:

> Some Westerners misinterpret Genesis chapter two verses 23 and 24, and say that "husband and wife are the one bone and flesh; they two are one flesh and the dearest persons. After marriage they are united into one, so they should leave their parents and no longer live together with their parents." The first half of these words is right, but the second half is wrong. We should know that Lord Jesus Christ never said that you should take care of your wife more than your parents. The purpose of husband and wife being united together is to love each other and to learn to live a holy life. "To leave parents" does not mean to dismiss or get rid of the parents, but only means to live not under the same roof. This is reasonable if the wealth allows and if the parents wish to live separately. It is also natural that in American society children often live far away from their parents because of the job. However, if one insists that old parents must live separately, that is a misinterpretation of the teaching of

> the Bible and forsakes the obligation of children to take care of the parents. We Chinese are a people who highly appreciate filial piety. We must think again and again over this issue. Mark 15:4 says, "For God said, 'Honor your father and mother' and 'Anyone who curses his father or mother must be put to death.'" If you are a Christian, you ought to take care of your parents, because taking care of the parents is one of the three behaviors of filial piety. Furthermore, the Bible also tells us this very clearly. Therefore, we must remember this all the time. . . . When we worship God the Creator we should remember our parents for their grace of giving birth to us and rearing us. . . . We who are parenting should be role models for our children. God is watching us from above. If we can do this every generation, our Chinese traditional principle of filial piety (*xiaodao*) will be forever preserved.

The "Westerners' misinterpretation" was a target of criticism. This essay also clearly shows the author's conviction of the complete compatibility of biblical teachings and Confucian notions.

The emphasis on filial piety is often accompanied by an emphasis on family life, including harmonious relationships between husband and wife, between parents and children, and among siblings. Living in modern American society and following the biblical traditions, Chinese Christians tend to regard the nuclear family as the basic unit of family life. This is different from the traditional Chinese way in which the family often means the extended family or even the clan. On the other hand, these Chinese Christians disapprove of what they perceive as the "breakdown" of the family in American society. They underscore the need to extend family life beyond the nuclear family. As shown in the above quotation, they regard taking care of old parents as part of the good Chinese tradition that Chinese Christians should preserve.

The Philosophy of Life

Chinese Christians believe that Confucianism and Christianity share many other social and moral values as well. Chapter 4 described several moral values that CCC members cherish and promote, which could be called the "Protestant ethic." Actually, most of these values are Confucian too. Both Protestantism and Confucianism maintain "this-worldly asceticism"—success, thrift, delayed gratification, practical rationalism, and so on. Indeed,

Christians at the CCC claim that the Confucian and Christian philosophies of life are very much alike. An article published in *Living Water* in 1989 reads:

> Learning to be a human person (*xue zuoren*) is the emphasis of Confucianism. To be a human person is to be free and independent. Wealth and rank will not make him wallowing, poverty and lowness will not make him shaking, and coercive forces will not make him bending. He will not give up moral principles no matter in what circumstances. The true freedom is not to be determined by circumstances. This central view of Confucianism is consistent with a biblical principle. Paul said in the Philippians 4:11–13, "I have learned to be content whatever the circumstances. I know what it is to be in need, and I know what it is to have plenty. I have learned the secret of being content in any and every situation, whether well fed or hungry, whether living in plenty or in want. I can do everything through him who gives me strength." . . . Therefore, no matter in what circumstances, we should always strive forward and upward, with full confidence, dynamism and strong will. We should trust the Lord to lead our life and receive His grace and gifts with joy and hope.

Here the compatibility of Confucianism and Christianity is affirmed with no doubt.

Confucian Deficiency and the Remedy

While pointing out many compatible teachings in Confucianism and Christianity, these Chinese Christians never say that they are the same. In fact, they frequently note various differences between Confucianism and Christianity. The fundamental difference, or the root of other differences, they claim, is the lack of a clear view of God and the spiritual world in Confucianism.

Confucius himself does not deny the existence of God or gods;[7] however, he is agnostic, believing that man cannot know things beyond this world. Confucius talks about no supernatural things and declares that "without knowing life, how can you know death" (*wei zhi sheng, yan zhi si*)! Most Confucian followers in dynastic China moved farther and farther away from acknowledging the existence of God or gods. However, agnosticism is not an essential element in Confucianism, these Chinese Christians argue. They point out that Confucius was fond of ancient classics and that in the classics that Confucius edited, there is no lack of the notion of God. All of the most ancient Chinese classics, including *Shi Jing* (the Book of Songs), *Shu Jing* (the Book of History), *Yi Jing* (the Book of Change), and *Li Ji* (the Book of Rites) have many verses about *Shangdi* or *Tian*. This idea of a supreme ruler who has power and personality is very close to the notion of God in the Judeo-Christian tradition.

Many contemporary Neo-Confucian scholars praise the agnosticism in Confucianism. To Chinese Christians, however, this lack of religious dimension is a fatal deficiency of Confucianism. Although it is true that Confucius cared little about the spiritual world and death, these questions have to be answered. Precisely because Confucianism failed to provide consistent answers concerning God, death, and the spiritual world, these Chinese Christians argue, various human-invented wrong religions have filled China ever since the Han Dynasty (206 B.C.–A.D. 220), when Confucianism became the orthodoxy. Religious Daoists developed a system of gods, spirits, and immortals. Buddhism brought China the doctrine of "soul transmigration." For these Chinese Christians, only Christian beliefs provide the right answer to the questions that Confucianism failed to address. As a member wrote in the church magazine,

> Confucianism did not negate the existence of the spiritual world. Daoist and Buddhist superstitions filled the empty space left by Confucianism, but the [Buddhist] soul transmigration is just absurd. Thank God for giving us a clear answer: after death there will be resurrection for Christians. We trust what the Bible says, that we will be resurrected.

To remedy what they perceive as the deficiency of Confucianism, these Chinese Christians call for a restoration of ancient Chinese culture prior to Confucius. They see that the pragmatic rationalism after Confucius blocked Chinese people from the transcendent or *Shangdi* (God), just like ancient Jews who sometimes betrayed Jehovah, God of their ancestors. Once we are reconnected with God as believed by our ancient ancestors, they say, we can expect the revival and revitalization of Chinese culture in the modern world. These Chinese Christians want to show that God is no alien to Chinese spirituality. Ancient Chinese ancestors believed and worshiped God, who is a universal God and is thus the Chinese God too. By pointing out the verses about God in the most ancient Chinese texts and by arguing that this God is the same God whom Christians believe in and worship, these Chinese Christians want to prove that believing in God is indeed very Chinese, very traditional (in ancient roots), rather than at odds with Chinese identity and Chinese traditions.

Moreover, Confucianism has to be complemented by Christianity in the modern world. These Chinese Christians believe that without believing in the living God many Confucian moral values would be devoid of meaning or impossible to practice. For example, *ren-ai* (love) is an ideal in Confucian morality. But people often fail to love others. This is because of the lack of godly love, these Christians believe. They claim that only if one receives love from God can one love others without utilitarian purposes. "We love because he [God] first loved us" (1 John 4:19) and "since God so loved us, we also ought to love one another" (1 John 4:11). Loving others has to be sustained by the love of God. In this sense, only through Christianity can Confucian moral ideals be fulfilled.

More important, Confucianism has to be complemented with Christianity in the modern world. Modernity has challenged the authority of traditions. In the past the Confucian orthodoxy was maintained by the dynastic state, but the dynastic state has collapsed. Another source of authority for Confucianism is traditionalism—upholding Confucian morals because the ancestors held them. In modern society, however, no traditional values can be preserved intact without passing rational reexamination. Appealing to tradition alone is insufficient to carry on Confucian moral values. In this regard, the absolute notion of God in Christianity can be a powerful source of authority. Because these Chinese Christians find the main Confucian values compatible with conservative Christianity, they find it natural to complement Confucianism with Christian beliefs and to maintain these values through the Christian institution. Christian beliefs provide the absolute foundation for the moral principles of Confucianism in the modern world, and this foundation has well survived various modern or postmodern challenges. Also, living in the United States as a minority, they see that no institution has better resources to implement and pass on Confucian values than the church.

Chinese Christians believe that without the Christian faith, Confucianism alone cannot protect the Chinese people from the rising tide of unhealthy developments in modern society. This is true both to Chinese as a minority in America and to Chinese societies in Asia. The so-called greater China has been in an economic boom. But social anomie and moral chaos are rampant along with the rise of materialism, consumerism, and eroticism. Many Chinese Christians in America share this burning concern about the breakdown of Chinese society and consequently strive hard to evangelize Chinese compatriots. In this process, they do not intend to replace

Confucianism with Christianity. Rather, they want to revitalize Confucianism through Christianity.

Confucian Orthodoxy Versus Christian Orthodoxy

The description above shows that these Chinese Christians are integrating Confucianism and Christianity. Their efforts have touched upon many Christian theological questions. To attain the Christian identity, these Chinese Christians adhere to evangelical Christianity. Meanwhile, to retain their Chinese identity, they want to inherit the Confucian orthodoxy. Because syncretism has been regarded as a danger to the Christian faith in the orthodox Christian theology, an unavoidable question is: Is it syncretic to mix Confucianism and Christianity?

How do these Chinese evangelical Christians uphold orthodox Christian beliefs while remaining truthful to the Confucian orthodoxy? Theological judgment is not the purpose of this sociological study. On the other hand, an empirical study of a Christian church cannot avoid asking questions with theological significance. "Syncretism" worries theologians and the subjects of this ethnographic study. The Chinese Christians at the CCC have made great efforts to prove the authenticity of their Christian faith as well as their Chinese identity.

First, for these Chinese Christians, Confucianism is a system of moral values, whereas Christianity provides transcendent beliefs and spiritual guidance. In other words, they regard the core of the Confucian orthodoxy as on the level of moral values or social ethics, whereas the essence of Christianity is on the level of spirituality concerning the transcendent. This is to say that Confucianism and Christianity do not compete on the same level. Therefore, these Chinese evangelical Christians can claim that they remain truthful to both Christianity and Confucianism without being syncretic. A frequent statement in talks and articles at the church is "Worship Jesus Christ as God, revere Confucius as a sage, and honor ancestors as human beings."

An article in *Living Water* tried to clarify proper names for the birthday of Christ and that of Confucius. The conventional Chinese translation of the word *Christmas* is *Shengdan* (*sheng*: sage, saint, holy, sacred; *dan*: birth, birthday). In the 1980s some newspapers in Taiwan adopted a new translation of *Christmas—Yedan* (birthday of Jesus). The article reads:

> Some Confucian apologists [in Taiwan] even have suggested calling the birthday of Confucius *Shengdan* and claim that only the birthday

of Confucius deserves to be called *Shengdan*. . . . Actually, the conventional use of the word *"Shengdan"* for the birthday of the Lord Jesus Christ has no competition with that of Confucius. The character *sheng* in *Shengdan* is not the *sheng* in *shengren*, but is the *sheng* in the word *shensheng*, which means Holy, Godly, or Divine. The *sheng* in the word *shengren* means sages or saints, who are persons of noble virtues and high prestige. [Chinese] Christians also revere Confucius as a sage, and have the greatest esteem for this great Chinese sage. However, he is a man, not God. He is a sage, but not the Holy Divinity. Jesus Christ differs categorically. He was given birth by the virgin Mary whom the Holy Spirit conceived. Jesus Christ is the incarnation of the Word (*Dao*), the Son in the triune Persons of God. Although He was a person when he was in the world, He was also God. Therefore, His birthday is and should be called *Shengdan*, the Holy Birth.

This article may look tedious, but is indicative that assuring the authenticity of both their Chinese identity and their Christian identity is important for these Chinese Christians. For them, calling Confucius a sage, rather than a god, is a restoration of Confucianism to its primary form. Confucius never claimed himself a god, or even a sage. Worshiping Confucius as a god is thus against Confucius himself. The feudal dynasties made Confucius a god for the purpose of social control. Chinese Christians call for going back to the original Confucianism and getting rid of the corrupted practices developed in dynastic times. They assert that only with this restoration can Confucianism be revived in the modern world.

Second, in their attempts to integrate Confucianism and Christianity, these Chinese Christians have simultaneously tried to differentiate primitive or essential Christianity from Western theologies. Western theologies have adopted Greek and Roman philosophies to understand and explain Christian notions. However, the Greek and Roman philosophies are only certain means to approach God and the gospel, not the essence of Christianity. Those theologies have helped Western Christians to understand God; they may be helpful for Chinese Christians; but they are not necessarily essential to the Christian faith. Chinese traditional philosophies are very different from Greek and Roman philosophies. These Chinese Christians hope that Chinese theologians will adopt thoughts of Chinese sages to develop a Christian theology so that Chinese people can easily accept Christian beliefs. In their view, an indigenous Chinese Christian theology should be rooted both in continuity with the historical church and in Chinese culture. They argue that the original Hellenic philosophies are not Christian but pre-Christ.

If Westerners could successfully integrate Greek and Roman philosophies with their Christian faith, the Chinese may do something similar by integrating Chinese philosophies with Christianity. A Chinese Christian thinker, who was a popular speaker at the CCC and other Chinese churches, proposed that Chinese theologians should pay more attention to the Chinese philosophical category of "relation" than the Western philosophical categories of "substance and attribute," pay more attention to the Chinese conviction of the goodness of human nature, and talk less about predestination and eschatology. When such a Chinese theology is established, it will be quite different from existing Christian theologies.

Traditional Chinese Heterodoxies: Daoism and Buddhism

Although Confucianism was the orthodoxy in China, Daoism (Taoism) and Buddhism had pervasive influences among the populace. As two major heterodoxies, Daoism and Buddhism complemented Confucianism and made lasting imprints in Chinese culture. Therefore, Chinese Christians must deal with them and take positions.

Appreciating Philosophical Daoism While Rejecting Religious Daoism

Daoism is a Chinese indigenous tradition with roots in ancient Chinese classics. Whereas philosophical Daoism emphasizes knowing or comprehending the Dao and reaching the Dao through inaction (*wu wei*) and spontaneity (*zi ran*), religious Daoism has a system of gods and spirits, religious rituals and symbols, and monasticism. For Chinese Christians the distinction between philosophical Daoism and religious Daoism is important. Generally speaking, Chinese evangelical Christians reject religious Daoism but selectively accept some notions of Daoist philosophy. They regard the Daoist rituals, spirits, and monastic system as superstitious and wrong, although they appreciate some life wisdom in *Dao De Jing* (*Tao Te Ching*) and other Daoist classics. A Chinese pastor stated the Christian position clearly:

> I accept Daoism like I accept Confucianism. I respect Laozi as the founder of Daoism, although I disagree with Daoist religionists who made Laozi the god *Taishang Laojun.*

The main link between Daoism and Christianity is the word *Dao*. In *Dao De Jing*, Dao is a mystic force. Many philosophers and religionists have tried to understand and interpret the meaning of this mystic Dao, which seems to be very close to the notion of Logos in Greek philosophy. Interestingly, the word *Logos* also appears in the beginning of the gospel of John in the New Testament. The English Bible translates *Logos* as 'Word,' whereas the most commonly used Chinese Bible translates *Logos* as 'Dao.' Therefore, the first verse of the gospel of John in Chinese reads like this:

> In the beginning was the Dao, and the Dao was with God, and the Dao was God. (*Tai chu you Dao. Dao yu Shen tong zai. Dao jiu shi Shen*).

To Chinese people who are familiar with *Dao De Jing*, reading these biblical verses can be enlightening. They seem to directly address the important question of Dao and to provide a clear interpretation of the mystic Dao. In light of the Christian scriptures, the Dao is a person of the Triune God. This Dao is God, who later was incarnated as Jesus Christ. The Chinese translation of *incarnation* is "the Dao took up the body of flesh" (*dao cheng rou shen*).

Rev. Moses Chow, the first pastor of the CCC, tells the story of how his Daoist father became Christian (1995, 8–12). After his clandestine conversion to Christianity, Moses brought home a copy of the gospel of John in Chinese, hoping his father, a fervent Daoist follower, would read it. At first his father angrily tossed the book aside because it was a book of a *foreign* religion. Later, when he was alone, he opened the book out of curiosity. Young Moses, hiding from his father's sight, watched closely his father's reactions. Upon reading the first verses, his father murmured, "Why, this book talks about *Taoism!*" "The Holy Spirit began to enlighten his heart as he read on," Chow reported. "I hardly dared breathe while watching father read through the gospel of John at one sitting" (1995, 9–10). Then, the senior Chow called Moses and asked to be taken immediately to the pastor. His father had a long conversation with the Chinese pastor. Chow reported that for the next few months after his father read the gospel of John, "he spent every waking hour intensely studying the Word [Dao] of God" (1995, 10). This was followed by the conversion of the whole family. Not surprisingly, Rev. Moses Chow continues to speak positively about the affinity between Daoism and Christianity.

The Dao as a link to the Christian gospel makes a reinterpretation of *Dao De Jing* possible. Yuan Zhiming, a popular speaker at the CCC and many other Chinese churches, has developed a systematic reinterpretation of *Dao De Jing* in light of Christianity. The manuscript, entitled *The Light of*

God (Shen Guang), was circulated among CCC members before its formal publication.[8] To Yuan Zhiming, a Christian convert, God is a universal God of all humankind, and the Dao (Word or Way) of God is the universal Dao. In his book, Yuan comes to the conclusion that more than twenty-six hundred years ago, when God prophesied the coming of Jesus Christ through the prophet Isaiah, God also shed light to ancient China through Laozi. Before the gospel came to China in more recent times, the Dao in *Dao De Jing* had been a myth puzzling generations of people. It was like a gorgeous cloud in the sky. Watching from below, many people have sensed the great superhuman wisdom in it, but they could not see the light above the cloud. The light was from God, Yuan asserts. It has always been there, but people could not see it; therefore, they could not understand Laozi in his own terms. Now with the light of God we can finally understand Laozi.

According to Yuan, Laozi prophesied the Dao of God. The Dao in Laozi is the same as the Dao (Word) in the Bible. Through interpreting various verses in the book, Yuan argues that *Dao De Jing* clearly articulates that the Dao is God, is Who He Is (YHW), is infinity, eternity, the creator, the transcendent, revelator, and savior. *Dao De Jing* also reveals that the Dao would be incarnated as a *Shengren* (sage), who would be a prophet, a priest, a king, and a savior. Because God's revelation to Laozi was only a "general revelation" (*yiban qishi*), *Dao De Jing* could not prophesy the incarnation of Dao as clearly as Isaiah in the Old Testament, for only Isaiah received God's direct and specific revelation (*zhijie tebie qishi*) at about the same time of Laozi. *Dao De Jing* is not a part of the Holy Scripture. However, reading *Dao De Jing* would help Chinese people to understand God and Christ. Simply put, the Dao of God is not alien to Chinese culture.

This reinterpretation of *Dao De Jing* by Yuan Zhiming is a novel one. It will stimulate debates both among Chinese Christians and among non-Christian scholars of Daoism. Reactions from CCC members during my field work there were positive and accepting, although Yuan has also been challenged at various Chinese Christian meetings. If his reinterpretation can be accepted, this may mark a new era in the development of Chinese Christian theology.

Rejecting Buddhism Without Reservation

Buddhism came to China about two thousand years ago. Chinese Christians acknowledge the great impact of Buddhism on Chinese culture and the continuous influence of Buddhism among Chinese people. However, they generally reject Buddhism without reservation. An article in *Living Water* in

1986 listed and articulated ten irreconcilable contrasts between Buddhism and Christianity:

(1) Buddhists worship many gods, whereas Christians worship the "One True God."

(2) Buddhists believe the world is meaningless and has no purpose, whereas Christians believe the world was created by God and it has God's wonderful purpose.

(3) Buddhists hold pessimistic and negative views of life, regard life as sufferings, whereas Christians hold optimistic and positive views of life, regard life as serving the family, the society, the country and the world [note the Confucian tone!] and to glorify God.

(4) Buddhists want to withdraw and escape from the world, whereas Christians affirm and engage in the world.

(5) Buddhists believe in fatalism—causes in the previous life have consequences in this life, whereas Christians seek God's will that can change our fate.

(6) Buddhists regard every and any being as equal, the soul transmigrates [through the forms of god, spirit, human, animal, ghost, and devil] according to cause-consequence retribution, whereas Christians regard man as the best of all beings who is created in the image of God.

(7) Buddhists advise people to do good for the purpose of escaping from the cause-consequence retribution, whereas Christians advise people to do good for the purpose of breaking away from evil by knowing God.

(8) Buddhists cultivate themselves by relying on their own virtuous work, whereas Christians regard man as unreliable. Just as a strong man cannot lift himself up, every person has to rely on God for salvation.

(9) Buddhists are vegetarians because they fear killing animals may cause retribution in the coming life, whereas Christians eat food to keep health.

(10) Buddhists cultivate themselves for the purpose of entering nirvana, whereas Christians believe in the Lord for the purpose of achieving eternal life. Buddhists cannot explain what nirvana is, which may simply mean nonbeing; whereas Christians have a clear explanation about life after death—eternal life and resurrection.

The writer of this article was not a trained theologian, but a lay believer whose profession was hydraulic engineering. His views on Buddhism are commonly shared by CCC members and other Chinese evangelical Christians. These Chinese Christians feel uncompromising competition with Buddhism. Some church members are adult converts from Buddhist backgrounds. They consistently criticize Buddhist beliefs and practices and try to persuade Chinese people to give up Buddhism for Christianity. In fact, some members even helped to convert a Buddhist abbot. In 1989 six or seven CCC members visited a Chan (Zen) Buddhist Center in the Greater Washington area. A person who had both Christian relatives and Buddhist relatives initiated and arranged this visit. The head monk of the Chan center and several Buddhist nuns welcomed these Christian visitors with a sumptuous vegetarian dinner. At the table they freely exchanged views about life and religion. The monk gave the guests some volumes of Buddhist Sutras and expressed a hope for more conversation in the future. As a reciprocal courtesy the guests later mailed the abbot some books on philosophy, Christianity, and Buddhism written by Christian scholars. Several months later this Buddhist head monk cast off his monastery *jiasha* and was baptized at a Christian church. He gave several testimonies at fellowship group meetings and a Sunday worship service at the CCC before moving to California. This event encouraged many CCC members to further evangelize Chinese Buddhists. Doubtless, the competition with Buddhist religion will continue.

Reflection: Types of "Chinese" Christians

To affirm their Chinese identity, CCC members have been making choices in their inherited Chinese cultural traditions. Overall, they consistently preserve Confucian moral values, selectively accept some Daoist notions, and categorically reject Buddhism. However, this general summary is not applicable to all individuals. First of all, many people change their attitudes toward traditional culture over time. A common pattern for Chinese converts is to at first distance themselves from Chinese cultural traditions as much as possible, and then gradually return to some traditions. Immediately following their conversion, their Christian identity takes priority. Anything that may jeopardize their newly achieved Christian identity is cast off. After they achieve a sense of security in their Christian identity, Chinese cultural traditions become less of a threat to their faith. Then they may look to the traditions for cultural values and religious inspiration. Secondly, Chinese cultural traditions are diverse. Depending on circumstances and personal choices, a Chinese Christian may inherit some Confucianism or some Daoism or some Buddhism or a mixture of elements from all three. I have been able to distinguish three types of "Chinese" Christians.

Most CCC members accept Confucianism, or Confucian moral values. Normally these "Confucian" Christians are conservative in theology, traditionalist in ethics, reserved in behavior, and rationalistic in beliefs. They emphasize family life, moral education of children, and successes in the world. Their religious life is very much family-centered or community-oriented. However, they would object to being called "Confucian" Christians for two reasons. First, Confucianism for them simply means "Chinese." They often refer to certain values as "Chinese" rather than "Confucian." An important reason for this is that the term *Confucianism* is a misnomer coined by Westerners. The Chinese term for Confucianism is the "scholarly tradition" (*rujia*), which is synonymous with Chinese culture. Second, they do not intend to preserve Confucianism per se. Their preservation is selective: preserving Confucian moral values while rejecting Confucian agnosticism. They also reject the ritualistic and state-sanctified version of Confucianism, such as worshiping Confucius and emphasizing imperial loyalty.

Some Chinese Christians at the CCC explicitly accept or appreciate some notions of Daoism. These "Daoist" Christians tend to place emphasis on spiritual cultivation through devotional prayers, direct relationship with God, and personal salvation through grace. Compared with "Confucian" Christians, these people are more pietistic than ethicistic, more individualistic than collectivistic, and more experientialistic than rationalistic. Some may have charismatic tendencies and like to be filled by the Holy Spirit, speak in tongues, conduct spiritual healing, and practice exorcism. "Daoist" Christians are few, less than ten percent at the most. In the Washington area, two of the twenty Chinese churches are obviously charismatic; their members might have more Daoist tendencies.

Buddhism is generally rejected by Chinese evangelical Christians. However, for some converts from Buddhist backgrounds, some habits of the heart may continue to affect their Christian practices. Some "Buddhist" Christians are very otherworldly oriented and like to proclaim the "void" of the world and worldly life. Furthermore, the habits of the heart with Buddhist traditions may have two different manifestations. Chan (Zen) Buddhism emphasizes enlightenment through one's own efforts; Pure Land Buddhism believes in "salvation" through the "other-power" and religious work (*gongde*, including religious observances and moral behaviors). Chan Buddhists prefer simplicity, whereas Pure Land Buddhists like elaborate rituals. At the CCC, very few members like elaborate rituals and observances.

One may find more of this type of Christian in Chinese Catholic churches. Meanwhile, I have not seen any Chan-like Christians at the CCC who would favor simple methods (*fangbian famen*) and self-nourished enlightenment. However, some may exist outside the church. For example, since the late 1980s some Chinese intellectuals in China have been called "cultural Christians" (*wenhua jidutu*). These people are scholars of Christian studies who may not join any church or participate in Christian rituals. Nonetheless they accept some Christian notions and beliefs. Some unchurched Chinese in the United States who nevertheless claim the Christian faith may be of this type as well. Overall, "Buddhist" Christians are very few, if any, in the evangelical Chinese churches.

The construction of Chinese identity is a complex process for Chinese immigrants in the United States because of the long history of Chinese civilization and its diverse cultural traditions, because of modern conflicts and divisions in Chinese society, and because of their migrating away from China. This is simultaneously a process of deconstruction and reconstruction.

6

Deconstructing the Chinese Identity, Reconstructing Adhesive Identities

Identity construction is a complicated process for Chinese Christians in America. It is a simultaneous process of both deconstruction and reconstruction. Chinese Christians undergo a two-way process of segregating various dimensions of the Chinese identity and integrating Chinese, Christian, and American identities. Three dimensions of the Chinese identity may be distinguished: political, cultural, and primordial (or biological). For Chinese Christians in America, the general tendency is moving away from Chinese political identity toward Chinese cultural identity, and moving from particularism toward universalism. Meanwhile, as immigrants and converts, they achieve American and Christian identities. Each of these identities is elusive and changing, and the three identities (Chinese, Christian, and American) are not always compatible and harmonious with each other. Integrating these multiple identities, like merging three separate circles, results in tensions, conflicts, and various patterns of combinations.

Three Types of Chinese Identities

Several Chinese words correspond to the English word *Chinese* when used to describe people (not the language), including the commonly used *zhongguoren, huaqiao, huaren,* and *huayi.* Semantically these words are not much different and are often used interchangeably in daily conversations. Sometimes, however, they are used to make distinctions between various Chinese people. For example, *zhongguoren* refers to a citizen or citizens of the Chinese state; *huaren* refers to a Chinese person or persons living outside China with or without Chinese citizenship; and *huayi* refers to a person or persons of Chinese descent, especially those born of Chinese parents outside China. Chinese governments, both the Republic of China and the People's Republic of China, often use the word *huaqiao* to refer to all overseas Chinese, which implies that these Chinese are "temporarily" living outside China as "sojourners." However, overseas Chinese themselves have been moving away from the sojourner or *huaqiao* mentality and becoming "Chinese in the diaspora" or *huaren* settling down permanently in the host society (see Lai 1992; Tu 1994a, 25; Wu 1994, 149–54).

To facilitate the analysis of the process of deconstruction and reconstruction of the Chinese identity, I will use three Chinese words to denote three distinctive types of Chinese identities: *zhongguoren* for national or political identification with the Chinese nation-state, *huaren* for cultural identification with the Chinese culture, and *huayi* for primordial or biological identification with the Chinese people. I use these three words for types of identities, not exclusive categories of persons. Thus defined, any person can concurrently have all three identities, although one identity may be more prominent than the other two. It is also possible to hold only one or two of the identities without the rest. For example, a person in China is a Chinese citizen (*zhongguoren*) but may completely reject the traditional Chinese culture and thus have no *huaren* identity. Some diasporic Chinese may hold strong cultural identity (*huaren*) but may not identify with China the state and thus have no *zhongguoren* identity. A person of Chinese descent may be far removed from any political identification with China and know almost nothing of Chinese culture, thus only *huayi* identity remains. These types of Chinese identity can be applied to organizations as well as to individuals. The Chinese Christian Church of Greater Washington, D.C., as a whole has experienced changes of moving away from *zhongguoren* identity, intensifying *huaren* identity, and shifting from *huayi* identity toward *huaren* identity.

Moreover, each type or dimension of identity has its own complexity. Politically, Chinese in the diaspora face challenges of choosing political loyalty to either China or the host country. But there are also separate political entities of China—the Communist People's Republic of China (mainland) and the Nationalist Republic of China (Taiwan)[1]—and different political parties and factions within these Chinese societies. Culturally, the Chinese have multiple and diverse traditions, as we have seen in Chapters 2 and 5. Without cultural and political Chinese identity, one can still remain Chinese simply because of Chinese blood or consanguine ties, with or without primordial affinities toward other Chinese.

Zhongguoren: The Waning Nationalist Identity

The *zhongguoren* identity of the CCC has been waning for two reasons: the political fragmentation of China and increasing identification with the United States. When the church was established in 1958, most participants were Chinese citizens, not U.S. citizens. Most were Chinese students who were supposed to return to China upon graduation. Only a few came to the United States as legal immigrants. The New Immigration Act of 1965 opened the possibility for more Chinese immigration, allowing many Chinese students to adjust from the student visa to permanent residence. Gradually, more people became permanent residents and more permanent residents achieved U.S. citizenship. However, the *zhongguoren* identity lagged some years behind citizenship status. Until the late 1970s, this church had an apparent *zhongguoren* identity. Specifically, they identified with the Republic of China (Taiwan), celebrated the "Double Tens" (October 10, the National Day of the ROC), and held a memorial service for the death of ROC President Chiang Kai-Shek in 1975. Because a majority of church members came from Taiwan and some ROC diplomats attended this church, this specific political identification is not hard to understand.

However, the church's political loyalty to the ROC was challenged from the outset. Not all church members were willing to identify with the ROC or the Guomindang (Nationalist) government. After the Chinese Communists took power in mainland China, some people fled to Hong Kong or Southeast Asian countries rather than following the Guomindang to Taiwan. Among them were people who disliked the Guomindang government for its corruption and other problems when ruling the mainland. Some church members were diasporic Chinese from the Philippines, Malaysia, Indonesia, Singapore, Thailand, and later from Vietnam. They had lived as an ethnic minority often in a hostile society, and some had suffered anti-Chinese violence. However, neither the ROC nor the PRC governments had provided protection to them. They thus moved farther away from the ancestral land to the United States to seek protection. Some of them wished for a strong Chinese nation and thus held on to certain aspects of a *zhongguoren* identity (nationalism in general), but they found both the ROC and PRC governments disappointing. Therefore, they had little interest in political alignments with the Guomindang government in Taiwan or the Communist government in the mainland. Consequently, they simply became less involved in Chinese politics. The presence of these people, although a minority in the CCC, propelled the church toward weaker *zhongguoren* identity.

The *zhongguoren* identity became more problematic after 1979 when the United States switched its formal diplomatic relations from the ROC in Taiwan to the PRC. This was followed by the coming of immigrants and students from mainland China. Since the 1980s, especially after 1989, many mainland Chinese have joined this Chinese church. These mainlanders often have strong Chinese nationalist sentiments. Politically, they often voice sharp criticisms of things in China under the Chinese Communist Party. However, when people from Taiwan make similar criticisms of the same things, they often resent it or get even by expressing negative opinions of the Guomindang government both before and after 1949. The increasing presence of these mainland Chinese has made some pro-ROC people at the church uncomfortable, but it has evidently constrained political activism either for the ROC or against the PRC. Overall, Chinese Christian churches in America today do not hold formal ties with Chinese governments or their respective consulates in the United States. In comparison, Chinese Buddhist temples that I have visited usually maintain close relationships with the ROC in Taiwan and its semi-official consulates. For example, Buddhist temples in Chicago, New York, and Houston often had Taiwanese government officials as honored greeters during important Buddhist festival celebrations.

The *zhongguoren* identity became very complicated in the 1990s. A recent crisis is an example. In March 1996 the ROC held its first direct presidential election in Taiwan. The most divisive issue in the campaign was unification with mainland China. While the main opposition party, the Democratic Progressive Party, openly campaigned for Taiwan independence, the ruling Guomindang split into two camps. One camp wanted to maintain the status quo without denouncing the ideal of unification in the indefinite future; the other camp called for taking positive steps toward unification. Eventually, some pro-unification people in the Guomindang split off and set up the New Party. People in Taiwan were generally divided into these three positions. Overseas Chinese who had once identified with the ROC in Taiwan were similarly divided. To complicate the issue further, the PRC conducted missile tests and military drills near Taiwan in the Taiwan Strait, showing its determination and capability for unification. While many Chinese in America denounced these military threats, some people, especially among mainland Chinese students and scholars, applauded it. At the church, people were divided into all these conflicting positions. The multiple *zhongguoren* identities made it impossible for the church to have a unified voice. Consequently, the church took no action, not even verbally condemning any party. Instead, at Sunday services church leaders offered prayers for all Chinese people across the Taiwan Strait and prayed for God to give leaders on both sides enough wisdom to avoid any bloodshed.

The *zhongguoren* identity of this church is therefore waning in part because of the multiple and diverse sociopolitical backgrounds of church members. To avoid division, the church stresses the cultural commonalities or the *huaren* identity over *zhongguoren* identity. In addition, generally speaking, the longer a Chinese immigrant stays in the United States, the more likely it is that he or she will identify with the United States. In other words, the longer a person stays away from China the weaker his or her *zhongguoren* identity is. Once settling down in this country, people become more concerned about things around them and get more involved in social political issues of this country. Naturally, they spend less time and energy on things in China. Among individual church members, a majority still hold an evident *zhongguoren* identity. Newcomers fresh from China have great attachment to China. Many longtime members who have become U.S. citizens still call China *zuguo* (ancestral land). Some ABCs and ARCs, after tourist trips or short-term teaching or mission trips to China, have also increased *zhongguoren* (nationalist) identity. The increasing transpacific and transnational activities, and the economic and political rise of Chinese societies are important factors holding up the *zhongguoren* identity among these Chinese people.

Huaren: The Strengthening Cultural Identity

The CCC is a Chinese church. Cultural homogeneity is a cement for the church. However, the cultural identity as *huaren* is also multiple and diverse, as we have seen in Chapter 5. First, there are several competing Chinese dialects—Mandarin, Cantonese, Taiwanese, and others. Second, there are different opinions concerning specific traditional rituals, festivals, and symbols. Third, there are several traditional value systems—Confucianism, Daoism, and Buddhism. More important, different individuals, depending on their personal experiences, would choose different combinations of elements from these three realms. Consequently, each person has a distinctly eclectic *huaren* identity. Even members in one family may make distinctive choices. Figure 2 attempts to depict the complexity of Chinese cultural identity.

On the first layer are different Chinese dialects: Mandarin is dominant, Cantonese is secondary, and there are also Taiwanese and other dialects. On the second layer are cultural symbols, rituals, and festivals: the church

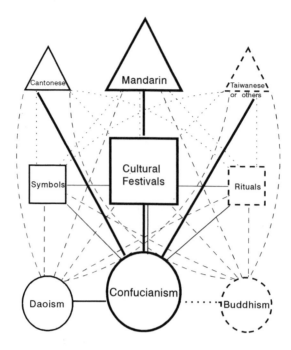

Fig. 2.   Chinese cultural identity at the Chinese
Christian Church of Greater Washington, D.C.

together celebrates those Chinese festivals that do not have clear religious
implications; church members selectively accept some Chinese cultural symbols but reject most traditional Chinese rituals. On the bottom are systems of
traditional values: most members commonly accept Confucianism, choose
some Daoist notions, but totally reject Buddhism. Within such a complex
matrix of multiple dialects, multiple traditional values, and multiple rituals,
we can say only this: Most people at this Chinese Christian church speak
Mandarin, hold Confucian values, celebrate Chinese New Year and appreciate some Chinese symbols; yet some church members do not follow these
"mainstreams."

Overall, despite the competing understandings of Chineseness, cultural
identity (*huaren*) is the most prevailing Chinese identity at the CCC. The
myth of the unique Chinese culture of five thousand years serves as the
basis for this cultural identity. People are proud of their cultural heritage.
Some believe that a constructive integration of Christian beliefs with Chinese culture would protect Chinese immigrants and their children from
the morally degenerating modern or postmodern society. Because Chinese

culture originated in geographical China, there is a certain degree of attachment to that land. While many immigrants who have achieved American citizenship continue to call China their *zuguo* (ancestral land), this *zuguo* may have less and less nationalist or political meaning. This word is becoming more religio-cultural in a sense. That land is consecrated as the Holy Land (*Shenzhou*), somewhat like Jerusalem is to the Jews. Although it is under the rule of the Chinese Communist Party, which they often dislike, their cultural roots come from it. This "holy land" sentiment is not the same as the political or nationalist *zhongguoren* identity.

Huayi: The Marginal and Unstable Primordial Identity

A few American-born people at the CCC hold little *zhongguoren* or *huaren* identity. They have no political or nationalist attachment to any Chinese government, have no particular concerns about current events in China, speak no Chinese, and have little knowledge of Chinese culture. Nevertheless they have come to join and stay in this Chinese church. Born of Chinese parents, they regard themselves as Chinese and feel Chinese in their hearts. Their primordial Chinese identity mostly comes from consanguineous or lineal ties. However, as members of this Chinese church, these *huayi* either become more *huaren* over time or remain marginal persons.

Daniel Yew is a good example of a *huayi* becoming more *huaren* over time. Daniel immigrated as a baby along with his parents from Hong Kong. He grew up in the United States without much exposure to Chinese culture or experience with a Chinese community. He went to public schools, attended white American churches, and worked among non-Chinese. Only after he renewed his commitment to serve the Lord did he feel the need to find a Chinese church, so he switched from a predominantly white church to the CCC. He said that in that white American church there were no service (leadership) opportunities for a Chinese American like him, although he had tried to get more involved in various activities. When Mr. Yew came to the CCC, he immediately found opportunities to serve. At first he taught youth Sunday school classes in English. Later he was elected as a deacon to the Official Board, the main leadership body of this church. When I interviewed him in 1995, Daniel said that he still had no particular concerns about political affairs in mainland China, Taiwan, or Hong Kong. All of his immediate family members and direct relatives were in the United States. At the time of his switching to the CCC, his Chinese identity was apparently out of primordial attachment to Chinese people. After more than ten years, however, he had learned many Chinese cultural values and had learned to speak Mandarin well. He also married a woman from Taiwan. His *huaren* identity has grown stronger and more evident over the years.

Another example of *huayi* identity is a young man called Randy Woo, a third- or fourth-generation Chinese descendant who grew up on the West Coast. Randy spoke no Chinese other than several Cantonese words and had no particular concerns about social-political affairs in China. In a casual conversation he told me, "I attend this church because this is a Chinese church. I am a Chinese anyway, although I don't speak any Chinese. . . . I like the English Sunday service."

Randy has attended this church regularly for about ten years, but did not apply to become a formal member until 1995. During this time he made no effort to learn the Chinese language or Chinese culture and did not interact much with the immigrants. He was content with his cultural identity as of Chinese descent (*huayi*) and comfortable to be with the English-speaking ABCs and ARCs in this church. In a sense he was still a marginal person. Nevertheless, he was accepted as a faithful Chinese Christian in this Chinese Christian church. When he becomes involved more in the Chinese New Year's *jiaozi* party and other cultural activities and in leadership teams that have immigrant members, he will probably learn more and more Chinese cultural customs, values, and behavioral patterns. The longer he stays in this church, the more he will probably gain a *huaren* identity.

At present very few people in the CCC are like Randy, who maintains *huayi* identity with little *huaren* identity. Chinese descendants who have lost the Chinese language and Chinese culture usually seek other options, such as attending a Caucasian-dominated church or forming an "Asian-American" church. In fact, so-called Asian-American churches have emerged in the last decade or so in some metropolitan areas, especially on the West Coast. These monolingual English churches are intentionally established for descendants of Asians, especially Chinese, Koreans, Japanese, and some Southeast Asians. The reasons given for establishing such churches, as revealed in their discussions on Internet forums, include (1) these people grew up in an ethnic (e.g., Chinese or Korean) church but want to speak English only in a less ethnically stiff environment; (2) as Asians they all look similar; (3) they share some residual Confucian or Asian values; (4) they have had similar experiences of being subtly or blatantly discriminated against by others in the larger society; and (5) some are children of inter-Asian marriages who find it hard to stick to a church of one particular ethnic group. These people disagree about whether there is or will be a distinct "Asian-American culture."

It is obvious to me that these pan-Asian churches constitute racial formation in process. The number of such churches is small, probably about a dozen or two at this time. How they construct their identities and how they evolve remain to be observed, but this alternative identity construction is theoretically and practically important.[2] Suffice it to say here that some Chinese descendants do not have either a *zhongguoren* identity or a *huaren* identity, and that even their *huayi* identity is weakened and replaced by a racial identity of "East Asians" or "Asian-Americans." However, these people are likely to leave the Chinese church. For those who stay, mingling with people who have *huaren* identity will exert some influence on them. Over time, they will probably be pulled toward a stronger *huaren* identity.

In brief, most CCC members still hold all three types of Chinese identities at present. However, the political identification with China is often specific, changing, and divisive. In contrast, the cultural identification with China tends to emphasize harmony, unity, and commonalities. The difficulties of *zhongguoren* identity propel the church toward a unifying *huaren* identity. Overall, this Chinese church in America encourages and nurtures the cultural *huaren* identity more than the other two identities and helps to pull the *zhongguoren* and *huayi* identities toward the cultural *huaren* identity. The church as a whole is experiencing changes in its Chinese identity construction. Along with the increase of the cultural identity (*huaren*), the political identity (*zhongguoren*) is being pushed out, and the primordial identity (*huayi*) is being pulled over toward *huaren* identity (see Figure 3).

Chinese Unity and Chinese Pride

The process of increasing *huaren* identity and waning *zhongguoren* identity is also a process of moving from particularism toward greater universalism; that is, it is moving away from specific political attachments to a common culture, and toward a religious identity that transcends political, cultural, and racial/primordial identities.

Chinese Unity and Harmony

Unity and harmony are highly valued in ancient Chinese classics.[3] The unity of the heterogeneous Chinese people in the past has fascinated many

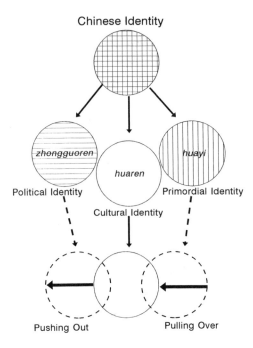

Fig. 3.   Reconstruction of Chinese identities
at the Chinese Christian Church of Greater
Washington, D.C.

Western observers.[4] However, modern China has been full of revolutionary
bloodshed, competing warlords, civil wars, violent political persecutions,
and uncompromising ideological struggles. China continues to be divided
geographically as well as sociopolitically. Overseas Chinese communities
are likewise notoriously fragmented (Lyman 1974; H-S Chen 1992). Sun
Zhongshan (Sun Yatsen), the father of the Republic of China who led the
revolution to overthrow the Qing Dynasty, criticized the Chinese as being
like "a plate of loose sand," a favorite sarcasm among the Chinese. Chinese
Christians in the United States are proud of being Chinese and strive to unite
Chinese people of different social, cultural, and political backgrounds. I met
a renowned Chinese Christian leader when he came as a guest preacher
at the CCC. Upon learning that I was doing sociological research on the
Chinese Christian church in the United States, he made this remark:

> Chinese people are always divided, no matter whether they are in
> China or in the United States. But the Chinese church has united all

kinds of Chinese people. No other kinds of Chinese organizations in the United States have achieved such a unity. If you don't believe it, go and find out for yourself.

I find this to be quite true. Most ethnic Chinese organizations and associations in the United States are internally homogeneous, based on a single denominator of either ancestral location (*tongxianghui*), surname, Chinese university (*tongxuehui*), or common political stand. In contrast, Chinese Christian churches usually have heterogeneous members of diverse backgrounds. These Chinese churches have achieved a high degree of unity out of multidimensional diversity. This unity is in part based on a common Chinese identity, mostly of the cultural or *huaren* type.

This Chinese cultural unity is supplemented by the Christian religion, which holds unity as an ideal as well.[5] Christian unity and Chinese cultural unity complement each other in this process of upholding unity out of diversity (see F. Yang 1998a). When some members show divisive tendencies, such as insisting on speaking a certain dialect or expressing assertive partisan views about Chinese politics, they are reminded, by church leaders and also themselves, that they are Christians after all and should be united in the same God, the same Christ, and the same Spirit. The Christian identity might appear to be limiting because it would exclude non-Christians. Because most Chinese are not Christians, this could mean an exclusion of most Chinese from this unity. However, because of the emphasis on Christian evangelism, the church treats every Chinese person as a prospective convert and thus opens its doors to welcome and actively invite all Chinese to come in. In fact, some individuals have regularly attended this church for years without being baptized. Compared with other types of ethnic Chinese organizations and associations, the church is one of the most open toward newcomers. While most other ethnic Chinese organizations set boundaries based on ascribed or fixed identities (e.g., a common ancestral place), Christian identity is achieved by individuals. For example, every individual can become a Christian, but a person from Hebei, like me, cannot become a Cantonese. As a most open ethnic organization, the church unites Chinese people of various backgrounds.

The Chinese Mission

Chinese people have been receivers of Christian missions. However, the meaning of "Chinese missions" is changing from missions *for* the Chinese to missions *by* Chinese Christians. A triennial "China Missions" conference has been organized since 1983 by Ambassadors for Christ, Inc., whose founders were leaders of the CCC. The conference, which is held in Washington, D.C., has had thousands of participants in the 1990s. It serves as a mechanism for mobilizing Chinese Christians for world missions. Meanwhile, several Chinese Christian missionary organizations have been established in the United States. The CCC has actively taken part in this change from "missions for the Chinese" to "missions by Chinese Christians." Evangelism has been the most important mission of this evangelical church, as we have seen in earlier chapters. Evangelistic home missions and overseas missions have been continuously promoted since the early years of the church, and it continues to engage in many missions with financial and human resources. In its evangelistic efforts the CCC, like many Chinese Christian churches in the United States, has held a "Chinese first" principle. A 1974 document, "Missions Department Working Principles," stated this clearly:

> Our primary concern of the Christian mission is for Chinese people. Because our church is a Chinese church in the U.S., naturally we have greater concerns for and understanding of the Chinese, as Paul had of the Jews (Romans 9:1–3). Under the principle of working together in division of labor, our work understandably is more toward the Chinese, who include a quarter of the world's population. Besides our concern for the Chinese in Southeast Asia, we must also be concerned for the many Chinese in South America (Peru, Cuba, Brazil, Trinidad, and Jamaica especially), in Africa (South Africa, East Africa, especially Tanzania), in Europe and in Australia. We must initiate and support evangelistic work among all these Chinese people.

The justification for the "Chinese first" principle is interesting. Since the early 1980s, in order to mobilize Chinese churches for evangelism missions, some Chinese Christian leaders and missionary organizations have raised a slogan: "Reaching the Chinese to reach the world." This is an inspiring vision for many Chinese Christians. Chinese have spread to many countries of all continents around the world, and Chinese continue to leave China in large numbers. Chinese Christian leaders claim that if everything is under the control of God, then the spread of Chinese people must have the purpose of God. For evangelical Christians, this purpose could not be anything else but to spread the gospel to all peoples of the world. They believe that diasporic Chinese not only occupy strategic geographic positions, but they also have a great advantage over European and American missionaries. Since the Chinese are not political or military aggressors, Chinese missionaries would meet less nationalistic resistance from native peoples. Diasporic Chinese could become the bridge of the gospel to all peoples in the world. Therefore, evangelizing Chinese in the diaspora is strategic to the mission of evangelizing all peoples. Many Chinese churches in North America share this vision and have been actively involved in implementing it.

The Chinese: An Almost-Elected People?

In mission mobilization, some Chinese Christian leaders claim that the Chinese must have a special position in God's salvation plan. This position, they believe, may be somewhat similar to the Jews—the elected people. There are many parallels between the Jews and the Chinese. Like the ancient Jews, ancient Chinese believed in God (*Shangdi*); like Judaic culture, Chinese traditional culture emphasized moral laws, filial piety, and traditionalism; like Jews in history, the Chinese have had many sufferings that, in the eyes of these Chinese Christians, were due to their denial of God and refusal of Jesus Christ; and like Jews who are God's elected people, God's grace has protected the Chinese, both in China and in the diaspora. About two thousand years ago the spread of Jews in the Roman Empire prepared for the spread of Christianity. Similarly, the spread of the Chinese in today's world must be a preparation for the completion of spreading the gospel to all peoples. Some Chinese Christian leaders claim that God's salvation plan is near completion. Therefore, they have been working in zeal to bring the gospel back to Jerusalem to fulfill biblical prophesies. Some efforts have been made to establish a Chinese church in Israel and to prepare to hold a missions conference in Jerusalem in the year 2000. Of course, not all Chinese Christians agree with the analogies between the Chinese and Jews. In the mobilization for Chinese Christian missions, however, such discourses have been very common.

To add to this analogue is the interesting Chinese word *waiguoren* for referring to non-Chinese people. *Waiguoren* means a person of a foreign nation. *Guo* in this word means "country, state, or nation." It would sound strange to hear a Chinese national in the United States referring to Americans as *waiguoren* (foreigners). In fact, when this is pointed out, the person who used this word often feels embarrassed. However, not only do Chinese immigrants continue to use this word frequently, but I have also heard some American-born and American-raised Chinese at the church using this word. Rev. Allan

Houston, a white American, was the assistant pastor of the CCC for about eight years. While CCC members often called him "the American pastor," some people liked to refer to him as "the *waiguoren* pastor." In an interview, Daniel Yew, the man who had a *huayi* Chinese identity as described above, referred to the white American churches he used to attend as *waiguoren* churches. Apparently, many Chinese people use the word *waiguoren* very much like the word *gentile* is used by Jews. It is a word to distinguish non-Chinese from Chinese, without necessarily any connotation of the modern nation-state (*guo*). The boundary is an ethnic or racial one, not a political one. This word is another evidence of the strong ethnic Chinese identity.

From Particularism to Universalism

Chinese identity is a particular one among ethnic/national groups. However, in their identity construction, Chinese Christians in the United States are moving from particularism to universalism. This is happening in three ways. First, Chinese unity moves from subcultural and subgroup identity to the overarching and unifying Chinese cultural identity. Second, when the Chinese identity becomes dominated by Chinese cultural identity rather than nationalistic identity, it expands the scale of inclusion beyond ethnic Chinese. Chinese traditions, especially Confucianism, are not exclusively Chinese. These traditions have had great influences in Korea, Japan, and some Southeast Asian countries. The cultural identity of this Chinese church could be expanded to include people from these Asian countries. Third, the Christian identity is even more inclusive. The "Chinese" particularism cannot limit the "Christian" universalism as has been shown in the expanding Chinese missions toward non-Chinese peoples.

Moreover, since 1995 some Chinese Christian leaders in the United States have been at the forefront in calling Chinese churches to drop the word *Chinese* from their church names in order to welcome non-Chinese. They believe that Chinese Christians as Christians should broaden their minds and hearts and go beyond their own ethnic boundaries in their evangelistic missions. Some Chinese churches have even experimented with putting this vision into action. For example, the Houston Chinese Church in Texas, a nondenominational evangelical church, planted a new church in 1997, which they intentionally named "Fort Bend Community Church." The pastors want to make it a church for people of all ethnic backgrounds in that neighborhood. Although many lay leaders and church members have doubts about its practicability because of cultural and racial reasons, their very experiment is a testimony of growing inclusiveness and universalism. At the present, however, Christian Chinese still have a great need to defend the authenticity of their Chineseness in spite of becoming Christian. This need is a priority because of the minority status of Christians among the Chinese and because of the vast evangelistic mission field among the Chinese in China and the diaspora.

Tensions and Conflicts of Integrating Multiple Identities

While reconstructing their Chinese identity, Chinese Christians in America are also in the process of achieving a Christian identity and an American identity. These three identities—Chinese, Christian, and American—are all indispensable on the primary level for the Chinese Christian church and its members. The process of integrating multiple identities that are often at odds with each other is full of internal tensions and conflicts.

Chinese Identity Versus American Identity

China and the United States are two modern nation-states and represent two largely distinctive cultures of the East and the West. Moreover, the Chinese were excluded from immigration and naturalization in the United States until the 1940s. Since World War II, Chinese immigrants have been treated equally with many other peoples from the Eastern Hemisphere; consequently, many Chinese immigrants have come to the United States. However, the Cold War kept the United States and Communist China in camps of opposition for several decades. Conflicts of national interests and ideologies continue to trouble the relations between China and the United States.

Meanwhile, immigrant and ethnic Chinese, the once unwelcome people in the United States, have become a "model minority" to the American public and their "successful assimilation" has been praised. However, tensions in political allegiance, racial identification, and cultural values continue to agitate Chinese immigrants and their children. Like other Chinese in the larger society, many Chinese church members have lived in these tensions. Some individuals finally returned to China, with or without a choice. For those who have stayed here, as time passes, their Chinese political identity wanes and political participation in American society increases. As this happens, identification with American culture and values also increases. They have achieved significant structural and cultural assimilation, to use the terms of Milton Gordon (1964) and classic theorists. However, the Chinese cultural identity persists and even intensifies for some people along with a waning Chinese political identity, as we have seen above. In other words, their American identity and Chinese identity coexist and may even grow simultaneously.

The coexistence of Chinese and American identities in the church brings tensions and conflicts into this community. American-born generations generally identify more with the United States and American culture, whereas recent immigrants are more Chinese. The "generation gap" in this Chinese church is largely due to conflicts of Chinese and American cultures. For example, the immigrants want the American-born young people to show deference and obedience, whereas the ABCs want more independence and respect. The immigrants want to pass on the Chinese language and Chinese traditional culture to their children, whereas the ABCs want to go their own way with liberty.

The presence of a non-Chinese assistant pastor helped to push this church toward greater Americanization, although this result was unexpected and probably undesired by the immigrant members. Because of Allan Houston's presence, English became the primary or even the only language at Official Board meetings. He also helped the English-speaking young people to achieve more independence from the immigrant leaders. But his presence also intensified the church's existing "clash" of Chinese and American cultures. For instance, in dealing with conflicts, Rev. Houston preferred frank confrontation and talking things out. He claimed that the American ways were more in line with biblical principles. However, Chinese immigrants wanted to maintain a harmonious atmosphere and often preferred to communicate in more indirect or nonconfrontational ways. Furthermore, Rev. Houston paid more attention to developing ministries, whereas Chinese lay leaders hoped he would pay more attention to personal relationships and show deference to the older people. When he tried to hire another white man as a youth pastor (which would have meant a Chinese church with two white American pastors and no Chinese-speaking pastor), some seniors finally approached him, indirectly, with a letter to the Official Board. With the consensus of lay leaders, the church subsequently confined Rev. Houston's leadership space. The interactions at some meetings of the Pastor Search Committee were also very indicative of the conflicts of American and Chinese cultural ways. In the process of searching for a new senior pastor, Rev. Houston suggested procedures based on written manuals and logical steps. However, other committee members, who were immigrants, dismissed them as impractical and insisted on using personal contacts and informal networks to find the new pastor.

Most church members are ambivalent about adopting American ways and values versus maintaining Chinese ways and values. The church as a whole agonizes in its efforts to accommodate all the different members, some of whom are more Chinese and others more American. While the passage of time and generations increases American identity, the continuous immigration and increasing transpacific contacts are factors for maintaining Chinese identity.

Facing the tensions between Chinese and American identities, some CCC members claim that their Christian identity transcends the earthly identities. They see that China and the United States are countries with concrete borders, that Chinese and American cultures have limited boundaries, but that the kingdom of God is not bounded. The universal faith is believed to be absolute, whereas all human cultures are relative. "Citizenship" in Christendom may not set these Chinese Christians in America completely free from earthly tensions and conflicts, but it does ease the anxiety of these tensions and conflicts to a certain extent. The Christian identity provides an absolute ground on which these individuals can selectively reject and accept certain things Chinese and certain things American. With their absolutist evangelical faith, they can justify their choices with psychological peace and theological assurance. Many CCC members expressed this view about the transcendence of their Christian identity over earthly identities. However, Christian identity also has its own tensions and conflicts with the other two identities.

Christian Beliefs Versus Chinese Values

Tensions and conflicts between Christian and Chinese identities are many. Historically, as we have seen, Christianity was not a Chinese traditional religion, and Chinese converts to Christianity were regarded as becoming non-Chinese. Even today many Chinese still regard Christianity as a foreign religion and the Christian God as a foreign god. Chinese Christians assure their Chinese identity by preserving Chinese cultural traditions and reinterpreting Chinese classics. They have made efforts to integrate Chinese values with Christian beliefs and to articulate the compatibility of the two; however, discrepancies remain.

For example, traditional Chinese culture is very family-centered, whereas Christianity is supposed to be God-centered. This discrepancy has contributed to some conflicts at the CCC. As a God-centered religion that highly emphasizes the evangelistic mission, Christians are expected to devote themselves to Jesus Christ. Such devotion may mean leaving home, going abroad, and evangelizing in a faraway mission field. In the early 1970s the church had an exciting period of missions work. Many young people committed themselves to serve their Lord for their whole lives; they entered seminaries and sought missionary opportunities. While the mission-oriented pastor was very pleased to see this zeal for missions, many Chinese parents disapproved of it, and some even openly objected to it. Some outspoken members accused the church of disturbing their family life by having too many gatherings and causing disagreements between husbands and wives and between parents and children. After years of suffering in wars, political violence, social turmoil, and immigration instabilities, many Chinese immigrants hoped for a stable and peaceful family life. They wanted the Christian faith and the church to strengthen and improve their family life. They wanted their children to succeed in school and careers. However, the mobilization for missions inspired the young people, who were children of the immigrants, to go to strange mission fields. Many church members opposed the pastor on this, along with many other issues. Eventually, the conflicts led to the schism in 1976. It was apparent to me that the schism was in part due to conflicts between the Christian religion and Chinese culture.

Christian Beliefs and American Values

There are also tensions and conflicts between American values and Christian beliefs. Many people assume that the United States is a Christian nation or that American culture is a Christian culture. However, conservative Christians do not share a number of normative values with mainstream America. Two continual controversies at the CCC show the tensions between the Christian religion and American culture. One concerns democracy, the other is about the status of women (both are discussed at length in Chapter 4).

The CCC has vigorously maintained a congregational democracy for most of its history. The congregational meeting has the highest authority in decision making. However, many Christians do not agree with this. We have already seen how in the early 1970s, Pastor Frank Chao succeeded in centralizing the power to ordained elders and pastors. After the 1976 schism, the church restored congregational democracy and imposed limits to the term and power of the pastor. However, there have always been some dissents about this democracy. Some members argue that the church should be a theocracy (ruled by God), not a democracy (ruled by people). They say that pastors are servants of God and only God can decide the staying and leaving of a pastor; a democratic vote on a pastor is thus unbiblical. The contrasting positions of the immigrants and the ABCs are very interesting. Most immigrant Chinese at the church have insisted on the principle of democracy. The justifications for this are that this is a Christian church and it is in the United States. In contrast, among those who dissented against voting on Rev. Tang in 1995 or on any pastor, many were American-born young people. Here the generational difference reflects not the conflict between Chinese and American cultures, but between Christian beliefs and American values.

Another controversy is about women's positions in the church and women's roles in general. Sermons and lectures often affirm the conservative Christian position about traditional gender division. Wives are expected to be subordinate to husbands; men are expected to take up leadership roles in the church. Again, it was a surprise when I heard the American-born young people voicing strong opposition to a candidate for the senior pastor position merely because his wife was also an ordained pastor. These young people argued that "If he [the candidate] compromises in any way on this important issue of a woman pastor, how can we expect him to stick to the absolute authority of the Bible?" In contrast, many immigrant Chinese showed more flexible attitudes. This controversy too reflects the conflict between Christian beliefs and American values.

The 1976 Schism: A Result of Complex Identity Conflicts

There were many controversies and problems leading to the 1976 schism, which I have mentioned at various points in this and earlier chapters. Some CCC members insisted that it was a result of personality conflicts or conflicts between true Christians versus false Christians. Looking at it from the perspective of identity construction, however, the evidence suggests that it was a result of the interlocking conflicts of all three identities, or conflicts between Chinese culture and American values, between Chinese culture and Christian beliefs, and between American values and Christian beliefs. There were conflicts between Chinese ways of making personal relationships and American ways of managing church business. There were generational conflicts between immigrant Chinese and ABCs due to Chinese and American cultural conflicts. Chinese immigrants wanted to maintain Chinese unity and preserve Chinese culture, whereas many ABCs wanted to have more independence and to have their own English Sunday services. There were conflicts between American democracy and Christian authority. There were also conflicts between Christian evangelism and Chinese family life and between Christian evangelism and ethnic community involvement. These conflicts were complicated and interlocked with personality and character conflicts, and eventually resulted in the bitter split.

Roughly speaking, those who split off and formed the Chinese Bible Church of Maryland put more emphasis on Christian identity. The radicals in this group wanted to focus exclusively on Christian devotion and evangelistic missions. Some of them later gave up well-paying jobs and went overseas as missionaries. They opposed church democracy, measures of cultural preservation, and involvement in ethnic community activities. On a scale from liberal to fundamentalist, the new church was obviously more fundamentalist.

After the schism the CCC restored congregational democracy, maintained the Chinese School, and continued Christian evangelism. I find that the remaining members at the CCC were not really in direct opposition to those who left to form the Bible Church. Those in extreme opposition to the fundamentalists also left the CCC, either before or after the schism, and stopped attending any church. These dropouts appeared to have a stronger Chinese identity. They had greater concerns about China-related affairs and ethnic Chinese community activities. In my telephone interviews with two of these ex-members, both said that they continued to be Christian believers but that "they found more important things to do [than fighting within the church]." Both were very active in ethnic Chinese organizations, such as various *tongxianghui* (same province associations), alumni associations of Chinese universities, and Chinese American civil rights organizations. For them, all Chinese churches are too conservative, too exclusively focused on religious affairs without concerns about social services, social justice, and political participation. These not-so-conservative Chinese Christians could not find a Chinese church with a theological fit. Neither did they want to join non-Chinese churches. Consequently, they became unchurched.

In brief, the more conservative people with a stronger Christian identity left for the Chinese Bible Church, and the not-so-conservative people with a stronger Chinese identity left for the nonreligious ethnic community. After this, the CCC became a church of people who wanted to maintain a balance of the three identities. Although tensions and conflicts continue, overall the church has maintained an equilibrium of Chinese, American, and Christian identities in the last twenty years.

Constructing Adhesive Identities

Despite tensions and conflicts, the three identities—Chinese, American, and Christian—are merging together in the church like three separate circles coalescing into one. The ideal pattern of identity integration for these Chinese Christians in America is not that one identity replaces another, but that three identities adhere together. CCC members hope that they can simultaneously claim Christianity and Chinese and American cultures in constructive ways. They want to select the good elements from the three systems while rejecting the bad elements of each of them. We have seen the selective assimilation and selective preservation processes in Chapters 4 and 5. Is it possible to hold these three identities at once? Apparently, there are people who hold one exclusive identity without the others (singular identity); some hold two identities without the third one (binary identity); and some people hold all three identities (trinary identity). Some people combine Chinese and American identities but are not very Christian; some combine Chinese and Christian identities but are not very American; some combine American and Christian identities but are not very Chinese; and some combine all three identities (see Figure 4).

Moreover, there are various patterns of integrating multiple identities. I find three major patterns for the people at the CCC. The first pattern is "fragmentary integration": a person may adopt some values or lifestyles from others while maintaining one dominant identity. For example, new immigrants are very Chinese overall, but may have adopted some American values or lifestyles. ABCs are very American overall, but many speak some Chinese language and like certain Chinese ways. Some acknowledge that they are "half-Chinese and half-American." Some people go to this church primarily because this is a *Chinese community* wherein they meet very friendly people on a regular basis, rather than because it is a church. Their Christian identity may be weak, and a few are non-Christian even though they have regularly attended this church for years. Many people follow this pattern of fragmentary integration in one way or another.

The second pattern may be called "fusive integration": blending together several cultures and melting out distinct characteristics. For the people who have "fusively integrated" Chinese and American cultures, their behavior

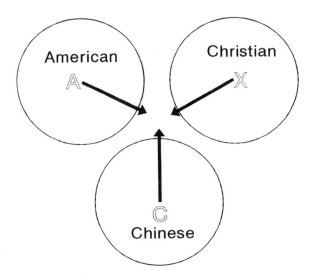

I: Three Identities Merging Together

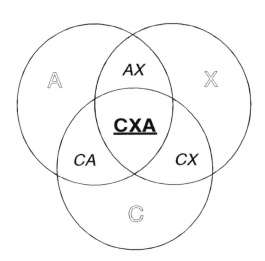

II: Coexistence of Singular, Binary, and Trinary Identities

Fig. 4.   Integration of multiple identities at the Chinese Christian Church of
Greater Washington, D.C.: Chinese, Christian, and American

appears to be "too American" to Chinese people, and yet "too Chinese" to Americans. They become marginal persons to either Chinese or American mainstreams. A few ABCs, but not many at present, have this type of Chinese-American identity.

The third pattern is "adhesive integration": adding multiple identities together without necessarily losing any particular one. People who follow this pattern speak two or three languages fluently, understand Chinese and American cultural values and social norms very well, and are knowledgeable and respected Christians. People who have adhesive identities can function well in various cultural settings. Depending on circumstances, they can freely choose to act like Americans among Americans and like Chinese among Chinese, or they can act like Chinese among Americans and like Americans among Chinese. Many leaders at the Chinese church enjoy adhesive identities. One example is Kevin Cheung, who was born in the 1940s in Shanghai of a Cantonese family, graduated from high school in Hong Kong, came to the United States to attend college, received a doctorate in engineering, and works in the aerospace industry. He speaks fluent English, Mandarin, and Cantonese and is a well-respected lay leader among Mandarin-, Cantonese-, and English-speaking congregants. In an interview, he illustrated the advantage of holding all three identities:

> Holding three identities is just like practicing *kungfu* [Chinese martial arts]. It is good to learn one style of *kungfu*, but it is even better to learn more styles. That will make you stronger and capable to defend against different kinds of *kungfu* masters. For me, holding three identities is really beneficial. When there is a problem, I can use Chinese culture to deal with it, or use American culture, or use Christianity, depending on the nature of the problem. For example, when being criticized, Chinese people often feel very bad for losing face. If I get criticized, I will use the American way to deal with it. I would say, "no big deal," and get over it. On the other hand, Americans want to move up every couple of years. If there is no promotion, Americans often get very frustrated. In this case, I will use the Chinese way to deal with it. We Chinese say *gongcheng shentui* [retire after a great accomplishment]. If the emperor trusts and uses me, I will continue to do my best. If not, it's fine. We don't have to become the *zaixiang* [prime minister, or the second man under the emperor]. Americans like to claim credit for their contribution. To me claiming credit is not that important. As a Christian, I believe God knows everything and will judge me accordingly. Also, as a Christian,

> I will not be afraid of capable persons. I can help my colleagues and even subordinates who are capable persons succeed or even surpass me. For this matter, no Chinese or American values will help. Only with the Christian faith can I do it. Of course, it is not always easy. We need to completely trust the Lord and submit ourselves to Him.

Like many CCC members, Kevin Cheung says that his Christian identity transcends the earthly Chinese and American identities. It provides him an absolute ground on which he can selectively reject or accept certain things Chinese and certain things American.

At the present, all three patterns of identity integration exist at this Chinese Christian church. The simultaneous coexistence of multiple identities and various patterns of integration presents great challenges to church members and church leaders. For individuals, they cannot escape from the difficult challenges of identity construction and have to sort out the options for themselves. For the leaders, to make their ministry effective, they need to understand the various patterns and variations of each pattern and adopt appropriate measures and strategies to help different people in different situations. However, this task is too challenging for many Chinese ministers who may themselves be undergoing the confusing process of identity reconstruction. It is common to hear frustrated Chinese ministers complain about the difficulty of their ministry work. It is also common to hear ordinary Chinese Christians complain about the lack of qualified pastors. Given the complexity of the identity reconstruction of multiple identities, it is inevitable that many Chinese Christians, both lay and clergy, feel confusion, puzzlement, frustration, anxiety, and alienation. This is the reality that Chinese Christian leaders and ordinary believers today have to face.

Conclusion

Pluralism and Adhesive Identities

Chinese Christians in immigrant and ethnic churches in the United States are undergoing identity construction and reconstruction. At the Chinese Christian Church of Greater Washington, D.C., as in many other Chinese churches, a majority of church members are adult converts. As converts, they have achieved a Christian identity; as immigrants, they have achieved an American identity. At the same time, their Chinese identity has been undergoing reconstruction as well.

These three identities are not easily compatible with each other. Tensions and conflicts are myriad in the process of identity reconstruction. However, the church helps its members, both immigrants and their American-born children, to attain and sustain multiple and adhesive identities. In this process, the immigrant church functions as a conversion agency, an assimilation agency, and an ethnic center for selectively preserving cultural traditions. In sum, the Chinese Christian church helps its members to construct an evangelical Protestant identity, a conservative American identity, and a cosmopolitan and cultural Chinese identity.

One Church, Three Identities

Chapters 3 through 5 described, one by one, the construction of three primary identities. However, none of these three identities stands alone. Church participants are Christians who are American Christians and Chinese Christians; as Americans they are Christian Americans and ethnic Chinese Americans; as Chinese they are Christian Chinese and American

Chinese. These three identities are interconnected. The construction of adhesive identities is both necessary and possible in the social contexts of pluralism and transnationalism.

Social, Cultural, and Religious Context

First of all, contemporary Chinese immigrants come to an increasingly pluralistic American society. Race relations may have changed since the Civil Rights movement, but race continues to divide Americans into subsocieties (Omi and Winant 1986, 1994). Moreover, rapid increases of Hispanic and Asian-American populations in the last few decades have problematized the previous racial dichotomy of whites and blacks (Moore and Pachon 1985; Takaki 1989; Espiritu 1992). Meanwhile the American core culture, with the dominance of white Anglo-Saxon Protestant values, has been eclipsed amid various social movements and revolutions since the 1960s (Glazer and Moynihan 1963; Kazal 1995). The ethnic revival movements since the 1970s have boosted the legitimacy of ethnic groupings and multiculturalism (Royce 1982; Fishman et al. 1985; Conzen et al. 1992). Religious pluralism has greatly expanded as well. While Protestantism continues to be dominant in American culture, Catholicism and Judaism have become equally American religions (Herberg 1960). Islam, Buddhism, Hinduism, and other nontraditional American religions have gradually increased in numbers of believers and become much more acceptable (Kosmin and Lachman 1993; Warner 1998). The New Age movement has given rise to various new religions and Oriental mystical practices. Also, "no religion" has become an acceptable answer, and the proportion of people with no religion has increased in the population (Greeley 1989; Gallup 1990; Kosmin and Lachman 1993). Within such a social, cultural, and religious pluralism, religious conversion becomes less an act of conformity to social pressures and more a matter of personal choice.

Second, these Chinese Protestants are establishing themselves in a time of restructuring of American Protestantism. The significance of denominationalism has been in decline since World War II (Wuthnow 1988), while culture wars between liberal and conservative Americans are on the rise (Hunter 1991). Sociological studies have consistently shown the conservative growth and the liberal decline among Protestant denominations and churches (Kelley 1972; Hoge and Roozen 1979; Roozen and Hadaway 1993). Within conservative Christianity there are further differences of fundamentalism, evangelicalism, and pentecostalism (Ammerman 1987; Warner

1988). Within this Protestant pluralism, new immigrants who had been converted by Protestants before immigration face the question of deciding their religious allegiance. Historical denominational ties are important, but other factors are also important in their consideration, including their socioeconomic status, their immigration experience, and the institutional policies of existing churches toward immigrant groups. About half of all Chinese churches established since the 1950s are nondenominational independent churches. The CCC is one of them. In the meantime, converts choose the kind of Protestantism that they find attractive and helpful, and they join those churches that welcome and actively recruit new arrivals. The CCC, like many other ethnic Chinese churches, has been effective in recruiting converts. There has been a rapid growth of independent and evangelical Chinese churches in the United States.

Third, these Chinese immigrants come from various societies of third-world countries. In their original countries they and their compatriots suffered colonialism and imperialism, wars and revolutions, natural disasters and human catastrophes. They also experienced the collapse of cultural traditions, the rise of nationalism, and the dramatic changes of modernization. Specifically, many Chinese immigrants experienced Japanese imperialism during World War II, the Chinese Civil War in the 1940s, Communist revolutions in mainland China and Indochina, and anti-Chinese violence in Southeast Asia. There has been rapid modernization in Taiwan, Hong Kong, and Singapore, followed by mainland China and other Southeast Asian countries. What is more important, Western imperialism and modernization have fiercely shaken and, to a large extent, fragmented Chinese cultural traditions. To save China and the Chinese race, an iconoclastic nationalism arose at the beginning of this century and flourished thereafter (Lin 1979; Tu 1987). Through unremitting struggles and sustained efforts, China as a modern nation-state has become stronger and stronger, but the reconstruction of Chinese culture and identity has become increasingly complicated and difficult.

Within this American and global context, the Chinese immigrants have made their efforts to construct and reconstruct their multiple identities.

The Christian Identity

The Chinese Christian Church of Greater Washington, D.C., is a nondenominational evangelical Protestant church. Its public rituals reflect strong influences of the Reformed tradition with a Baptist tone. As we have noted, evangelism has been *the* mission of the church, and the church as a whole has no political involvement and few social service ministries.

The church was founded by a group of Chinese students and new immigrants who had been Christians before coming to the United States. They were then joined by Chinese new immigrants with very diverse social, cultural, and denominational backgrounds. About half of all past and present church members were adult converts from non-Christian backgrounds. The CCC has maintained a congregational polity that insists on equal participation in the congregational democracy. The continuous growth of this and other similar Chinese churches coincides with the trends of conservative growth, declining significance of denominationalism, and increasing congregationalism in American Protestantism (Warner 1994), although the reasons may not be all the same.

In contemporary pluralistic American society, why have so many Chinese immigrants converted to conservative Protestantism? Through examining conversion testimonials and reviewing the historical changes, we can see three important reasons. First, third-world experiences of the immigrants before coming to America and immigration experiences as a racial minority in the United States intensified the desire for religious interpretations about the meaning of life and the world. Many people were ruthlessly uprooted from China and other home places, then suffered loneliness and difficulties as immigrants in this strange land. Facing the rapidly changing and increasingly relativized society, many people longed for order, purpose, and rules. Second, they find conservative Protestantism attractive because it proclaims absoluteness, love, and certainty. The church has become a haven for the homeless sojourners. Third, although Chinese cultural traditions have been broken down, these immigrants continue to cherish many traditional values, especial Confucian moral values. In conservative Christianity, these Chinese find a good match for their cherished social-ethical values. Fourth, the Christian identity also provides a universal and absolute ground on which these Chinese can selectively reject or accept certain cultural traditions, either Chinese or American. Overall, their construction and attainment of evangelical Protestant identity in the independent ethnic church have important contextual factors of both modern China and America (Yang 1998b).

The American Identity

Most CCC members have become American citizens and adapted to life in American society. However, cultural assimilation or Americanization began before immigration for many people because many new immigrants came from urban areas where American values and lifestyles were not totally strange. In the United States the most important assimilation agencies are mass media, schools, and workplaces. Most new Chinese immigrants came to the United States as students at first and studied among non-Chinese, then found professional jobs and worked among non-Chinese. They also send their children to public schools. In its forty-year history, the church has had some change toward more English usage and more American styles. However, these changes were not brought about by the church; they simply reflect the growing acculturation of church members. While individuals are structurally assimilated in public spheres, mainly schools and work, the church provides an ethnic community for private life—religious and fellowship activities.

In the meantime, the church has been effective in proclaiming a particular American value system—conservative Protestantism. The church assimilates its members by promoting those values of the "Protestant ethic" or "this-worldly asceticism": success, thrift, delayed gratification. It also proclaims conservative gender roles. More important, the church heralds the conservative Christian version of American civil religion, which emphasizes the Christian foundation of the United States. Like other evangelical or fundamentalist Christians, CCC members often express worries about what they see as the erosion of this Christian foundation and the degeneration of moral values. The church fosters a community that supports efforts to guard against American eroticism, consumerism, and materialism. The members' evangelical Christian faith, their Confucian cultural heritage, and their experiences of turbulent and unstablizing sufferings hold them back from political participation and social service involvements. CCC members believe in education and hard work. They are grateful for American acceptance and proud of their tangible contributions to this society as scientists and engineers.

For these immigrants, assimilation does not mean simply blending themselves as individuals into the American society or melting into the big American pot. Rather, they choose to congregate with fellow Chinese while studying and working among non-Chinese. Living in suburbs of racially mixed neighborhoods and working or studying among non-Chinese, they find that the ethnic church provides a warm community environment for supporting immigrants and nurturing American-born youth. The church has made many efforts to preserve the Chinese language and certain Chinese cultural values. It helps to pull American-born Chinese toward more Chinese cultural identity.

The independent ethnic church may appear to be a willingly segregated ethnic ghetto. However, ethnic grouping has become normal and acceptable in contemporary American society. Ethnicization itself is a process of Americanization (Higham 1981; Gerber, Morawska, and Pozzetta 1992). Immigrants do not just become Americans—they become ethnic Americans. Historically, Chinese Christian immigrants could claim their equal American identity with white Christians mostly through the independent ethnic church rather than through racially integrated churches. This Chinese ethnic church is independent but not really isolated. Church members are structurally assimilated in American public institutions. Although not affiliated with a denomination, the church selectively networks with some non-Chinese Christian organizations and individuals. This Chinese church even hired a white American as its assistant pastor. But these mutually voluntary relationships can be maintained only if they are mutually beneficial.

Like evangelization, Americanization is a continuous process. While many newcomers have become American citizens and adopted American lifestyles, Chinese students, new immigrants, and other sojourners have always comprised a significant proportion of the church membership. Some of these church members adjust to the immigrant status, some return to Asia, and some others become truly transnational persons who travel back and forth between Asia and America frequently. In short, their becoming American does not mean giving up the Chinese identity. Instead, the church helps them to retain and reclaim Chinese cultural identity within American pluralism.

The Chinese Identity

Most participants in the CCC are ethnic Chinese. These immigrants did not come to America to give up their Chinese identity. On the contrary, many came to America with the explicit intention of better preserving their Chinese identity (Tu 1994). This is not only true of those Chinese re-migrants from Southeast Asian countries, but is also true of some Chinese from China. Postcolonial nationalism in Southeast Asian countries sometimes encouraged discrimination and violence against ethnic Chinese because of their economic status and their social, cultural, or political attachments to China. At the same time, China itself has had many waves of antitraditionalism, from the radical May Fourth Movement (1919) to the even more radical Cultural Revolution (1966–76). Communist revolutions swept mainland China and Indochina and caused many Chinese to flee from political persecution and suppression. Many new Chinese immigrants have the sense of spiritual as well as terrestrial homelessness as a result of their sufferings in imperialism, colonialism, nationalism, communism, and modernization. Arriving in the new land, they are making efforts to reconstruct their Chinese identity.

The CCC clearly asserts its common Chinese identity. However, church members come from very different places and have very different socio-cultural and sociopolitical backgrounds. They speak different dialects and languages; they are sympathetic to different political parties in China; and they have different understandings of Chineseness. But they congregate with other Chinese despite the differences. Subgroup tensions and conflicts have been many, yet Chinese unity has been tenaciously preserved in the church. Church members are proud of their Chinese unity in diversity. At the same time, this cosmopolitan reality forces these people to redefine their Chinese identity and expand the meaning of Chineseness. The Christian faith and the American setting provide both strains and latitudes for their reconstruction of Chinese identity.

In their reconstruction of Chinese identity, they examine Chinese cultural traditions for compatibility with their evangelical Protestant faith. While maintaining the universality of their Christian faith, these Chinese Christians also claim their Chinese cultural heritage. They have made efforts to differentiate nonreligious Chinese traditions from religious ones. To assure their Chinese identity they have selectively preserved nonreligious traditional values, rituals, and symbols. They have tried hard to preserve the Chinese language, to preserve Confucian moral values and some notions of philosophical Daoism, and to continue celebrating Chinese New Year as a Chinese cultural festival. To protect the integrity of their Christian faith, they reject Buddhism and religious Daoism. The Christian faith provides them with a basis on which they can selectively preserve traditional Chinese culture.

In their missions of Christian evangelism, they set the priority principle of "Chinese first." In a sense, this principle of Chinese first is also an effort to assure their Chinese identity. First of all, it shows their basic commitment to fellow Chinese. Second, it can be seen as an effort to extend their particular Christian experiences to fellow Chinese. Without such sharing or extension, their experiences risk becoming completely un-Chinese. Actually, the Christian faith does not obstruct their Chinese identity. Rather, it helps their efforts to save Chinese people and to revitalize Chinese culture.

Like evangelism and assimilation, the construction of Chinese identity is a continuous process. The definition of Chineseness is not fixed, and the identity of Chinese descent is not taken for granted. The church helps to renegotiate, redefine, and reconstruct the Chinese identity. Living far away from China, some may become non-Chinese, whereas others recover or rediscover their Chineseness. Ironically, racist discrimination in the past helped Chinese immigrants to maintain their Chinese identity, as it did for Jews and blacks. Now, the declining racism and growing cultural pluralism in America give immigrants freedom to preserve their ethnicity. Modern technologies of transportation and communication are shrinking the world into a global village. The increasing contacts with China and Chinese people in Asia make it possible for Chinese in America to connect closely with their distinctive cultural roots in China.

Chinese identity may be distinguished into three types—political identity (*zhongguoren*), cultural identity (*huaren*), and primordial or racial identity (*huayi*). After nearly forty years, the CCC as a whole still holds all three identities. However, it has been changing in the process of identity reconstruction. The change is pushing away Chinese political identity, increasing Chinese cultural identity, and pulling over Chinese primordial identity toward Chinese cultural identity. The change toward more Chinese cultural identity is also a process of changing from particularism toward universalism. These Chinese Christians in America are moving away from specific political attachments toward a common Chinese culture, then into a Christian identity that transcends political, cultural, and racial/primordial identities.

Integrating Multiple Identities

The three primary identities—Chinese, Christian, and American—are not always compatible with each other, but are often in tension and conflict. However, many Chinese Christians at the church claim that the Christian identity as the universal faith transcends their earthly Chinese and American identities. They believe that the Christian identity provides them with an absolute ground for selectively rejecting and accepting certain things Chinese and certain things American.

The integration of multiple identities has several patterns. "Fragmentary integration" is the process of maintaining one dominant identity while adopting some elements of the other identities; "fusive integration" is blending together two or three identities and melting out distinct characteristics of previous identities; "adhesive integration" is adding two or three identities together without losing distinct characteristics of each identity. People who have adhesive integration can function fully in two or three cultures. The classic understanding of assimilation that regards American society as a "melting pot" would favor the fusive integration (see Gordon

1964); but adhesive integration is probably the ideal pattern for many new immigrants since the 1960s. In 1971 anthropologist Francis L. K. Hsu called for "creative adjustment" and positive approach to the inescapable "double identity" (chaps. 10 and 11).[1] In 1982 anthropologist Bernard P. Wong found that post-1965 new Chinese immigrants commonly hoped for maintaining multiple identity (81–83).[2] In the 1990s at least some Chinese Americans—Chinese Christians in the Chinese church—are functionally holding adhesive identities. This is not a uniquely Chinese phenomenon. Kim and Hurh (1993) find an "adhesive pattern of adaptation" among some Korean immigrants; a Korean American theologian made a Christian plea for retaining multiple identities (Lee 1995). Further empirical studies are necessary to determine which immigrant and minority groups are constructing adhesive identities.

Theoretical Implications

A prominent characteristic of contemporary American society is pluralism, which has challenged existing sociological theories of assimilation and ethnicity (Kazal 1995). Some scholars have tried to develop new concepts to integrate "assimilation" and "ethnicity" (e.g., Kim and Hurh 1993; Mittelberg and Waters 1992; Portes and Zhou 1993). While I did not intend to test old or new theories, I have been very much informed by these recent theoretical developments. Nonetheless, this study has some implications for the theoretical development of immigrant assimilation in several respects.

Identity Construction in the Pluralist Context

Pluralism in America is not a new reality, but it has intensified since the 1960s and has achieved qualities of postmodernism. This is seen in two ways. First, the society has entered the postindustrial age, and the economic structure has changed dramatically. In the past, assimilation of immigrants could be achieved gradually through climbing ladders of social mobility. However, these ladders are no longer available to many of the new immigrants. Instead, many face a situation that may be called, to use a Chinese metaphor, the "dragon gateway." Those people who can jump over the high gateway will become powerful "dragons," and they will have prosperity and freedom. Those people who fail to jump over the gateway will remain to be "carps," and they will be trapped in underclass situations. This structural change leads to what some scholars have called "segmented assimilation" (Portes and Zhou 1993). Instead of the uniform process of acculturation preceding structural entrance to the mainstream society, there are several distinct forms of adaptation among new immigrants. "One of them replicates the time-honored portrayal of growing acculturation and parallel integration into the white middle-class; a second leads straight in the opposite direction to permanent poverty and assimilation into the underclass; still a third associates rapid economic advancement with deliberate preservation of the immigrant community's values and tight solidarity" (Portes and Zhou 1993, 82).

Second, human history has entered the information age. Communication and transportation technologies are shrinking the world into a global village. Both cross-national information exchange and cross-national migration are increasing. Two results are relevant to identity construction (Beyer 1994). On the one hand, globalization brings greater homogenization across borders on various levels. A local event may become news, instantly spreading to the whole world and consequently causing immediate reactions in other parts of the world. In this process of change, some universal and transnational standards are emerging. On the other hand, diversity becomes an unavoidable reality. In this increasingly cosmopolitan society, people of diverse cultures become next-door neighbors, both literally and in the shrunken time-space.

In such a situation, individuals have to continuously negotiate their boundaries with others, or construct and reconstruct their distinctive identity. They are constantly in search of group belonging and in need of learning to live with people of other cultures. They face challenges of defining their distinctiveness and yet finding commonness with others. Moreover, transnational identity becomes not only a possible option because of communication and transportation technologies, but increasingly it becomes a necessity for success in the integrated world market. In brief, in this postmodern information age, homogenization and diversification coexist at once, and individuals constantly adjust or renegotiate their identities.

Selective Assimilation and Selective Preservation

Within the increasing pluralism, assimilation of immigrants becomes more complicated. Structurally, assimilation has become "segmented." From the standpoint of immigrants, assimilation is selective. The choices newcomers make will greatly influence their degree of success in the host society. To maximize the chance of socioeconomic success, immigrants need to select the subsystem into which they want to assimilate in the host society, control the pace of assimilation, and maintain a cohesive ethnic community.

Selective assimilation means negotiating the people category assigned by the host society and its agents. The host society, represented by the government and existing civic organizations, will assign newcomers to their respective "proximal hosts" or categories of people who may share some features with the newcomers (Mittelberg and Waters 1992). However, newcomers will make their own choices, consciously or unconsciously. The establishment of the CCC was a conscious choice. Before the arrival of new Chinese immigrants, most Chinese lived in the ghetto Chinatown. Those Chinatown Chinese were immigrants from rural areas of Guangdong and laborers or small shop owners in Chinatown. In comparison, most new Chinese immigrants after World War II had a better education and higher social status before coming to the United States. They attended American universities and became professionals in mainstream American institutions. There was a Chinatown church in Washington, D.C., which was founded in 1935 as a mission to Chinatown Chinese by mainline Protestant churches; however, new Chinese immigrants were reluctant to join that the church. Instead, they established their own new church. At its beginning CCC adopted one distinctive marker—it was Mandarin-speaking. This was an efficient boundary distinguishing it from the Cantonese-speaking Chinatown church. At the same time, these new Chinese immigrants also made a religious choice—to be an evangelical independent church without denominational affiliation.

Selective assimilation means exercising control over the pace and aspects of assimilation. Within the new economic structure where intermediate mobility ladders are lacking, educational investment and strict moral ethics become crucial in order to jump through the "dragon gateway." New Chinese immigrants generally trust the education system, so they send their children to public schools and prestigious universities; they trust the economic system, so they work hard and invest wisely to gain tangible rewards; they trust the social-legal system, so they seek gradual changes toward equality. However, they do not trust the media and entertainment industry for encouraging liberal moral values and unconventional lifestyles. Instead, these Chinese Christians choose evangelical Christianity because its value system fits their desire for order and success. They choose to congregate in the evangelical Christian church because it provides material and social capital for Chinese immigrants and their children. The immigrants have made themselves into middle-class citizens, and through the church community they have also secured a good future for their children. They have managed to achieve the structural assimilation in school and work, but are trying to assimilate only certain American cultural values.

Selective assimilation simultaneously means selective preservation of traditional culture. Immigrant individuals of a minority race cannot simply leave the ethnic culture behind and immerse themselves in mainstream white society. To avoid being assigned to a disadvantaged racial category or otherwise marginalized, they need to maintain a strong ethnic community. Within the favorable environment of pluralism, these new immigrants have fostered an ethnic group consciousness to guard against what they believe to be undesirable assimilation to bad American subsocieties of the underclass; the anticultural disorder; and the immorality of drugs, violence, and liberal sexuality. Some traditional Chinese values became assets for achieving ethnic cohesion and maintaining a success-oriented ethic.

Selective assimilation also means constructing adhesive identity. For many Chinese new immigrants and their descendants, bi-culturalism becomes desirable, practical, and advantageous. They are fully assimilated, yet without being deprived of their ethnic culture and identity, and thus they have more resources and options in life. Therefore, they could function well either in a Chinese situation or an American situation, or in even more complicated situations.

Christian Conversion and Chinese Identity

Past studies of European and some Asian immigrants show that transplanted religious organizations help to preserve traditional culture and maintain ethnic identity (Vecoli 1969; Dolan 1972; Abramson 1973; Choy 1979; Kim 1981; Williams 1988; Hurh and Kim 1990; Min 1992). Traditional religions provide continuity of identity among many changes in the new land. My study suggests that the immigrant church of religious converts like the CCC also helps to preserve traditional culture and construct ethnic identity. Hence, conversion to Christianity should not be seen as simply an act of completely giving up cultural roots. It should be understood in the context of postmodern pluralism.

Religious conversion in postmodern pluralism can be an act of preserving traditional culture. Postmodern pluralism has a tendency to relativize traditions. The Chinese highly value their cultural traditions, especially Confucian moral values, but traditionalism alone cannot justify the authority of such a system of ethics. These Chinese immigrants find a good match between Confucian moral values and evangelical Christian beliefs, and the conservative Christian faith provides an absolute foundation for their cherished social ethics. Therefore, religious conversion to evangelical Christianity indeed helps these people to maintain their Chinese identity. Without the institution of the Christian church, the preservation of traditional Chinese culture could have been more difficult within postmodern pluralism.

This conclusion, that religious conversion helps to preserve cultural traditions, may be extendable to some other ethnic groups, but not to all. The nature of Chinese identity and Chinese culture make this identity reconstruction possible. Traditionally, Chinese identity is not inseparably attached to certain religions. The orthodoxy of Confucianism is not a religious one. Confucianism is mostly a system of social ethics, and it allowed coexistence of many religions in the past. Moreover, the tendencies of orthopraxy further disclaimed Chinese identity of particular religions. Chinese unity has been a *cultural* unity. Therefore, Chinese converts to Christianity could claim their Chinese identity by preserving their nonreligious Chinese cultural heritage, rejecting traditionally religious elements of the culture, and sometimes reinterpreting the meaning of certain cultural traditions. For these Chinese, Christian conversion becomes an integral part of the general identity reconstruction of Chineseness.

Religious conversion in the postmodern era has to deal simultaneously with both universalism and particularism. For third-world countries the modernization process often means Westernization to a great extent. However, many third-world countries with highly developed cultural traditions have also rejected Western colonialism, imperialism, and Christianization. Nationalism rose to liberate third-world peoples from this cohesive Western universalization. Many countries have experimented with Marxist communism—a kind of universalism that ironically affirmed nationalist particularism in practice. In China, communist experiments became very destructive to traditional culture and society. Christianity is an alternate universalism with which many Chinese today have become interested in experimenting. Both in China and in the diaspora, the number and proportion of Christians among the Chinese have risen rapidly in the last few decades.

This study of a Chinese church in America shows that this form of Christian universalism can be constructive, rather than destructive, to traditional Chinese culture. Christian conversion does not mean complete denial of Chinese culture. Rather, traditional values find a more solid foundation in the midst of postmodern pluralism. While universalism is achieved, particularism is also affirmed.

Chinese conversion to Christianity also shows that the clash of civilizations between Christian and Confucian worlds, which was prophesied by Samuel

Huntington (1993), is not the unavoidable destiny. This study shows that Chinese Christians have constructively integrated Confucianism with Christianity. Modernism may have presented exclusivist conflicts of cultures in favor of Western culture. However, postmodernism is opening possibilities for cultural pluralism as well as for cultural integration in a constructive and harmonious way. Difficulties abound, as we have seen in the various tensions and conflicts in this ethnic church. However, there is also the hope of constructive integration and dynamic equilibrium.

Appendix

The Chinese Christian Church of Greater Washington, D.C.: An Annotated Chronology

Year	Pastor(s)	Significant Events and Organizational Changes
1958		Began Sunday worship services in Mandarin in the office building of the International Students, Inc. (ISI), in downtown Washington, D.C. The initial participants were Chinese students in a Bible study fellowship started by a Chinese evangelist affiliated with the ISI.
1959		Held the first Congregational Meeting, which refused ISI's invitation for affiliation, named the church "Chinese Mandarin Church of Washington, D.C.," and democratically elected three lay "coworkers" as leaders.
1962	MC	Hired Moses Chow from Shanghai/Indonesia/U.S./Japan as the pastor.* Began formal membership registration; organized the choir; formed the "committee of coworkers" with seven elected lay people.
1963	MC	Elected seven deacons to form the "Deacons Board," which was chaired by a layman; began discussing about electing elders but could not reach agreement. Formed the "Women's Group" and the "Men's Group"; began to have Sunday lunch at the church, which persists today.
1966	MC	Elected five lay members as trustees to form the Trustees Board alongside the Deacons Board.
1967	MC/KL	Hired Kevin Lee from Hong Kong as assistant pastor.
1968	MC/KL	Both Chow and Lee resigned at the end of the year. Chow devoted himself to a Chinese student ministry

Year	Pastor(s)	Significant Events and Organizational Changes
		organization and Lee moved to a Southern state for evangelism opportunities and later founded a Chinese Baptist church.
1969	FC	Hired Frank Chao from Hong Kong/Midwest as the pastor in January. Sunday services became bi-dialectal (Mandarin and Cantonese), later trilingual (Mandarin, Cantonese, and English).
1970	FC	Changed the church name to "Chinese Christian Church of Greater Washington, D.C." Dissolved the Deacons Board and the Trustees Board, and formed the Official Board with eleven elected lay deacons, chaired by a layman; ordained two lay elders; formed the Elders Board with the pastor as the natural chairman. The eldership was permanent and elders were natural members of the Official Board.
1971	FC	Purchased a piece of land in a suburb of Maryland and built a sanctuary building without external fund-raising or mortgage. Established the Chinese Language School, the first one in this area. Formed task forces to plan a child-care center and an elder-care home (never realized). Began the "Annual Missions Conference" and "faith pledge" of donations. In the following years, the number of church members grew quickly, both by baptism and by membership transfer. The church discouraged subgroups based on homogeneous backgrounds. The missions fund grew rapidly, even superseding the general fund in 1974 and 1975; many people were inspired to seek seminary education and do overseas missions.
1974	FC	Ordained the third permanent lay elder. The Elders Board became the goal-setting and decision-making body, whereas the Official Board of deacons became the administrative board.

Year	Pastor(s)	Significant Events and Organizational Changes
1975	FC/PL	Paul Liu, a young seminary graduate who spoke little Chinese, was ordained, and the church hired Paul Liu as the assistant pastor for the youth ministry at the insistence of Pastor Frank Chao. Began sponsoring ethnic Chinese out of Vietnamese refugee camps and experimented with a Sunday service in Vietnamese for the refugees. Sunday attendance peaked at over 400. Various dissatisfactions, complaints, and conflicts among leaders and members became overt. Held many congregational meetings and special meetings to clarify misunderstandings, but the conflicts escalated.
1976	FC/PL	Began a separate English service for the young people in January. Frank Chao resigned in April amid tensions and conflicts. Schism in August: Assistant Pastor Paul Liu, two elders, most deacons, the church secretary, and half of the members walked out and formed the Chinese Bible Church of Maryland. The English service stopped.
1977		Debated and revised the church constitution and bylaws, restoring the highest authority to the congregational meeting; the Official Board, composed of the remaining elder and elected deacons, became the executive board; imposed a term limit of one year to the pastorship.
1978	SC	Hired Simon Chang from Hong Kong as the pastor in January, but a year later the congregational meeting voted him out. Simon Chang, along with a couple of families from the CCC, left to establish the Chinese Baptist Church of Maryland.
1980–81		Debated and revised the church constitution and bylaws: changed the term limit of the pastorship to two years, renewable upon congregational approval by at least two-thirds of positive votes.
1982	PH	Hired Philip Hung from Hong Kong/Canada as the pastor.

Year	Pastor(s)	Significant Events and Organizational Changes
		Began publishing the church quarterly magazine *Living Water*.
		Began holding annual summer retreat for the whole church on a weekend in a remote place.
		In the following years, a dozen fellowship groups based on language/dialect and other social and cultural backgrounds were formed, including the Teens (English, high school students), Emmanuel (English, college students and young professionals), Evergreen (Mandarin, senior people), Living Water (Mandarin, young professionals, 1986), Carmel (Cantonese, young professionals, 1987), Canaan (Mandarin, middle-aged, 1987), Elim (Cantonese, middle-aged, 1988), Ark (Mandarin, evangelizing mainland Chinese, 1989).
1985	PH/MH	Hired Murray Hwang, an American-born Chinese, as the youth pastor. In the following year, started the English Sunday service alongside the Chinese service, and a combined communion service held on the first Sunday of each month.
1988	PH/MH	Murray Hwang resigned to enter law school.
1989	PH/AH	Hired Allan Houston, a white man from the South, as the assistant pastor to minister to the English-speaking congregants.
		Philip Hung resigned.
1990	AH	Allan Houston, the de facto pastor to the whole church of about 250 people, recommended hiring another white man to be a pastor, but the Chinese-speaking people strongly opposed it.
1991	DT/AH	Hired Daniel Tang from the PRC/Hong Kong/California as the senior pastor.
1993	DT/AH	The English congregation gained more independence.
1995	DT/AH	Daniel Tang was fired by the congregational meeting.
1997	SY/HS	Allan Houston resigned.
		Hired Solomon Yuen from Hong Kong/New York as the senior pastor.
		Hired Harry Smith, a white man, as the associate pastor.
1998	HS	Solomon Yuen resigned because of Harry Smith.

* Pseudonyms are used for personal names of church members throughout the book except for Moses Chow and Ted Choy, who have published autobiographies.

Notes

Introduction

1. The year of 1989 was an eventful year in China. From April to June college students and people from all walks demonstrated in Beijing and other cities for democracy. Then the government sent tanks to the Tiananmen Square on June 4 and violently crushed the prodemocracy movement. The "June Fourth Incident" (*liusi shijian*) as it is called by the Chinese, or the "Tiananmen Massacre" as it is known by the American public, was the last stroke in smashing Communist idealism or disillusion among Chinese intellectuals. The turbulent changes in China and around myself in 1989 and the following years also substantially altered my own journey, a life journey entangled with temporal, academic, and spiritual dimensions. Instead of returning to China and resuming my teaching at the People's University of China at the end of 1989, I registered as a graduate student in sociology in the fall of 1989. My wife came to join me in the summer of 1990. Thanks to some presidential executive orders and the Chinese Students Protection Act of 1992, I have stayed in the United States until now and completed my Ph.D. in early 1997. Also, at the end of 1992 I was baptized into the Chinese Christian Church of Greater Washington, D.C.

2. Hurh and Kim (1990) cite the number from a survey of Asian-Americans in the Chicago area conducted in the 1970s. The *Los Angeles Times* (Dart 1997) reports results of a survey of 773 ethnic Chinese in six Southern California counties conducted in May 1997. Among the respondents, 19 percent said they were Protestant, 7 percent answered simply Christian, and 6 percent said they were Roman Catholic. At the same time, 20 percent identified themselves as Buddhists, and 44 percent said "none." An unpublished survey of Chinese-Americans in the Seattle area in the 1980s indicates similar patterns. The General Social Survey has too small a sample of ethnic Chinese (total N = 78 in the 1972–94 cumulative data) for accurate estimates. Nonetheless, it is interesting to list its numbers here: 27 percent of the Chinese in the sample were Protestants, 22 percent Catholics, and only 14 percent other religions (including Buddhism). It is important to note that Chinese Protestant leaders tend to put much lower estimates of Christians among ethnic Chinese. Based on counting heads during typical Sunday services in Chinese Protestant churches in the San Francisco area, Rev. James Chuck concludes that "Chinese youth and adult participation in Protestant churches is probably more near the 5% range" (1996, 15). Wing Ning Pang, an elder at a Chinese church in the Los Angeles area, gave a "generous" estimate of 10 percent of Protestants in the Chinese population in the United States (Pang 1980, 36). These low estimates include people who

regularly attend Chinese churches every week. However, not every active church member is able to attend church every Sunday, and some Chinese Christians attend non-Chinese churches.

3. Statistics of Chinese Christians in China are hard to come by. Thompson Brown (1986, 78) cited numbers of 936,000 baptized Protestants, 3,274,740 baptized Catholics, 600,000 Protestant catechumens, and 194,712 Catholic catechumens, totaling 5,005,452 in 1949. This total would comprise about 1 percent of the total Chinese population of 450 million at that time. Jonathan Chao (1981, 356) suggests a number of 834,909 Protestants in China in 1949, which is less than 0.2 percent of the total population. Overall, by 1949, when the Chinese Communist Party took power in mainland China, it had "become evident that few of the Chinese people were likely to become Christians and that the missionaries' long-continued effort, if measured in numbers of converts, had failed" (Fairbank 1974, 1). Since the late 1970s Christianity has been the fastest growing religion in mainland China, but there is no informed and consistent estimate. Government sanctioned statistics report about four million Catholics and ten million Protestants, which would comprise about 1 percent of the total population of 1.3 billion. Some Christian organizations outside China claim that there are as many as ten million Catholics and sixty million Protestants, which would be about 5 percent of the population. In Taiwan and Hong Kong, Christians are about 5 percent at the maximum (Law 1981; Swanson 1981).

Chapter 2

1. There are discrepancies in estimates of total Chinese in the United States based on U.S. censuses. Barringer, Gardner, and Levin (1993, 39) report the Chinese population in 1920 as 85,202; whereas many works (J. Chen 1980, 268; Daniels 1988, 69; Mangiafico 1988, 119; B. P. Wong 1994, 235–37) list the number as 61,639. No notes or explanations regarding the sources of these figures could be found in these books. I suspect the lower number could be the U.S. census count excluding Hawaii and Alaska.

2. According to Chinn (1969, 28–29), approximately 6,000 Chinese women came under the War Brides Act of 1945 and the GI Fiancées Act of 1946; 3,465 "stranded" Chinese students, visitors, and seamen adjusted status under the Displaced Persons Act of 1948; 2,777 Chinese adjusted status under the Refugee Relief Act of 1953; and 15,111 Chinese refugees in Hong Kong entered the United States under the Refugee Escapee Act of 1957 and the Presidential Directive in 1962. Also, the *1970 Annual Report* of the Immigration and Naturalization Service (table 6E) reports a total of 17,630 refugees from China between 1946 and 1966.

3. Actually, there were complicated reasons. Bernard P. Wong pointed out that identifying with Taiwan had many advantages: "In so doing, one avoided being labeled a communist, and gained much prestige. Leaders of the *old overseas* were invited to visit Taiwan and were decorated by high-ranking officials in Taiwan. In addition, pro-Taiwan Chinese community leaders often got better value on export/import merchandise and were able to obtain permits and visas for business activities more readily" (1982, 77). But also important is that "some *old overseas Chinese* also suffered from the revolutionary activities of the Chinese communists. Their relatives, and sometimes even they themselves suffered from the various purges, land-reform, and other movements in China. Some had been imprisoned and later had the opportunity to escape to America. These old immigrants, needless to say, are anti-Communist" (1982, 77).

4. The word *joss* is a corruption of the Portuguese word *deos*, meaning 'God.' A "joss house" is thus a house of god or gods. "It is hard to define a Joss House in Occidental terms," wrote Charles Caldwell Dobie in 1936. "It is neither a church, nor a temple, nor a mosque.

But it could easily have elements of all three. A Joss House is not a thing of sect and dogma. It is, to quote the Chinese themselves, simply a 'place of worship.' Into it may be poured any and all the religious faiths and influences that the Chinese have absorbed and modified in the sixty centuries of their civilization" (289–90). "All Joss Houses hold forth on the topmost floor of any building which harbors them in order to be as near Heaven as possible" (297). In the second half of the nineteenth century, many joss houses were built. However, by the 1930s the only two joss houses left in San Francisco Chinatown had become show places for sightseers (287).

5. For example, Melford S. Weiss notes that in a "Valley City" in California, where the first Christian missions for the Chinese started in the 1850s, "Chinese churches did not have representation in the Chinese Benevolent Association" in the 1930s (1974, 93) and they "are not represented in the C.B.A." in 1970 (1974, 228). In New York a Chinese Christian minister, Rev. Lee To, served as the chairman of the CCBA in 1919–21 (Lai 1992, 143). Under his influence, "the members of the Chinese Consolidated Benevolent Association decided to cast out the 'Joss' (their idol) from their council hall" (J. I. H. Chen 1941, 43). However, an anthropological study focusing on various voluntary associations in New York's Chinatown (Kuo 1977) does not even mention Christian churches. Among the studies of Chinatown communities, Betty Lee Sung (1967), in an unusual exception, devotes a full chapter to positive influences of Christian missions in the Chinese community, but that chapter starts with the Chinese Community Church of Washington, D.C. She has no discussion of how well the Chinese church integrated into the power structure of other Chinatowns.

6. Including *Yi Jing* (*I Ching*, or *The Book of Change*), which is the most well-known Chinese classic in the West, *Shi Jing* (*Shih Ching*, or *The Book of Songs*), *Shu Jing* (*Shu Ching*, or *The Book of Documents*), and *Li Ji* (*The Book of Rites*).

7. James Watson outlines the standardized and absolute structures of Chinese funeral rites: In the performative domain are (1) public notification of death by wailing and other expressions of grief; (2) donning of the appropriate white attire for mourners; (3) ritualized bathing of the corpse; (4) the transfer of food, money, and goods from the living to the dead; (5) the preparation and installation of a soul tablet for the dead; (6) the ritualized use of money and employment of professionals who perform ritual services; (7) music to accompany the corpse and settle the spirit; (8) sealing the corpse in an airtight coffin; and (9) expulsion of the coffin from the community (1988, 12–15).

8. It is interesting to note the anachronism of the Catholic Church. "Almost two centuries after *Ex quo singulari*, during the Second World War, Pope Pius XII in 1939 reversed the decision of 1742, authorizing Christians to take part in ceremonies honoring Confucius and to observe the ancestral rites. By then, however, the veneration of Confucius had been largely discontinued, since the country had put in a modern school system to replace the traditional Confucian-oriented 'temple-related' institutions" (J. Ching 1993,195).

9. Anthropologist Bernard P. Wong (1982) notes that pre-1965 Chinese immigrants identified themselves as "overseas Chinese": "They practice traditional customs, observe traditional Chinese holidays and festivals, and follow the social interaction pattern of the Old World. . . . [T]he sojourners had little or no communication with the larger society. They live, work, and socialize in the areas of Chinatown. . . . They were known to be the strong supporters of the Republic Revolution led by Dr. Sun Yat-Sen" (1982, 74).

10. L. Ling-chi Wang (1994) summarizes "five basic types of Chinese American identity. Each is connected to a different notion of *gen* [roots]; none is static": (1) *luoye guigen*: the sojourner mentality, (2) *zhancao-chugen*: total assimilation, (3) *luodi shenggen*: accommodation, (4) *xungen wenzu*: ethnic pride and consciousness, and (5) *shigen qunzu*: the uprooted. "Although each type emerged from a distinct historical setting, all five are found among the

Chinese in the United States today, and all are still changing and interacting constantly with one another, sometimes in peaceful coexistence and at other times in conflict. Depending on the circumstances, a person may move from one identity to another" (1994, 198).

Chapter 3

1. Biographical information is taken from the published autobiography of Ted Choy with Leona Choy (1997).

2. Few published works have studied the diverging changes between liberal and conservative missionaries to China. However, some writings discuss certain aspects of these changes. For example, Lian (1997) describes the shifts of some influential missionaries toward liberalism, and Armitage's (1993) biography of David Adeney, a China Inland Mission missionary, illustrates the active proselytization of conservative missionaries in China during the wars and among the Chinese in Southeast Asia after 1950.

3. Many articles first appeared in the Chinese Christian magazine *Ambassadors*, a bimonthly published by the Ambassadors for Christ in Paradise, Pennsylvania, then collected in a book edited by Edwin Su (1994).

4. Many Chinese have complained about the confusing Western denominationalism. In 1877 a Chinese American, Wong Chin Foo, published an article in *North American Review* entitled "Why Am I a Heathen?" He was bewildered by the multiplicity of Christian denominations. "He examined the major denominations of Christianity and was attracted to none, not 'merciless' Presbyterianism, 'divided' Baptism, 'noisy' Methodism, 'elitist' Congregationalism, 'skeptical' Unitarianism, or 'eccentric' Quakerism" (see Zhang 1998, 46). Anthropologist Francis L. K. Hsu remarked, "One of the most difficult things for Western missionaries to explain to the Chinese is denominationalism. If there is one true God who created and loved all mankind, why should there be Protestants, Catholics, Methodists, Presbyterians, and even Northern and Southern Baptists? In the end, very few Chinese in China ever accepted Christianity" (1971, 54). These words are echoed in the debate of denominationalism among Chinese American Christian leaders.

5. Biographic information is from his autobiography (Chow 1995) and a phone interview.

6. Pseudonyms are used for individuals at the CCC except for Theodore Choy and Moses Chow who have published autobiographies.

7. In 1993 the Fuller Seminary invited Bishop Ting, the chairman of the "Three Self Patriotic Association" in China, for the inauguration of the new Fuller president. Chinese seminarians at Fuller and Chinese pastors in America mobilized to make a protest. They requested the Fuller Board of Directors to withdraw their invitation to Bishop Ting or to extend an invitation to a leader of underground churches in China. After failing to get these requests, they raised protest banners and walked out of the hall during the inauguration ceremony. During and after this event, some Chinese Christian leaders in the United States circulated words about the declining conservativeness of the Fuller Seminary. This incident illustrates the overall conservative tendencies of Chinese Christians in the United States.

8. Most studies of Chinatowns or histories of Chinese communities have no discussion of Chinese churches in the Chinese community (see, e.g., Nee and Nee 1972; J. Chen 1980; B. P. Wong 1982; Kinkead 1992; Fong 1994), or merely mention them in passing (e.g., Dobie 1936; Hsu 1971). Loo (1991) and S. S. Wang (1993) focused on social services in Chinatowns,

and neither of them mentions Chinese churches. These scholars' biases against Christian churches could be a reason, but the lack of social influences of Chinese churches on the ethnic community is probably also an important factor. Betty Lee Sung (1967) is exceptional in devoting a whole chapter to praising positive contributions of Christian missions and pastors in their community services.

9. In conventional use in the literature of Chinese immigrants, the word *sojourner* refers to someone who sees his emigration as temporary and wants to go back to China. I use this word in a different way here, to refer to a person in a special cohort of Chinese new immigrants who has lived in various places in Asia and America.

10. Christiana Tsai (Cai Shujuan), born and converted in China, suffered terrible diseases but her Christian faith remained firm. She was brought to the United States by missionaries and lived in Paradise, Pennsylvania, until her death. She became well known among both Chinese and non-Chinese Christians. Her autobiography, *The Queen of the Dark Chamber*, influenced many people.

11. In a study of recent, rapid Christian conversion among the Akha people in Thailand and Burma, anthropologist Cornelia Ann Kammerer argues that the intensification of missionary proselytization among the Akha people "is as much a reaction to as a cause of the increasing responsiveness to the Christian message" (1990, 279). Robin Horton (1971, 1975) also argued that internal changes of African society and culture were more important in explaining African conversion to Christianity.

12. For example, the Overseas Missionaries Fellowship published a booklet entitled "Christian Missionaries and the Anti-Opium Movement in China" (date unknown). A catalogue introduction reads, "A brief history of how opium entered China, how China's anti-opium movement started, and how missionaries reacted to the opium trade to China." Some historians have done in-depth research on this subject too (see Lodwick 1996).

13. For more theoretically systematic arguments about Chinese conversion to evangelical Christianity, see F. Yang (1998b).

Chapter 4

1. Contemporary immigrant Chinese exhibit a bipolar structure of socioeconomic status. Occupationally, many are in high-paying professional and managerial occupations, while many are also in low-paying service jobs. There are "Downtown Chinese" of waiters and seamstresses as well as the affluent and professional "Uptown Chinese" (Takaki 1989, 425). The middle-class and upper-middle-class Chinese immigrants often live in metropolitan suburbs, where many "new Chinatowns" have emerged (Kwong 1987; H. Chen 1992; Fong 1994).

2. In their critical review of the interpreted history of earlier European immigrants and their descendants, Perlmann and Waldinger (1997) summarize it like this: "The descendants of the last great migration started out at the very bottom; but, they have now either caught up with—or surpassed—their WASP betters of yore. . . . The old factory-based economy also allowed for a multigenerational move up the totem pole. Immigrant children could do better if they just hung on through the high school years, after which time well-paid manufacturing jobs would await them. The third or fourth generation would continue on through college and beyond, completing the move from peddler to plumber to professional" (894).

3. The immigration laws since 1965 give high preferences for professionals (occupational immigration). Other two main categories are close relatives of U.S. residents and citizens, and political and religious refugees.

4. Sucheng Chan argues that Asian Americans suffer double problems in their adaptation: they are immigrants and they are racial minorities: "As immigrants, many of their struggles resemble those that European immigrants have faced, but as people of nonwhite origins bearing distinct physical differences, they have been perceived as 'perpetual foreigners' who can never be completely absorbed into American society" (1991, 187). Her examination of the identity construction among earlier second-generation Chinese Americans (1998) shows that while attending public schools mixed with non-Chinese, many American-born Chinese children first sought to identify as just "Americans." "As they became adolescents, however, they increasingly experienced rejection from their former Euro-American friends. They were stunned to discover that the identity imposed on them as 'Chinese' (or worse, as 'Chinks' and 'Chinamen') was far more powerful, in terms of determining their 'place' in American society, than whatever labels they might have fashioned for themselves. . . . Only after they had received their college degrees and entered the adult world of work did American racism hit them full force. Job discrimination was something that their parents had always warned them about, but they never realized its impregnable power until they sought employment outside their own ethnic communities. Under such circumstances, they paradoxically began to look to *China* as a place where their *American* ambitions might best be fulfilled" (1998, 157–58).

5. In 1998 the Chinese senior pastor, Solomon Yuen, from Hong Kong, also resigned from the CCC, openly citing problems of working with the assistant pastor, Harry Smith, a Caucasian who spoke no Chinese.

6. Chinese churches in the United States usually do not have Chinese-style buildings. In other words, there is no "Chinese look" for most Chinese churches. However, Chinese American churches built by Chinese Christians commonly show features of simplicity, austerity, and practical functionality. Although these features are not uniquely Chinese, they nevertheless follow a frugal Chinese ethic. Meanwhile, these features are also traditional in the puritanical Protestantism that most Chinese American churches follow.

7. Many pre–World War II American-born children of earlier Chinese immigrants "became ashamed of their personal appearance, the values and behaviors they were taught by their parents, and the communities from which they had emerged; self-hatred and the need to be accepted by white society became their primary obsession. In practice, this meant the rejection of their parents' language and culture, and the pursuit of white values in an attempt to become thoroughly Americanized." Some even "went so far as to anglicize their Chinese family names, suppress their Chinese language ability and accent, dissociate themselves from their relatives and Chinese friends, move out of Chinatowns if possible, and take advantage of modern cosmology, some by dyeing their hair, others by undergoing plastic surgery to alter their eyelids, nose, and lips" (L. Wang 1994, 202–3).

8. Will Herberg's "The American Way of Life" includes beliefs in democracy, free enterprise, and a social egalitarianism. Many contemporary scholars also believe that common ideology is the basis of American national identity. See Chapter 2.

9. "During the early 1900s, attending church was often the only acceptable outside activity allowed girls by immigrant parents. In 1920, almost all of the Chinese children (close to one thousand) attended Sunday school in Chinatown. In addition, many young people participated in choirs and church-sponsored debates and athletic events. By 1930 there were ten churches in Chinatown competing against each other to attract the second generation into their folds. . . . Catering to the interests of the young people, the various churches offered a range of activities, including Bible classes, club activities, Saturday night socials, discussion groups, and summer recreational programs" (Yung 1995, 151). Most of the exceptional Chinese American women who graduated from college and entered professions in the 1920s did so with the support of Christian parents or benefactors (Yung 1995, 133).

10. A Chinese pastor in a Houston church claimed that the over-representation of men in his church council was a positive sign of this Chinese church's vitality. In traditional Chinese society, he said, religion, especially Buddhism, was the women's sphere. Men usually let women do religious things while they focused on feeding the family. Therefore, if more women had taken leadership roles at the church, many men might stop actively participating in church activities because they would not want to compete with women.

11. There are very few Chinese women ministers in the United States, and most of them serve older churches or mainline churches. For example, the Chinese Community Church of Washington, D.C., has had women as associate pastors. New Chinese immigrant churches, who are mostly evangelical, tend not to accept women ministers.

Chapter 5

1. Roughly speaking, Chinese dialects spoken by people in southeastern provinces south of the Yellow River (e.g., Guangzhou, Fujian, Shanghai, Hunan) are often mutually unintelligible for their close neighbors as well as for people in other parts of the country. Meanwhile, dialects spoken by people in the vast land north of the Yellow River (e.g., Shandong, Shaanxi, Helongjiang, and also Sichuan) are distinctive variants of Mandarin. Although Northern Chinese can usually understand each other, their distinctive accents are often used as traces to identify their place of origin. For example, a man from Shandong would find affinity immediately upon hearing another man speaking in Shandong dialect.

2. In a *Los Angeles Times* news report, Tran (1998) reports that about 85,000 to 90,000 students nationwide attend Chinese language schools on Saturdays or Sundays. There are also many Korean, Vietnamese, and Japanese schools. These schools usually operate from rented public schools or are affiliated with churches, Buddhist temples, and Chinese community centers. They commonly offer instruction in reading, speaking, and writing as well as some cultural activities, ranging from martial arts to brush painting to music lessons.

3. "Stone" is a translation of the Chinese character *shi*.

4. Bernard Wong provides brief illustrations of festivities in New York Chinatowns (1982, 88–90).

5. It is inaccurate to call the traditional Chinese calendar system a lunar system and the Chinese New Year a Lunar New Year.

6. Francis L. K. Hsu described Qingming activities among the Chinese in Hawaii: "In front of graves both new and old are clusters of Chinese men, women, and children paying homage and making offerings to their dead. The offerings may be slim or abundant, including pigs and chickens roasted whole or simply sliced meats and plates of fruit. But cups of alcohol are poured on the ground in front of the tombs, bundles of burning incense placed before them, and large or small quantities of specially made paper money and papier-mâché life-like figures are burned for the benefit of the dead. The entire assemblage kneels down in twos and threes to kowtow to the dead. There are always offerings of flowers. And finally, in front of many of the tombs, a large string of firecrackers is exploded" (1971, 60). In contrast, these traditional Chinese rituals were not seen in a Chinese Christian cemetery in Hawaii: "Instead there is more of the usual type of observance common among white Christian Americans such as flowers and silent prayers on Easter, Memorial Day, Christmas, birthdays of the dead, Father's Day, Mother's Day, and so on" (1971, 63).

7. "Respect gods and spirits, but keep a distance from them" (*jing guishen er yuan zhi*) is a commonly quoted saying of Confucius.

8. Yuan's book was later published in Taiwan in 1997, entitled *Laozi vs. The Bible: A Meeting Across Time and Space.*

Chapter 6

1. There were also the British colony Hong Kong (until 1997) and the Portuguese colony Macao (until 1999).

2. Since the Civil Rights movement in the late 1960s, some descendants of Asian immigrants have been politically active in advocating for pan-Asian solidarity (see Espiritu 1992; Wei 1993). They want to see themselves as truly Asian-Americans rather than Chinese-Americans, Japanese-Americans, Korean-Americans, and so forth. In other words, they emphasize not their distinctive ethnic cultures, but common status and destinations in American society. Although evangelical Christians among descendants of Asian immigrants usually seem at odds with the activists of the pan-Asian American movement, their departure from their parents' ethnic churches and congregating with other Asian descendants nonetheless puts them in the same grand process of racial formation.

3. See, for example, *Yi Jing (Book of Change)*, Qian: Zhuan; *Lun Yu (Analects)* 1:12; *Zhong Yong (Doctrine of the Mean)* 1:4–5.

4. Anthropologist James L. Watson writes, "I began with a question that has preoccupied Western observers since the early Jesuits first began to write about the Central Kingdom: What held Chinese society together for so many centuries? Put another way, how was it possible for a country of continental dimensions, inhabited by people who speak mutually unintelligible languages and exhibit an amazing array of ethnic differences, to be molded into a unified culture?" (1993, 81).

5. For example, according to the gospel of John in the New Testament, Jesus prayed "May they be brought to complete unity to let the world know that you sent me and have loved them even as you have loved me" (John 17:23). Also, Paul said that Christians ought to become one organic body in Christ: "The body is a unit, although it is made up of many parts; and though all its parts are many, they form one body. So it is with Christ. For we were all baptized by one Spirit into one body—whether Jews or Greeks, slave or free—and we were all given the one Spirit to drink" (1 Corinthians 12:12–13).

Conclusion

1. Hsu believes that "*complete* Americanization to the extent of total similarity with white Americans is impossible" because Chinese are physically distinguishable from whites and will always experience rejection as minority people in the United States (1971, 129). "This means that the Chinese in America, in common with other minority groups, will have a continuing problem of double identity. But the effective way of dealing with it is not to deny its existence but to face it squarely" (130). He thinks that by consciously maintaining their Chinese culture

and identity, Chinese Americans can bring distinctive contributions to American society and enrich the American Dream in a pluralist society.

2. Wong reports that earlier Chinese immigrants commonly stick to Chinese traditional culture and want to "isolate themselves from the mainstream of American life. Living in ghetto-like Chinatown, they are in America, but exist as Chinese. This ghetto-like environment gives them a sense of separation. They read only the Chinese newspaper, listen to Chinese music, eat Chinese foods, and socialize with other Chinese. They are highly ethnocentric and see no worthwhile reason to assimilate into American society" (1982, 77). Meanwhile, the American-born children of the earlier Chinese immigrants "have little knowledge of Chinese culture or language" (78). In comparison, post-1965 new Chinese immigrants commonly have multiple identities. They "lament the fact that many American-born Chinese have lost their cultural heritage, and they express the hope that their children will grow up with a dual identity: Chinese and American. . . . Unlike the sojourners of the past, the new immigrants long for naturalization" (83).

Bibliography

Abramson, Harold J. 1973. *Ethnic Diversity in a Catholic America*. New York: John Wiley.

AFC (Ambassadors for Christ, Inc.). 1984, 1994. *Directory of Chinese Churches, Bible Study Groups and Organizations in North America*. Paradise, Pa.: Ambassadors for Christ, Inc.

Alba, Richard D. 1985. *Italian Americans: Into the Twilight of Ethnicity*. Englewood Cliffs, N.J.: Prentice-Hall.

————. 1990. *Ethnic Identity: The Transformation of White America*. New Haven: Yale University Press.

Alba, Richard D., and Victor Nee. 1997. "Rethinking Assimilation Theory for a New Era of Immigration." *International Migration Review* 31(4): 826–74.

Alexander, June Granatir. 1987. *The Immigrant Church and Community: Pittsburgh's Slovak Catholics and Lutherans, 1880–1915*. Pittsburgh: University of Pittsburgh Press.

Ammerman, Nancy T. 1987. *Bible Believers: Fundamentalists in the Modern World*. New Brunswick: Rutgers University Press.

————. 1991. "North American Protestant Fundamentalism." In *Fundamentalisms Observed*, ed. Martin E. Marty and R. Scott Appleby, 1–65. Chicago: University of Chicago Press.

Armitage, Carolyn. 1993. *Reaching for the Goal: The Life Story of David Adeney*. N.p.: OMF IHQ, Ltd.

Bainbridge, William S. 1992. "The Sociology of Conversion." In *Handbook of Religious Conversion*, ed. H. Newton Malony and Samuel Southard, 178–92. Birmingham, Ala.: Religious Education Press.

Bankston, Carl L., III, and Min Zhou. 1995. "Religious Participation, Ethnic Identification, and Adaptation of Vietnamese Adolescents in an Immigrant Community." *Sociological Quarterly* 36(3): 523–34.

Barkan, Elliott R. 1995. "Race, Religion, and Nationality in American Society: A Model of Ethnicity—From Contact to Assimilation." *Journal of American Ethnic History*, 14(2): 38–75.

Barringer, Herbert R., Robert W. Gardner, and Michael J. Levin. 1993. *Asians and Pacific Islanders in the United States*. New York: Russell Sage Foundation.

Barth, Gunther. 1964. *Bitter Strength: A History of the Chinese in the United States, 1850–1870.* Cambridge: Harvard University Press.

Basch, Linda, Nina Glick Schiller, and Cristina Szanton Blanc. 1994. *Nations Unbound: Transnational Projects, Post-colonial Predicaments, and De-territorialized Nation-States.* Langhorne, Pa.: Gordon and Breach.

Bays, Daniel H., ed. 1996. *Christianity in China: From the Eighteenth Century to the Present.* Stanford: Stanford University Press.

Beckford, J. A. 1978. "Accounting for Conversion." *British Journal of Sociology* 29: 249–62.

Bellah, Robert N. 1968. "Civil Religion." In *The Religious Situation: 1968*, ed. Donald R. Cutler, 388–93. Boston: Beacon Press.

Bellah, Robert N., et al. 1985. *Habits of the Heart: Individualism and Commitment in American Life.* Berkeley and Los Angeles: University of California Press.

Berger, Peter. L. 1969. *The Sacred Canopy.* Garden City, N.Y.: Doubleday, Anchor Books.

Berger, Peter L., and T. Luckmann. 1966. *The Social Construction of Reality.* Garden City, N.Y.: Doubleday, Anchor Books.

Beyer, Peter. 1994. *Religion and Globalization.* London: Sage Publications.

Bodnar, John E. 1985. *The Transplanted: A History of Immigrants in Urban America.* Bloomington: Indiana University Press.

Brown, G. Thompson. 1986. *Christianity in the People's Republic of China*, rev. ed. Atlanta: John Knox Press.

Buczek, Daniel S. 1976. "Polish-Americans and the Roman Catholic Church." *Polish Review* 12(3): 39–61. Also in *Immigrant Religious Experience*, ed. George E. Pozzeta. New York: Garland, 1991.

Bulluck, Pam. 1995. "Healthy Korean Economy Draws Immigrants Home," *New York Times* (22 August).

Busto, Rudy V. 1996. "The Gospel According to the Model Minority? Hazarding an Interpretation of Asian American Evangelical College Students." *Amerasia Journal* 22(1): 133–47.

Caplow, Theodore, Howard M. Bahr, John Modell, and Bruce A. Chadwick. 1991. *Recent Social Trends in the United States: 1960–1990.* Montreal: McGill-Queen's University Press.

Cayton, Horace R., and Anne O. Lively. 1955. *The Chinese in the United States and the Chinese Christian Church.* New York: Bureau of Research and Survey, National Council of the Churches of Christ in the United States.

Chan, Sharon Wai-Man. 1996. *The Dynamics of Expansion of the Chinese Churches in the Los Angeles Basin.* Ph.D. Dissertation. Fuller Theological Seminary.

Chan, Sucheng. 1991. *Asian Americans: An Interpretive History.* Boston: Twayne Publishers.

———. 1998. "Race, Ethnic Culture, and Gender in the Construction of Identities Among Second-Generation Chinese Americans, 1880s to 1930s." In *Claiming America: Constructing Chinese American Identities During the Exclusion Era*, ed. K. Scott Wong and Sucheng Chan. Philadelphia: Temple University Press.

Chan, Wing-Tsit. 1967. "On Translating Certain Chinese Philosophical Terms." In *Reflections on Things at Hand.* New York: Columbia University Press.

Chao, Jonathan. 1981. "Cong Huaren Jiaohui Fazhan Shi Kan Jiao Hui Zeng-zhang" (Church Growth in the History of Chinese Churches). In *Jindai Zhongguo Yu Jidujiao Lunwen Ji* (Essays on Modern China and Christianity), ed. Lin Zhiping, 345–62. Taipei: Yuzhouguang Press.

Chen, Hsiang-Shui. 1992. *Chinatown No More: Taiwan Immigrants in Contemporary New York.* Ithaca: Cornell University Press.

Chen, Jack. 1980. *The Chinese of America.* San Francisco: Harper & Row.

Chen, Julia I. Hsuan. 1941. *The Chinese Community in New York: A Study in Their Cultural Adjustment 1920–1940.* Ph.D. Dissertation. Washington, D.C.: American University. Reprinted in 1974 by R and E Research Associates, San Francisco.

Child, I. L. 1943. *Italian or American? The Second Generation in Conflict.* New Haven: Yale University Press.

Ching, Julia. 1993. *Chinese Religions.* Maryknoll, N.Y.: Orbis Books.

Chinn, Thomas W., ed. 1969. *A History of the Chinese in California: A Syllabus.* San Francisco: Chinese Historical Society of America.

Chow, Moses C., with Leona Choy. 1995. *Let My People Go! Autobiography.* Paradise, Pa.: Ambassadors for Christ, Inc.

Choy, Bong Youn. 1979. *Koreans in America.* Chicago: Nelson-Hall.

Choy, Ted, with Leona Choy. 1997. *My Dreams and Visions: An Autobiography.* Winchester, Va.: Golden Morning Publishing.

Chuck, James. 1996. *An Exploratory Study of the Growth of Chinese Protestant Con-gregations from 1950 to Mid-1996 in Five Bay Area Counties: San Francisco, San Mateo, Contra Costa, Alameda, and Santa Clara.* Berkeley: American Baptist Seminary of the West.

Cohen, Myron L. 1994. "Being Chinese: The Peripheralization of Traditional Identity." In *The Living Tree: The Changing Meaning of Being Chinese Today,* ed. Tu Wei-ming, 88–108. Stanford: Stanford University Press.

Condit, Ira M. 1900. *The Chinaman as We See Him and Fifty Years of Work for Him.* Chicago: Missionary Campaign Library.

Constable, Nicole. 1994. *Christian Souls and Chinese Spirits: A Hakka Community in Hong Kong.* Berkeley and Los Angeles: University of California Press.

Conzen, Kathleen Neils, David A. Gerber, Ewa Morawska, George E. Pozzetta, and Rudolph J. Vecoli. 1992. "The Invention of Ethnicity: A Perspective from the U.S.A." *Journal of American Ethnic History* 12 (Fall): 3–41.

Covell, Ralph R. 1986. *Confucius, the Buddha, and Christ: A History of the Gospel in Chinese.* Maryknoll, N.Y.: Orbis Books.

Daniels, Roger. 1988. *Asian America: Chinese and Japanese in the United States Since 1850.* Seattle: University of Washington Press.

Dart, John. 1997. "Poll Studies Chinese Americans, Religion," *Los Angeles Times* (5 July): B5.

de Bary, Wm. Theodore. 1981. *Neo-Confucian Orthodoxy and the Learning of the Mind-and-Heart.* New York: Columbia University Press.

Dobie, Charles Caldwell. 1936. *San Francisco Chinatown.* New York: D. Appleton-Century Company.

Dolan, Jay P. 1972. "Immigrants in the City: New York's Irish and German Catholics." *Church History* 41(3): 354–68. Also in *American Immigration and*

Ethnicity: A 20-Volume Series of Distinguished Essays: Volume 19: The Immigrant Religious Experience, ed. George E. Pozzetta. New York: Garland, 1991.

———. 1975. *The Immigrant Church: New York's Irish and German Catholics, 1815–1865*. Baltimore: Johns Hopkins University Press.

Durkheim, Emile. 1947. *Elementary Forms of the Religious Life*. Glencoe, Ill.: Free Press.

———. 1973. *On Morality and Society: Selected Writings*, ed. Robert N. Bellah, Chicago: University of Chicago Press.

Espiritu, Yen Len. 1992. *Asian American Panethnicity: Bridging Institutions and Identities*. Philadelphia: Temple University Press.

Fairbank, John King, ed. 1974. *The Missionary Enterprises in China and America*. Cambridge: Harvard University Press.

Fenton, John Y. 1988. *Transplanting Religious Traditions: Asian Indians in America*. New York: Praeger.

Fingarette, Herbert. 1972. *Confucius—the Secular as Sacred*. New York: Harper & Row.

Finke, Roger, and Rodney Stark. 1992. *The Churching of America, 1776–1990: Winners and Losers in Our Religious Economy*. New Brunswick: Rutgers University Press.

Fishman, Joshua A., et al. 1985. *The Rise and Fall of the Ethnic Revival: Perspectives on Language and Ethnicity*. New York: Mouton.

Fong, Timothy P. 1994. *The First Suburban Chinatown: The Remaking of Montery Park, California*. Philadelphia: Temple University Press.

Fuchs, Lawrence H. 1992. "Comment: 'The Invention of Ethnicity': The Amen Corner," *Journal of American Ethnic History* 12 (Fall): 53–58.

Fung, Karl. 1989. *The Dragon Pilgrims: A Historical Study of a Chinese-American Church*. San Diego, Calif.: Providence Price.

Gallup. 1990. *Religion in America, 1990—Approaching the Year 2000*. Princeton: Princeton Religious Research Center.

Gans, Herbert. 1979. "Symbolic Ethnicity: The Future of Ethnic Groups and Cultures in America." *Ethnic and Racial Studies* 2:1–20.

———. 1992. "Comment: Ethnic Invention and Acculturation, a Bumpy-Line Approach." *Journal of American Ethnic History* 12 (Fall): 42–52.

———. 1994. "Symbolic Ethnicity and Symbolic Religiosity: Toward a Comparison of Ethnic and Religious Acculturation." *Ethnic and Racial Studies* 17(4): 577–92.

———. 1997. "Toward a Reconciliation of 'Assimilation' and 'Pluralism': The Interplay of Acculturation and Ethnic Retention." *International Migration Review* 31(4): 875–92.

Geertz, Clifford. 1973. *The Interpretation of Cultures: Selected Essays*. New York: Basic Books.

Gerber, David A., Ewa Morawska, and George E. Pozzetta. 1992. "Response [to comments on "The Invention of Ethnicity" paper]." *Journal of American Ethnic History* (Fall): 59–63.

Gitlin, Todd. 1995. *The Twilight of Common Dreams: Why America Is Wracked by Cultural Wars*. New York: Metropolitan Books.

Glazer, Nathan. 1993. "Is Assimilation Dead?" *Annals of the American Academy of Political and Social Science* 530 (November): 122–36.

Glazer, Nathan, and Daniel Patrick Moynihan. 1963. *Beyond the Melting Pot.* Cambridge: M.I.T. Press.

Gleason, Philip. 1980. "American Identity and Americanization." In *Harvard Encyclopedia of American Ethnic Groups*, ed. Stephan Thernstrom, Ann Orlov, and Oscar Handlin, 31–58. Cambridge: Harvard University Press.

———. 1992. *Speaking of Diversity: Language and Ethnicity in Twentieth-Century America.* Baltimore: Johns Hopkins University Press.

Gordon, Milton M. 1964. *Assimilation in American Life: The Role of Race, Religion, and National Origins.* New York: Oxford University Press.

Greeley, Andrew M. 1971. *Why Can't They Be Like Us? America's White Ethnic Groups.* New York: E. P. Dutton.

———. 1974. *Ethnicity in the United States: A Preliminary Reconnaissance.* New York: John Wiley.

———. 1989. *Religious Change in America.* Cambridge: Harvard University Press.

Green, John C., James L. Guth, Corwin E. Smidt, and Lyman A. Kellstedt. 1996. *Religion and the Culture Wars: Dispatches from the Front.* Lanham, Md.: Rowman & Littlefield.

Hammond, Phillip E., and Kee Warner. 1993. "Religion and Ethnicity in Late-Twentieth Century America." *Annals of the American Academy of Political and Social Science* 527 (May): 55–66.

Handlin, Oscar. 1951. *The Uprooted.* New York: Grosset and Dunlap.

Herberg, Will. 1960. *Protestant-Catholic-Jew: An Essay in American Religious Sociology*, 2d ed. Garden City, N.Y.: Doubleday.

Higham, John. 1981. *Strangers in the Land: Patterns of American Nativism, 1860–1925*, 2d ed. New Brunswick: Rutgers University Press.

Hoge, Dean R., and David A. Roozen, eds. 1979. *Understanding Church Growth and Decline: 1950–1978.* New York: Pilgrim Press.

Horton, R. 1971. "African Conversion." *Africa* 41: 85–108.

———. 1975. "On the Rationality of Conversion." *Africa* 45: 219–35, 373–99.

Hsu, Francis L. K. 1971. *The Challenge of the American Dream: The Chinese in the United States.* Belmont, Calif.: Wadsworth.

Hunter, James Davison. 1991. *Cultural Wars: The Struggle to Define America.* New York: Basic Books.

Huntington, Samuel P. 1993. "The Clash of Civilizations?" *Foreign Affairs* 72(3): 22–49.

Hurh, Won Moo, and Kwang Chung Kim. 1990. "Religious Participation of Korean Immigrants in the United States." *Journal for the Scientific Study of Religion* 29(1): 19–34.

Hurh, Won Moo, Hei Chu Kim, and Kwang Chung Kim. 1978. *Assimilation Patterns of Immigrants in the U.S.: A Case Study of Korean Immigrants in the Chicago Area.* Washington, D.C.: University Press of America.

Iannaccone, Laurence R. 1994. "Why Strict Churches Are Strong." *American Journal of Sociology* 99: 1180–1211.

INS (Immigration and Naturalization Service). 1996. *Statistical Yearbook of the*

Immigration and Naturalization Service. Washington, D.C.: U.S. Government Printing Office.

Isaacs, Harold Robert. 1975. *Idols of the Tribe: Group Identity and Political Change.* New York: Harper & Row.

Johnson, Rita. 1976. "Chinese Communities and the Catholic Church." In *The Chinese in America,* ed. Paul K. T. Sih and Leonard B. Allen, 25–33. New York: St. John's University Press.

Kallen, Horace Meyer. 1956. *Cultural Pluralism and the American Idea.* Philadelphia: University of Pennsylvania.

Kammerer, C. A. 1990. "Customs and Christian Conversion among Akha Highlanders of Burma and Thailand." *American Ethnologist* 17 (May): 277–91.

Kazal, Russell A. 1995. "Revisiting Assimilation: The Rise, Fall, and Reappraisal of a Concept in American Ethnic History." *American Historical Review* 100(2): 437–71.

Kelley, Dean M. 1986 [1972]. *Why Conservative Churches Are Growing: A Study in Sociology of Religion with a new Preface for the Rose edition.* Macon: Mercer University Press. (Originally published by Harper & Row).

Kim, Illsoo. 1981. *New Urban Immigrants: The Korean Community in New York.* Princeton: Princeton University Press.

Kim, Kwang Chung, and Won Moo Hurh. 1993. "Beyond Assimilation and Pluralism: Syncretic Sociocultural Adaptation of Korean Immigrants in the US." *Ethnic and Racial Studies* 16(4): 696–713.

Kinkead, Gwen. 1992. *Chinatown: A Portrait of a Closed Society.* New York: Harper-Collins.

Kohn, Hans. 1957. *American Nationalism: An Interpretative Essay.* New York: Macmillan.

Kosmin, Barry A., and Seymour P. Lachman. 1993. *One Nation Under God: Religion in Contemporary American Society.* New York: Crown.

Kuo, Chia-ling. 1977. *Social and Political Change in New York's Chinatown: The Role of Voluntary Associations.* New York: Praeger.

Kwon, V. H., H. R. Ebaugh, and J. Hagan. 1997. "The Structure and Functions of Cell Group Ministry in a Korean Christian Church." *Journal for the Scientific Study of Religion* 36(2): 247–56.

Kwong, Peter. 1987. *The New Chinatown.* New York: Hill and Wang.

Lai, Him Mark. 1992. *Cong huaqiao dao huaren* (From Huaqiao to Huaren: Social History of the Chinese in the United States in the Twentieth Century). Hong Kong: Joint Publishing Co.

Lau, Yuet Shing. 1933. *Meizhou Huaqiao Jiaohui* (Chinese Churches in America). San Francisco: The Convention of Chinese Christian Churches.

Law, Gail, ed. 1981. *Chinese Churches Handbook.* Hong Kong: Chinese Coordination Center of World Evangelism.

Lee, Jung Young. 1995. *Marginality: The Key to Multicultural Theology.* Minneapolis: Fortress Press.

Lenski, Gerhard. 1961. *The Religious Factor.* Garden City, N.Y.: Doubleday.

Leong, Russell. 1996. "Racial Spirits: Between Bullets, Barbed Wire, and Belief." *Amerasia Journal* 22 (Spring): vii–xi.

Lian, Xi. 1997. *The Conversion of Missionaries: Liberalism in American Protestant*

Missions in China, 1907–1932. University Park: The Pennsylvania State University Press.

Lieberson, Stanley, and Mary C. Waters. 1988. *From Many Strands: Ethnic and Racial Groups in Contemporary America*. New York: Russell Sage Foundation.

Lin, Irene. 1996. "Journey to the Far West: Chinese Buddhism in America." *Amerasia Journal* 22 (Spring): 106–32.

Lin, Yu-sheng. 1979. *The Crisis of Chinese Consciousness: Radical Antitraditionalism in the May Fourth Era*. Madison: University of Wisconsin Press.

———. 1996. " 'Chuangzao xing zhuanghua' de zai si yu zai ren" (Rethinking the 'Creative Transformation'). *Cultural China* 3(2): 21–34.

Link, Perry. 1994. "China's 'Core' Problem." In *China in Transformation*, ed. Tu Wei-ming, 189–205. Cambridge: Harvard University Press.

Liu, Kwang-Ching, ed. 1990. *Orthodoxy in Late Imperial China*. Berkeley and Los Angeles: University of California Press.

Lodwick, Kathleen L. 1996. *Crusaders Against Opium: Protestant Missionaries in China, 1874–1917*. Lexington: University of Kentucky Press.

Loewen, James W. 1971. *The Mississippi Chinese: Between Black and White*. Cambridge: Harvard University Press. (Reprint Prospect Heights, Ill.: Waveland Press, 1988).

Lofland, J., and R. Stark. 1965. "Becoming a World-Saver: A Theory of Conversion to a Deviant Perspective." *American Sociological Review* 30: 862–75.

Loo, Chalsa M. 1991. *Chinatown: Most Time, Hard Time*. New York: Praeger.

Lyman, Stanford M. 1974. *Chinese Americans*. New York: Random House.

Malony, H. Newton, and Samuel Southard. 1992. *Handbook of Religious Conversion*. Birmingham, Ala.: Religious Education Press.

Mangiafico, Lucian. 1988. *Contemporary American Immigrants: Patterns of Filipino, Korean, and Chinese Settlement in the United States*. New York: Praeger.

Marty, Martin E. 1972. "Ethnicity: The Skeleton of Religion in America." *Church History* 41(1): 5–21. Also in *American Immigration and Ethnicity: A 20-Volume Series of Distinguished Essays: Volume 19: The Immigrant Religious Experience*, ed. George E. Pozzetta. New York: Garland, 1991.

Miller, Stuart Creighton. 1969. *The Unwelcome Immigrants: The American Image of the Chinese, 1785–1882*. Berkeley and Los Angeles: University of California Press.

Min, Pyong Gap. 1992. "The Structure and Social Functions of Korean Immigrant Churches in the United States." *International Migration Review* 26 (Winter): 370–94.

———, ed. 1995. *Asian Americans: Contemporary Trends and Issues*. Thousand Oaks, Calif.: Sage.

———. 1998. *Changes and Conflicts: Korean Immigrant Families in New York*. Boston: Allyn and Bacon.

Mittelberg, David, and Mary C. Waters. 1992. "The Process of Ethnogenesis Among Haitian and Israeli Immigrants in the United States." *Ethnic and Racial Studies* 15 (July): 412–35.

Mohl, Raymond A., and Neil Betten. 1981. "The Immigrant Church in Gary, Indiana: Religious Adjustment and Cultural Defense." *Ethnicity* 8(1): 1–17. Also in *American Immigration and Ethnicity: A 20-Volume Series of Distinguished*

Essays: Volume 19: The Immigrant Religious Experience, ed. George E. Pozzetta. New York: Garland, 1991.

Moore, Joan W., and Harry Pachon. 1985. *Hispanics in the United States.* Englewood Cliffs, N.J.: Prentice-Hall.

Moore, R. Laurence. 1986. *Religious Outsiders and the Making of Americans.* New York: Oxford University Press.

Morawska, Ewa. 1990. "The Sociology and Historiography of Immigration." In *Immigration Reconsidered: History, Sociology, and Politics,* ed. Virginia Yans-McLaughlin, 187–238. New York: Oxford University Press.

Mullins, Mark. 1987. "The Life-Cycle of Ethnic Churches in Sociological Perspective." *Japanese Journal of Religious Studies* 14(4): 321–34.

Myrad, Gunnar. 1944. *An American Dilemma: The Negro Problem and Modern Democracy.* New York: Harper & Row.

Nee, Victor G., and Brett de Bary Nee. 1973. *Longtime Californ: A Documentary Study of an American Chinatown.* Boston: Houghton Mifflin.

Ng, David, ed. 1996. *People On the Way: Asian North Americans Discovering Christ, Culture, and Community.* Valley Forge, Pa.: Judson Press.

Niebuhr, Richard. 1929. *The Social Sources of American Denominationalism.* New York: Henry Holt.

Novak, Michael. 1972. *The Rise of the Unmeltable Ethnics: Politics and Culture in the Seventies.* New York: Macmillan.

Omi, Michael, and Howard Winant. 1986. *Racial Formation in the United States: From the 1960s to the 1980s.* New York: Routledge & Kegan Paul.

———. 1994. *Racial Formation in the United States: From the 1960s to the 1990s.* New York: Routledge.

Ong, Aiwha. 1996. "Cultural Citizenship as Subject-Making: Immigrants Negotiate Racial and Cultural Boundaries in the United States." *Currently Anthropology* 37 (5): 737–62.

Ong, Aiwha, and Donald Nonini, eds. 1997. *Ungrounded Empires: The Cultural Politics of Modern Chinese Transnationalism.* New York: Routledge.

Palinkas, Lawrence A. 1989. *Rhetoric and Religious Experience: The Discourse of Immigrant Chinese Churches.* Fairfax: George Mason University Press.

Pan, Lynn. 1994. *Sons of the Yellow Emperor: A History of the Chinese Diaspora.* New York: Kodansha International.

Pang, Wing Ning. 1980. "Build Up His Church for My Kinsmen's Sake: A Study of the North American Chinese Church." Paper for the North American Congress of Chinese Evangelicals, 23–28 June, Pasadena, California.

———. 1985. "The Chinese and the Chinese Church in America: A Preliminary Report for the Asian Ethnic Committee." Paper presented to the National Convocation on Evangelizing Ethnic America, April 14–18, Houston, Texas.

———. 1995. "The Chinese American Ministry." In *Yearbook of American and Canadian Churches, 1995,* ed. Kenneth B. Bedell, 10–18. Nashville, Tenn.: Abingdon Press.

Park, Robert Ezra. 1950. *Race and Culture.* Glencoe, Ill.: Free Press.

Perlmann, Joel, and Roger Waldinger. 1997. "Second Generation Decline? Children of Immigrants, Past and Present—A Reconsideration." *International Migration Review* 31(4): 893–922.

Portes, Alejandro, and Ruben Rumbaut. 1996. *Immigrant America: A Portrait*, 2d ed. Berkeley and Los Angeles: University of California Press.

Portes, Alejandro, and Min Zhou. 1993. "The New Second Generation: Segmented Assimilation and Its Variants." *Annals of the American Academy of Political and Social Science* 530 (November): 74–96.

Pozzetta, George E. 1991. "Introduction." In *American Immigration and Ethnicity: A 20-Volume Series of Distinguished Essays: Volume 19: The Immigrant Religious Experience*. New York: Garland.

Quan, Robert Seto. 1982. *Lotus Among the Magnolias: The Mississippi Chinese*. Jackson: University Press of Mississippi.

Rambo, Lewis R. 1993. *Understanding Religious Conversion*. New Haven: Yale University Press.

Roediger, David R. 1991. *The Waves of Whiteness: Race and the Making of the American Working Class*. New York: Verso.

Roozen, David A., and C. Kirk Hadaway, eds. 1993. *Church and Denominational Growth*. Nashville, Tenn: Abingdon Press.

Royce, Anya Peterson. 1982. *Ethnic Identity: Strategies of Diversity*. Bloomington: Indiana University Press.

Rumbaut, Ruben G. 1997. "Assimilation and Its Discontents: Between Rhetoric and Reality." *International Migration Review* 31(4): 923–60.

Schiller, Nina Glick, Linda Basch, and Cristina Blanc-Szanton. 1992. *Toward a Transnational Perspective on Migration: Race, Class, Ethnicity, and Nationalism Reconsidered*. New York: New York Academy of Sciences.

Siu, Paul. 1952. "The Sojourner." *American Journal of Sociology* 58 (July): 34–44.

Skeldon, Ronald, ed. 1994. *Reluctant Exiles? Migration from Hong Kong and the New Overseas Chinese, with a foreword by Wang Gungwu*. New York: M. E. Sharpe.

Smith, Timothy L. 1978: "Religion and Ethnicity in America." *American Historical Review* 83 (December): 1155–85. Also in *Modern American Protestantism and Its World, Ethnic and Non-Protestant Themes*, Vol. 8, ed. Martin Marty. New York: K. G. Saur, 1993; and in *American Immigration and Ethnicity: A 20-Volume Series of Distinguished Essays: Volume 19: The Immigrant Religious Experience*, ed. George Pozzetta. New York: Garland, 1991.

Snow, D. A., and R. Machalek. 1984. "The Sociology of Conversion." *Annual Review of Sociology* 10: 167–90.

Sollors, Werner, ed. 1989. *The Invention of Ethnicity*. New York: Oxford University Press.

Stark, Rodney, and William Sims Bainbridge. 1985. *The Future of Religion: Secularization, Revival, and Cult Formation*. Berkeley and Los Angeles: University of California Press.

Stout, Harry S. 1975. "Ethnicity: The Vital Center of Religion in America," *Ethnicity* 2(2): 204–24. Also in *American Immigration and Ethnicity: A 20-Volume Series of Distinguished Essays: Volume 19: The Immigrant Religious Experience*, ed. George E. Pozzetta. New York: Garland, 1991.

Su, Edwin, ed. 1994. *Jiaohui fazhan de luxiang* (The Direction of Church Growth). Paradise, Pa.: Ambassadors for Christ, Inc.

Sung, Betty Lee. 1967. *Mountain of Gold: The Story of the Chinese in America.* New York: Macmillan.

Swanson, Allen J. 1981. *Taiwan Jiaohui Mianmian Guan* (Aspects of Churches in Taiwan: Retrospective and Prospective in 1980). Taipei: Taiwan Jiaohui Zengzhang Cujin Hui.

Swidler, Ann. 1986. "Culture in Action: Symbols and Strategies." *American Sociological Review* 51(2): 273–86.

Takaki, Ronald. 1987. *From Different Shores: Perspectives on Race and Ethnicity in America.* New York: Oxford University Press.

———. 1989. *Strangers from a Different Shore: A History of Asian Americans.* Boston: Little, Brown.

Tsai, Shih-Shan Henry. 1986. *The Chinese Experience in America.* Bloomington: Indiana University Press.

Tseng, Timothy. 1994. *Ministry at Arms' Length: Asian Americans in the Racial Ideology of American Mainline Protestants, 1882–1952.* Ph.D. Dissertation. Union Theological Seminary, New York.

———. 1996. "Chinese Protestant Nationalism in the United States, 1880–1927." *Amerasia Journal* 22(1): 31–56.

Thompson, Lawrence G. 1989. *Chinese Religion: An Introduction.* Belmont, Calif.: Wadsworth.

Thomas, William I., and Florian Znaniecki. 1918–20. *The Polish Peasant in Europe and America.* Chicago: University of Chicago Press.

Tran, Tini. 1998. "Asian Language Schools Introduce Kids to Ancestors." *Los Angeles Times* (8 June).

Tu, Wei-ming. 1985. *Confucian Thought: Selfhood as Creative Transformation.* Albany: State University of New York Press.

———. 1987. "Iconoclasm, Holistic Vision, and Patient Watchfulness: A Personal Reflection on the Modern Chinese Intellectual Quest." *Daedalus* 116 (Spring): 75–94.

———. 1989. *Centrality and Commonality: An Essay on Confucian Religiousness.* Albany: State University of New York Press.

———. 1992. "Intellectual Effervescence in China." *Daedalus* 121 (Spring): 251–92.

———. 1994a. "Cultural China: The Periphery as the Center." In *The Living Tree: The Changing Meaning of Being Chinese Today,* ed. Tu Wei-ming, 1–34. Stanford: Stanford University Press.

———, ed. 1994b. *The Living Tree: The Changing Meaning of Being Chinese Today.* Stanford: Stanford University Press.

Vecoli, Rudolph J. 1964. "*Contadini* in Chicago: A Critique of *The Uprooted.*" *Journal of American History* 51 (December): 404–17.

———. 1969. "Prelates and Peasants: Italian Immigrants and the Catholic Church." *Journal of Social History* 2(3): 217–68. Also in *American Immigration and Ethnicity: A 20-Volume Series of Distinguished Essays: Volume 19: The Immigrant Religious Experience,* ed. George E. Pozzetta. New York: Garland, 1991.

———. 1970. "Ethnicity: A Neglected Dimension of American History." In *The State of American History,* ed. Herbert J. Bass. Chicago: Quadrangle.

———. 1985. "Return to the Melting Pot: Ethnicity in the United States in the Eighties." *Journal of American Ethnic History* 5 (Fall): 7–20.

Wang, Gungwu. 1981. *The Chineseness of China: Selected Essays.* Hong Kong: Oxford University Press.

———. 1991. *Community and Nation: Essays on Southeast Asia and the Chinese.* Singapore: Heinemann Educational Books.

———. 1994. "Among Non-Chinese." In *The Living Tree: The Changing Meaning of Being Chinese Today,* ed. Tu Wei-ming, 127–47. Stanford: Stanford University Press.

Wang, L. Ling-chi. 1994. "Roots and the Changing Identity of the Chinese in the United States." In *The Living Tree: The Changing Meaning of Being Chinese Today,* ed. Tu Wei-ming, 185–212. Stanford: Stanford University Press.

Wang, Shirley Shek. 1993. *Chinese Ethnic Organizations in California: The Social Network and Support System for Chinese Immigrants.* Ph.D. Dissertation. University of California, Los Angeles.

Warner, R. Stephen. 1988. *New Wine in Old Wineskins: Evangelicals and Liberals in a Small-Town Church.* Berkeley and Los Angeles: University of California Press.

———. 1993. "Work in Progress Toward a New Paradigm for the Sociological Study of Religion in the United States." *American Journal of Sociology* 98(5): 1044–93.

———. 1994. "The Place of the Congregation in the Contemporary American Religious Configuration." In *American Congregations* 2: 54–99. Chicago: University of Chicago Press.

———. 1998. "Introduction: Immigration and Religious Communities in the United States." In *Gatherings in Diaspora: Religious Communities and the New Immigration,* ed. R. Stephen Warner and Judith G. Wittner, 3–34. Philadelphia: Temple University Press.

Warner, W. Lloyd, and Leo Srole. 1945. *The Social Systems of American Ethnic Groups.* New Haven: Yale University Press.

Waters, Mary C. 1990. *Ethnic Options: Choosing Identities in America.* Berkeley and Los Angeles: University of California Press.

Watson, James L. 1988. "Remembering the Dead: Graves and Politics in Southeastern China." In *Death Ritual in Late Imperial and Modern China,* eds. James L. Watson and Evelyn S. Rawski, 203–27. Berkeley and Los Angeles: University of California Press.

———. 1993. "Rites or Beliefs? The Construction of a Unified Culture in Late Imperial China." In *China's Quest for National Identity,* ed. Lowell Dittmer and Samuel S. Kim, 80–103. Ithaca: Cornell University Press.

Watson, James L., and Evelyn S. Rawski, eds. 1988. *Death Ritual in Late Imperial and Modern China.* Berkeley and Los Angeles: University of California Press.

Weber, Max. 1961. "Ethnic Groups." In *Theories of Society, I,* ed. Talcott Parsons et al. New York: Free Press of Glencoe.

Wei, William. 1993. *The Asian American Movement.* Philadelphia: Temple University Press.

Weiss, M. S. 1974. *Valley City: A Chinese Community in America.* Cambridge, Mass.: Schenkman Publishing Company.

Whyte, W. F. 1955. *Street Corner Society: The Social Structure of an Italian Slum*, 2d ed. Chicago: University of Chicago Press.

Wickberg, Edgar. 1994. "Overseas Chinese Adaptive Organizations, Past and Present." In *Reluctant Exiles? Migration from Hong Kong and the New Overseas Chinese*, ed. Ronald Skeldon, 68–84. Armonk, N.Y.: M. E. Sharpe.

Williams, Raymond Brady. 1988. *Religions of Immigrants from India and Pakistan: New Threads in the American Tapestry*. New York: Cambridge University Press.

Wirth, Louis. 1928. *The Ghetto*. Chicago: University of Chicago Press.

Wong, Bernard P. 1982. *Chinatown: Economic Adaptation and Ethnic Identity of the Chinese*. New York: Holt, Rinehart and Winston.

———. 1994. "Hong Kong Immigrants in San Francisco." In *Reluctant Exiles? Migration from Hong Kong and the New Overseas Chinese*, ed. Ronald Skeldon, 235–55. Armonk, N.Y.: M. E. Sharpe.

Wong, Kevin Scott, and Sucheng Chan, eds. 1998. *Claiming America: Constructing Chinese American Identities During the Exclusion Era*. Philadelphia: Temple University Press.

Wong, Morrison G. 1995. "Chinese Americans." In *Asian Americans: Contemporary Trends and Issues*, ed. Pyong Gap Min, 58–94. Thousand Oaks, Calif.: Sage.

Woo, Wesley. 1983. *Protestant Work Among the Chinese in San Francisco Area, 1850–1920*. Ph.D. Dissertation. Graduate Theological Union, Berkeley, California.

———. 1991. "Chinese Protestants in the San Francisco Bay Area." In *Entry Denied: Exclusion and the Chinese in America, 1882–1943*, ed. Sucheng Chan, 213–45. Philadelphia: Temple University Press.

Wu, David Yen-ho. 1994. In *The Living Tree: The Changing Meaning of Being Chinese Today*, ed. Tu Wei-ming, 148–67. Stanford: Stanford University Press.

Wuthnow, Robert. 1988. *The Restructuring of American Religion*. Princeton: Princeton University Press.

Yancey, William L., Eugene P. Ericksen, and Richard N. Juliani. 1976. "Emergent Ethnicity: A Review and Reformulation." *American Sociological Review* 41(3): 391–402.

Yang, C. K. 1967 [1961]. *Religion in Chinese Society: A Study of Contemporary Social Functions of Religion and Some of Their Historical Factors*. Berkeley and Los Angeles: University of California Press.

Yang, Fenggang. 1995. "Chinese Protestant Churches in the United States: Explanations for Their Growth, and Their Conservative and Independent Tendencies." Paper presented at the Annual Meeting of the Society for Scientific Study of Religion, St. Louis, Missouri, October 1995.

———. 1998a. "Tenacious Unity in a Contentious Community: Cultural and Religious Dynamics in a Chinese Christian Church." In *Gatherings in Diaspora: Religious Communities and the New Immigration*, ed. R. Stephen Warner and Judith G. Wittner, 333–61. Philadelphia: Temple University Press.

———. 1998b. "Chinese Conversion to Evangelical Christianity: The Importance of Social and Cultural Contexts." *Sociology of Religion: A Quarterly Review* 59(3): 237–57.

Yoo, David. 1996. "For Those Who Have Eyes to See: Religious Sightings in Asian America." *Amerasia Journal* 22 (Spring): xiii–xxii.

Yu, Lingbo. 1996. *Mei jia huaren shehui fojiao fazhan shi* (A History of Chinese Buddhism in the United States and Canada). Taipei: Xin Wen Feng Publishing Co.

Yuan, Zhiming. 1992. "Shangdi yu Minzhu" (God and Democracy). *Zhongguo zhi Chun* (China Spring, a dissident Chinese magazine published in New York) 6: 40–43.

———. 1997. *Laozi vs. Shengjing: kua shikong de yinghou* (Laozi vs. the Bible: A Meeting Across Time and Space). Taipei: Yuzhouguang Press.

Yung, Judy. 1995. *Unbound Feet: A Social History of Chinese Women in San Francisco.* Berkeley and Los Angeles: University of California Press.

Zhang, Qingsong. 1998. "The Origins of the Chinese Americanization Movement: Wong Chin Foo and the Chinese Equal Rights League." In *Claiming America: Constructing Chinese American Identities During the Exclusion Era,* ed. K. Scott Wong and Sucheng Chan, 41–63. Philadelphia: Temple University Press.

Zhou, Min, and Carl L. Bankston. 1994. "Social Capital and the Adaptation of the Second Generation: The Case of Vietnamese Youth in New Orleans." *International Migration Review* 28 (Winter): 821–45.

Index

ABCs. *See* American-born Chinese
acculturation, 97
  before immigration, 97–98, 190–92
adhesive integration of identities, 17–18,
  27–28, 183, 185–86, 194–95, 198
adhesive pattern of adaptation, 24–25, 27
AFC. *See* Ambassadors for Christ,
  Incorporated
alcohol use, 111, 112
Ambassadors for Christ, Incorporated (AFC),
  64–65, 174
American-born Chinese (ABCs), 40
  attitudes toward speaking Chinese, 138–39
  Chinese identity, 167, 169
  converts at the CCC, 72, 74, 75, 88–89
  ethnic and racial consciousness, 99
  increasing population, 36, 37
  members of the Chinese Christian Church,
    58, 102, 104–5, 107, 130–31, 139, 178,
    181–82
  proportion in Chinese American
    population, 101
  rejection of Chinese identity, 210 n. 7
American identity, 9, 190–93. *See also*
  assimilation
  acculturation before immigration, 97–98,
    190–92
  adhesive attachment to ethnic identity,
    27–28
  Anglo-Saxon culture, 22–23
  changing definition of, 20
  of Chinese Christians, 121–22, 129

Christian aspects of, 121, 122–25, 191
civil religion, 23, 24
democracy, 63–64, 116–18, 180–81, 182
integration with other identities, 183–86,
  187–88, 194–95, 198
melting-pot model, 18, 20, 194
tensions with Christian identity, 116,
  177–79, 180–81
unity, 23–24
American-raised Chinese (ARCs), 40
  attitudes toward speaking Chinese, 138–39
  Chinese identity, 167, 169–70
  converts at the CCC, 72, 75, 88–89
  English language knowledge, 107
  members of the Chinese Christian Church,
    58, 130–31, 139
Ammerman, Nancy, 94
ARCs. *See* American-raised Chinese
Ark Fellowship, 4, 13, 67–68, 86, 87
art, Chinese, 145–46
Asian-Americans, 21–22, 28, 210 n. 4, 212 n.
  2. *See also* Chinese Americans
  churches, 170–71
  Koreans, 27, 28, 91, 195
assimilation. *See also* American identity
  core culture, 22–23, 24
  cultural, 26, 97–98, 178, 190–92, 210 n. 4
  economic factors, 25
  maintaining original language, 133
  as motive for Christian conversion, 90–91
  racial differences and, 21